THE FIGHT FOR ETHICAL FASHION

The Mobilization Series on Social Movements, Protest, and Culture

Series Editor

Professor Hank Johnston
San Diego State University, USA

Published in conjunction with *Mobilization: An International Quarterly*, the premier research journal in the field, this series disseminates high quality new research and scholarship in the fields of social movements, protest, and contentious politics. The series is interdisciplinary in focus and publishes monographs and collections of essays by new and established scholars.

Other titles in this series

Understanding the Tea Party Movement
Edited by Nella Van Dyke and David S. Meyer

Dynamics of Political Violence
A Process-Oriented Perspective on Radicalization and the
Escalation of Political Conflict
Edited by Lorenzo Bosi, Chares Demetriou and Stefan Malthaner

Beyond NGO-ization
The Development of Social Movements in Central and Eastern Europe
Edited by Kerstin Jacobsson and Steven Saxonberg

Violent Protest, Contentious Politics, and the Neoliberal State
Edited by Seraphim Seferiades and Hank Johnston

Student Activism and Curricular Change in Higher Education
Mikaila Mariel Lemonik Arthur

The Fight for Ethical Fashion

The Origins and Interactions of the
Clean Clothes Campaign

PHILIP BALSIGER
European University Institute, Italy

Routledge
Taylor & Francis Group

LONDON AND NEW YORK

First published 2014 by Ashgate Publishing

2 Park Square, Milton Park, Abingdon, Oxfordshire OX14 4RN
52 Vanderbilt Avenue, New York, NY 10017

Routledge is an imprint of the Taylor & Francis Group, an informa business

First issued in paperback 2020

British Library Cataloguing in Publication Data
A catalogue record for this book is available from the British Library

The Library of Congress has cataloged the printed edition as follows:
Balsiger, Philip.
The fight for ethical fashion : the origins and interactions of the clean clothes campaign / by Philip Balsiger.
    pages cm
Includes bibliographical references and index.
ISBN 978-1-4094-5805-0 (hardback : alk. paper)
1. Clothing trade--Moral and ethical aspects—Europe.
2. Anti-sweatshop movement—Europe. 3. Consumer behavior--Europe. I. Title.
TT496.E85B35 2014
338.4'7687—dc23

                                                                  2014006819

ISBN 978-1-4094-5805-0 (hbk)
ISBN 978-0-367-60044-0 (pbk)

To my parents

Contents

List of Figures, Tables and Documents

Preface

This book is the result of a long research journey and it would not be the same without the many people I encountered along the way. Its chapters were written and re-written in Lausanne, Zurich, State College, Pittsburgh, Cologne and Florence, and the fieldwork that it is based on was done in libraries, offices, cafes, shops and squares in Zurich, Paris, and a few other cities in Switzerland and France. It is impossible to mention everyone who has contributed, in one way or another, to this project, which goes back to the year 2006 when I first heard of a thing called 'political consumption' and decided to study the collective actors behind it: how social movements mobilize consumers and target corporations.

My gratitude goes firstly to the activists working or volunteering for the Swiss and French Clean Clothes Campaigns (CCC) and some of the organizations contributing to it. Without their generosity, their willingness to share their stories and to respond to my questions, the research on which this book builds would not have been possible. My recognition especially goes to Nayla from the French *Collectif Ethique sur l'étiquette*, who helped me greatly in getting in touch with former campaign officials in France and granted me access to the campaigns' internal archives. I am also especially grateful to the people at the Zurich office of the Bern Declaration and the volunteers from one of its regional groups, who welcomed me to participate in their activities. Attending their meetings and contributing to their actions was very rewarding and it opened my eyes to many aspects of mobilization that I would have otherwise overlooked. I also want to thank all the other people who agreed to be interviewed for this study—those working for clothing firms, government programs, and organizations pursuing the goal of making fashion more ethical.

Intellectually, the book owes much—if not everything!—to Olivier Fillieule, who is and has been a great mentor and friend, ever questioning existing theories of social movements and pushing me on the track towards a more interactionist and dynamic perspective on mobilization processes. The *Centre de recherche sur l'action politique* of the University of Lausanne (CRAPUL) was an immensely inspiring place to develop this research and exchange ideas with fellow political sociologists and friends. With her poignant remarks and suggestions, Nonna Mayer from the *Centre d'études européennes* at Sciences Po Paris also played a not insignificant role in improving this manuscript over the years.

When I left the University of Lausanne, I enjoyed the great privilege of being welcomed into two of the most outstanding European institutions to do social research, where I was granted generous fellowships which enabled me to rethink the structure of this book and complete its writing. First, the Max-Planck Institute for the Study of Societies in Cologne, Germany, provided me with a postdoctoral fellowship; I am especially grateful to the Institute's co-director, Jens Beckert, who invited me to join the 'sociology of markets' group and whose interest in the role social movements play in the rise of 'moral markets' has opened up new perspectives in my work. I then had the pleasure of becoming a 'Max Weber Fellow' for a year, joining the Max Weber Programme of the European University Institute (EUI) in Florence. The inspiring intellectual encounters on the hills overlooking Florence, and the new friends found at the EUI made this time productive and unforgettable. I was also warmly integrated into the vibrant community of social movement scholars at the EUI led by Donatella della Porta, to whom I am particularly indebted. Following this time at the EUI, I also want to thank the Swiss National Science Foundation for awarding me a postdoctoral mobility grant, allowing me to continue my stay at the EUI and finish the last revisions for this book. In this last stage, the comments and suggestions by Hank Johnston, editor of the Mobilization series, were extremely helpful in improving and tightening this manuscript. I also want to thank Susan Garvin for her very careful language editing, and Claire Jarvis from Ashgate for her efficient work.

Finally, I want to dedicate this book to the people who mean the most to me and whose presence has helped me through all the ups and downs such a long research endeavor inevitably gives rise to. To Danny, who makes me smile every day and has fed me through many difficult moments with his marvelous Tuscan meals. To my brother, who is always high on my list. And, most of all, to my parents who have instilled me with intellectual curiosity and have always been there for me, supportive of my choice of pursuing academic research. At last their patient yet persistent questions about the progress of this book get a final answer.

Chapter 1

Introduction: Contentious Markets

The Fight for Ethical Fashion

On a Thursday evening sometime in the spring of 2007, a few activists, staff members of an NGO, and invited guests gathered at a small clothing store in the center of a big Swiss city to celebrate the publication of an 'ethical shopping map.' It listed all the shops where interested consumers could buy clothes produced according to ethical criteria: fashion made with organic or fair trade cotton, t-shirts and jeans produced by workers getting a living wage and working in factories that respected basic safety standards, second-hand dresses or jackets made of recycled materials. The map also featured detailed information on different certification schemes and monitoring initiatives on the social standards in the clothing industry. To the activists' great excitement, it was widely reported on in the media, with newspapers and TV celebrating the rise of ethical fashion as a new trend.

Almost a decade earlier, the same NGO that was behind the 'ethical shopping map' had been part of a coalition that launched a campaign targeting the biggest Swiss clothing retailers. Through a postcard petition and regular evaluations of the retailers' practices, the campaign put pressure on the firms and asked them to guarantee the respect of minimal social standards in their supply chains. According to the makers of the campaign, around 70.000 such postcards were sent to different clothing companies over the next few years by concerned consumers all over Switzerland, bringing some of the leading Swiss retailers to join a pilot project on the monitoring of codes of conducts.

Both of these actions—the map from 2007, and the petition from 1999—were part of a collective 'fight for ethical fashion,' taking place not only in Switzerland but in many Western countries at around the same time. Today clothing comes not only in all kinds of colors, fabrics and cuts, but also comes as organic, fair trade, or carbon neutral. Consumers now find ethical brands and clothing lines on the fashion market, and these market changes would not have been possible without the work of social movement entrepreneurs launching campaigns and targeting corporations. Through petitions, evaluations, maps and many other tactics, activists put the question of the social and environmental conditions in the garment industry on the agendas of clothing retailers and in the minds of consumers. They mobilized consumers at the same time as they raised their awareness of labor abuses and companies' responsibility for them. And they directly targeted and publicly exposed firms to make them acknowledge the problem and change their policies and practices.

Over the past twenty years, the global anti-sweatshop movement has mobilized citizens all over Europe and North America. Social movement coalitions with third-world advocacy groups, unions, consumer organizations and student groups have fought together in various campaigns for the rights of factory workers in a globalized world, allying consumers in the West to their cause (Featherstone 2002, Sluiter 2009). They have attracted the media's attention to cases of labor abuses and thus shamed global companies for the way their clothes are produced. They have also collaborated with firms and governments to experiment with novel forms of control and regulation. In the course of this process, firms have come to develop counter-strategies, adopt certifications, join monitoring systems elaborated in collaboration with NGOs and/or governments, or launch 'ethical' product lines. New niche markets have developed around ethical clothing, inspired by and sometimes originating from actors belonging to the anti-sweatshop movement. Together, these developments have provided a variety of ways for citizens and consumers to mobilize, by protesting and by expressing their solidarity with workers through their consumption behavior.

How did social movements come to use the market place for their struggles? How does contention in markets work—how do activists and firms interact? And how can we explain the rise, dynamics and consequences of anti-sweatshop movements and campaigns? Through a comparative inquiry into the origins and interactions of this movement in Switzerland and France, this book sheds light on protest in the market place, and shows how contexts and strategic interactions shape the unfolding of professionalized movement campaigns. It delves into the history and unfolding of the fight for ethical fashion in those two contrasting cases. To describe, compare and explain the rise, strategies, interactions and outcomes of anti-sweatshop campaigns, it builds on a wide range of sources and methods, from archives and the analysis of internal and published campaign material, to interviews and participant observation.

The anti-sweatshop movement has been one of the most visible movements targeting corporations over the past few decades; it has innovated tactics adapted to the marketplace, but it has been only partially successful in pushing clothing firms to accept tougher social standards in their supply chains. In Europe, it is the European-wide coordinated network called the Clean Clothes Campaign (CCC) that mostly stands for this mobilization on behalf of working rights in the globalized clothing industry. The CCC was founded in the Netherlands in the early 1990s (Sluiter 2009). Over the last two decades, coalitions have formed in as many as 14 European countries to give voice to the CCC's claims, each one of them constituting a national branch of the network. Built around NGOs, unions, consumer organizations, or third world advocacy groups, these national coalitions have developed professionalized campaigns using a variety of action forms in order to enforce the CCC's main claims, namely that corporations adopt the specifically developed Clean Clothes code of conduct and participate in multi-stakeholder initiatives to monitor the code's implementation.

In spite of their transnational coordination, the campaigns were very much shaped by the national contexts of the states they took place in. They were carried by nationally distinct coalitions, developed a distinct tactical repertoire, and chose national (clothing) retailers as their targets. Interaction dynamics between campaigns and corporations were thus taking place primarily at the level of nation-states, and the campaigns' outcomes depended on those interactions. Of course, the CCC's (and also the broader anti-sweatshop movement's) ultimate goal was to improve working conditions in developing countries, and social standards, codes of conducts and their independent monitoring were means to achieve this. However, assessing the impact of the movement for workers in producing countries is not part of this study, which focuses instead on the interactions between campaigners and clothing retailers in the countries where the campaigns mobilized (for assessments on outcomes for factory workers in developing countries, see for instance Brooks 2009, Friedman 2009, Locke 2013). While the articulation of local struggles and transnational campaigns is thus out of this study's scope, it sheds light on the 'national' shaping of transnational mobilizations, analyzing the interaction dynamics between historically and geographically located movement actors and firms. The study reveals that although campaigners and their targets were inserted into global networks (transnational advocacy networks and global supply chains (Keck and Sikkink 1998)) they primarily opposed themselves on national stages.

The dynamics of the CCC in these two countries were very different. In France, a broad coalition campaigned from 1994 to 2005, launching several petitions and rankings that rated the 'social performances' of retailers, and mobilizing a large network of local grassroots coalitions. The targeted French retailers, for their part, did not remain inactive in the face of this mobilization. They fought back by founding a monitoring scheme based on social auditing called Initiative Clause Sociale to counter the coalition's claims, denouncing the campaign's strategy and questioning its legitimacy. In Switzerland, at about the same time, a joint pilot-project on the monitoring of working conditions in the production of clothes came to its end and was to be renewed thanks to state funding. This initiative involved three Swiss retailers selling clothes, and three organizations from the sector of development aid and third world advocacy: the Bern Declaration, Lenten Fund, and Bread for All. These three organizations had, in 1999, launched the Swiss 'Clean Clothes Campaign' through a postcard petition and regular evaluations of the Swiss clothing retailers' social records and reactions to the campaign's claims. But the initiative coming out of the pilot project of collaboration had mixed success, and firms gradually developed other strategies to counter the campaign's demands.

How did the campaigns emerge, how did they target corporations, and how can we explain their impact? In more than one way, movements targeting corporations constitute a conceptual challenge to social movement studies, a challenge that has to be addressed in order to answer these questions. Drawing on and expanding the rising literature on the 'contentiousness of markets' (King and Pearce 2010), the study develops a theoretical framework that attempts to combine the insights from structural approaches in movement research with the recently renewed interest in more dynamic accounts of movements. At the core of these accounts stands a focus on strategic interactions (Jasper 2004, 2006, Fligstein and McAdam 2012).

The Conceptual Challenge of the Contentiousness of Markets

The anti-sweatshop movement, with its campaigns, falls into a particular category of protest: it did not primarily seek legislative change by contesting national or supranational state institutions, but directly addressed its claims to clothing brands and retailers such as Nike, Carrefour, or Migros in Switzerland. For a long time, movement scholars were primarily interested in the contentious interactions between protestors and the state, and neglected other arenas of protest (Van Dyke et al. 2004, Armstrong and Bernstein 2008). But in recent years, the study of movements and markets has rapidly developed as an emerging field of studies at the intersection between social movement scholars and scholars coming from organization studies and economic sociology (Davis et al. 2005, Schneiberg and Lounsbury 2008, Soule 2009, King and Pearce 2010). In parallel, scholars of political participation have taken to studying 'political consumerism' (Micheletti 2003, Micheletti et al. 2004), that is boycotts, and 'buycotts' (i.e. buying products for ethical or political reasons) as increasingly frequent forms of citizen involvement in politics.

    Why this sudden interest in the marketplace as an arena for movement politics? Perhaps scholarly interest reflects the growth of market contention. Some authors suggest that with the growing power of corporations, movements increasingly target firms directly (Klein 2002, Micheletti 2003, Soule 2009). But the empirical evidence for such a shift in contentious repertoires is not conclusive; Soule (2009), who has the most systematic data available, cannot show a clear trend over time. If anything, many *historical* studies suggest that markets have always been sites of protest (see for instance Chatriot et al. 2006, Cohen 2003, Glickman 2005, 2009, Trentmann 2006). That movements target corporations and provoke market change is thus nothing new; social movements often play a crucial role in creating, establishing, or transforming markets and organizational forms. Polanyi (1985 [1944]) pointed to the social and political 'embeddedness' of markets and their contention. The rise of economic sociology since the early 1980s has further shown how the functioning and structures of markets are shaped by politics and policies (Fligstein 1996, 2001), and how social movements can be important actors in processes of market change (Rao 2009). The recent 'discovery' of market protest has thus more to do with evolutions within the social sciences studying markets and movements. A change of research focus from market stability to market change has led organizational scholars to discover social movement organizations (SMOs) and processes as an object of study (Davis et al. 2005, Lounsbury and Ventresca 2002, Rao 2009); at the same time, many social movement scholars have criticized the state centeredness of movement studies (Van Dyke et al. 2004) and have started to move towards the study of movements in multi-institutional contexts (Armstrong and Bernstein 2008; for examples of such studies, see Davis et al. 2005, Soule 2009, Rojas 2007, Walker et al. 2008).

Thus, parallel and sometimes common developments in both fields have produced a number of studies on the 'contentiousness of markets' (King and Pearce 2010; similar overviews can be found in Schneiberg and Lounsbury 2008, Soule 2012, Walker 2012). This literature has shown the various ways through which movements (try to) change corporations and markets. Some tactics resemble classic forms of protest: situated outside of corporations, movements use extra-institutional tactics in order to pressure their corporate targets (Soule 2009). Examples include anti-corporate protest (King and Soule 2007); boycotts (King 2008a) and tactics of public shaming, when corporate practices are publicly denounced by social movement organizations (Bartley and Child 2011). So, movements develop contentious frames against given corporate practices (den Hond and de Bakker 2007, Lounsbury 2005, Lounsbury et al. 2003, Raeburn 2004). Such frames are also used to mobilize consumers and shape demand within markets. While consumer studies and studies of political participation have observed an increased trend towards individual practices of boycott and buycott (Micheletti 2003, Micheletti et al. 2004, Harrison et al. 2005, Forno and Ceccarini 2006), a social movement perspective can illustrate the role of collective mobilizations in shaping consumer preferences and behavior (Balsiger 2010, Dubuisson-Quellier 2013b). Other studies have shown that movements also challenge corporations from within, using insider tactics such as shareholder activism (Davis and Thompson 1994, Giamporcaro-Saunière 2004) or promoting change through employee groups who use creative, yet usually quite moderate forms of mobilization adapted to the characteristics of the organizational setting (Raeburn 2004, Scully and Segal 2002, Kellogg 2011).

Besides contesting corporate practices, movements also seek to collaborate with firms, and have thus contributed to putting in place novel forms of private regulation. Sometimes, movements which start off as anti-corporate campaigns evolve into systems of private regulation (Bartley 2003, 2005), such as certification schemes for fair trade or environmental labels. In such instances, the boundaries between insiders and outsiders, claim-makers and targets, become blurred, as new entities emerge where corporations and movements work together. Finally, movements also contribute to the creation of new markets and categories. Movements give symbolic and material resources to the creation of new niche markets, either indirectly, such as in the temperance movements' role in opening entrepreneurial opportunities for the development of the soft drink industry (Hiatt et al. 2009); or directly such as when movements promote solar energy, windmills, organic food or grass-fed meat, and movement actors themselves become producers (Sine and Lee 2009, Vasi 2009, Weber et al. 2008). In these instances, movements use forms of prefigurative politics: instead of challenging power holders, they directly adopt the changes they are fighting for by developing alternative practices and building up new institutions.

This review and classification of studies on the 'contentiousness of markets' reveals the conceptual challenges this kind of protest poses to traditional definitions of social movements. Two points stand out. First, a clear-cut distinction between insiders and outsiders, challengers and members, seems inept to capture the empirical realities of contentious markets, where movement organizations collaborate with firms to establish forms of private regulation and where social movement actors may become economic actors themselves. Second, but linked to the first point, studies on movements in markets make a strong empirical case for the need for a broad definition of tactical action repertoires, beyond the common focus of social movement studies on collective, public, and contentious action forms. The analysis of tactical action repertoires must also include non-contentious, private, and individual actions[1] and examine how different contentious and non-contentious, individual and collective tactics are articulated with one another and used to provoke change in different settings. In sum, studying protest in markets must lead us to bring together three perspectives on movements: the focus of the political process paradigm on contentious and collective protest, the acknowledgment that movements also use institutionalized means to fight for change, and a Meluccian perspective on new social movements as 'challengers of codes' (Melucci 1996) in everyday lives.

Contexts and Strategic Interactions

Some of the main studies on 'movements and markets' adopt the language of opportunity structures to markets and apply the concepts of the political process model (McAdam et al. 1996) to the new environment. Authors have suggested different terms to denote these opportunity structures, each time associated with a different conceptualization. Opportunity structures are industrial (Schurman 2004), institutional (Raeburn 2004), economic (Wahlström and Peterson 2006, Luders 2006), or corporate (King 2008b, Soule 2009). The factors constituting these opportunity structures should grasp what influences movement dynamics in market arenas. Those studies thus highlight many different factors that determine the responsiveness of targets (see Table 1.1). Some of those factors are situated at the level of the industry or organizational field, often putting to use neo-institutional theories of organizations and markets to explain the interactions between firms and movements. Neo-institutionalist approaches conceptualize firms as part of organizational fields (DiMaggio and Powell 1983, Scott 1995). Coercive, normative and cognitive isomorphic pressures lead to the development of identical practices by all organizations part of the same field. This means that

---

1   Similar observations have been made by authors studying other movements that do not target the state in a traditional way (Armstrong and Bernstein 2008), but aim for instance also at personal change such as the movement against child sexual abuse (Whittier 2009) or target the spheres of science and health (Epstein 1996, Klawiter 2009).

the rise of new norms, adopted by professional corps such as human resource managers, triggers new practices. When large firms, or firms widely viewed as conservative change practices, this can be a strong signal and may lead other members of the organizational field to do the same (Briscoe and Safford 2008). Movements can try to take advantage of such isomorphic pressures by targeting specific firms and by using examples of firms that have made changes in their framing strategies (Raeburn 2004). Other studies adopt a perspective which is more attentive to power dynamics within fields, where incumbents are opposed to challenger actors (Fligstein 2001). The position of firms within fields may explain their reaction to movement demands. Schurman (2004) holds that challenger firms may respond positively to movement demands because they see it as a strategy to improve their position vis-à-vis bigger firms. The opposite hypothesis can be made, too: incumbent firms embrace change to maintain their dominant position. More generally, intense competition may favor reactivity by firms (King 2008b). Some conceptualizations also highlight the relation of an industry sector to the political arena—some sectors such as nuclear energy may be particularly sensitive and therefore protected by the state, while others are less subject to government actions (Schurman 2004, King 2008b. Wahlström and Peterson 2006). The existence of an industry association can also be an important feature channeling corporate reactions (Wahlström and Peterson 2006). Finally, the structure and the cultural characteristics of the product and of its 'global value chain' (Gereffi and Korzeniewicz 1994) also shapes corporate reactions to movements (Schurman and Munro 2009). For technologically complex products, suppliers are usually quite powerful actors in supply chains because their know-how and high skills cannot easily be dropped for cheaper competitors. But for a low-technology industry such as apparel, the opposite is the case, and clothing brands and retailers are the dominant actors (Locke 2013). This means that they can potentially put pressure on their suppliers to impose changes. Finally, building on the varieties of capitalism literature (Hall and Soskice 2001), authors have pointed to differences in the national organization of capitalism that can influence corporate reactions to pressure from social movements (Bair and Palpacuer 2012). In coordinated market economies, in particular, industry self-regulation and negotiations between companies and unions are common, and this may have spillover effects on the attitudes of companies to demands coming from other civil society actors.

At the level of single corporations, authors have singled out the instability of firms (for instance provoked by government action taken against it in an anti-trust case) as a first factor impacting responsiveness (King 2008b). Luders (2006) examines the cost structure that characterizes businesses, distinguishing between concession costs and disruption costs (i.e., how costly it is for a business to concede to movement demands vs how costly disruptions are for its operations). Zald et al. (2005) highlight a firm's organizational capacity and commitment, the latter factor being close to Schurman's invocation of corporate culture (2004). The higher its organizational capacity and commitment to change, the more likely a company will be to respond to movement demands. One can also further open up the 'black

Table 1.1   Major factors shaping reactiveness of firms to movement demands

Level of industry or field	Level of corporation
Isomorphic processes (Raeburn 2004) Incumbent vs challenger dynamics (Schurman 2004) Intense competition (King 2008) Relation of industry to political arena (Schurman 2004), Existence of industry association (Wahlström and Peterson 2006) Supply-chain structure (Schurman 2004, Schurman and Munro 2009, Locke 2013), Varieties of capitalism (Bair and Palpacuer 2012)	Vulnerability, instability (King 2008) Cost structure (concession and disruption costs) (Luders 2006) Organizational Capacity (Zald et al. 2005) Organizational commitment (Zald et al. 2005), corporate culture (Schurman 2004) Internal factions, elite allies and internal advocates (King 20008, Weber et al. 2009, Raeburn 2004)

box' of firms and conceive of them as arenas or 'open polities' (Rao et al. 2000). Internal power networks and struggles between factions within a firm can also shed light on a business's reactiveness. The existence of 'internal advocates,' elite allies of movement causes within firms, can be a decisive asset (Raeburn 2004, King 2008b); in a different process, movements may dissuade internal sponsors of a new contested practice from pursuing their goal (Weber et al. 2009).

Overall, studies using largely compatible theoretical frameworks—some putting emphasis on the determination of corporate practices at the field-level, others at the corporate level itself—have thus come up with a long list of factors that can be considered as part of the opportunity structure that movements targeting corporations face—a context that can be seen, following Soule (2009), as being composed of a series of nested opportunity structures, from the firm level to the industry and further on to domestic and transnational opportunities. But the criticism that has been levelled against approaches based on political opportunity structures (Fillieule 1997, 2006, Goodwin and Jasper 1999, 2011) can also be applied to the use of the concept of economic opportunity structures. It makes movement dynamics and outcomes depend too strongly on external factors and thus denies movement actors the capacity to shape dynamics themselves through their actions. Because movements pursuing changes in corporations and markets as their goal often also use tactics that do not target specific firms but rather aim at establishing alternative forms of trade or changing consumer preferences, the autonomy of movement players in shaping dynamics should be particularly stressed in this context. Furthermore, the multiplication of factors suggests that, just as with political opportunity structures, the concept is in danger of becoming a sponge that absorbs ever new aspects, depending on the theoretical preferences of researchers and the cases at hand (Gamson and Meyer 1996). As a consequence, structural features such as field position and corporate culture may often give contradictory signals concerning the reactiveness of a given firm and may therefore be of little help.

The classic structuralist model also fails to build on a trend of theoretical renewal in the study of social movements over the last decade. I have in mind strategic approaches to movement development (Jasper 2004, 2006, Maney et al. 2012) and a focus on strategic interactions (Fillieule and Tartakovsky 2008, Fillieule et al. 2010, Fligstein and McAdam 2012, Jasper 2011, Duyvendak and Jasper 2014). It breaks with conceptions where a movement's opponent is reduced to simple context, passively 'receiving' the moves of the movement but incapable of developing its own moves, its own strategy. Instead, a strategic interactions approach conceives of the interactions between movement actors and their targets as an open-ended game of moves and counter-moves, where actors on both sides take strategic decisions. The fight for ethical fashion in Switzerland and France strongly reflects just such a back-and-forth game among the players.

Strategic action can be defined as the "attempt by social actors to create and sustain social worlds by securing the cooperation of others," willing or otherwise (Fligstein and McAdam 2012, p. 17). Movements raise claims and use diverse action repertoires to give voice to their demands and bring targets to yield. Their targets, in turn, also have to be conceptualized as strategic actors, capable of reacting to these claims in different ways: for instance, by giving in, making some concessions, or fighting back using strategies such as dividing or delegitimizing their opponents. The dynamics of contention, then, are the contingent result of this back and forth between action and reaction. Thus contentious politics resembles more a cat-and-mouse game, although in this case, it is the tiny mouse that chases the much bigger cat. As in Tom and Jerry, the mouse (Jerry) finds all kinds of ruses to anger the cat (Tom); but Tom fights back, and their chases and battles can go on for a long time, for every move of one character leads to a reaction by the other one, and settlements may be difficult to find.

This is not to say that structural characteristics of both movements and their opponents do not play any role at all. Depending on such characteristics, some actions and claims will be materially and culturally available. According to contexts, certain strategies will be possible options or not, attractive or not, more or less likely. Structural characteristics, in other words, can help explain the strategies pursued by movement actors and their opponents. But they do not on their own determine movement dynamics. For this, one has to analyze the strategic interactions over time. Indeed, in this interaction, structural features may get changed, as for example when a strategic 'blunder' weakens a movement opponent (Jasper and Poulsen 1993), when movements achieve a change in the rules of the game, for example through a court decision; or when opponents coalesce and thus gain access to new resources.

Field perspectives are particularly useful to contextualize the dynamics of strategic interactions. While the heterogeneity of movement actors has been acknowledged for a long time through concepts such as 'multi-organizational fields' (Curtis and Zurcher 1973), movement industries and sectors (McCarthy and Zald 1977) or movement areas (Melucci 1985), scholars have recently re-discovered field approaches within a more strategic framework. Such conceptualizations can help make sense of the strategic interactions of movement actors with each other and with their targets. Drawing on Bourdieu (1985, 1989), field perspectives have notably been central in French social movement studies (Agrikolansky et al. 2005b, Mathieu 2012, Péchu 2006), but also in Crossley's (2003) explicitly Bourdieusian approach. In the US context, too, authors have recently suggested more dynamic conceptualizations of the contexts within which actors interact, speaking of arenas (Jasper 2011, Duyvendak and Jasper 2014) or strategic action fields (Fligstein and McAdam 2012).

Fields are constructed social orders within which actors compete, cooperate, or use coercion to maintain or improve their position in an on-going struggle (Fligstein and McAdam 2012). The peculiarity of social movement actors is that while they are routinely part of fields (such as the field of international solidarity organizations or the broader social movement field), they can operate as challengers in a variety of fields such as policy arenas or markets. When they launch challenges, they open up new arenas of strategic interaction, with the goal of forcing established actors in this field to react. Field perspectives thus allow for a very dynamic understanding of social movements and their interactions, and field structures and actors' positions and goals can conceptualize the contextual factors that explain strategic actions and interactions.

The Rise, Dynamics, and Outcomes of a Professionalized Social Movement Campaign

An approach centering on movement actors' strategic interactions has implications for the research strategies used to shed light on the classic questions of emergence, dynamics and consequences of social movements. Using a genealogical perspective on movement emergence, interaction processes within different fields can explain the rise of new causes, repertoires, and movements. Emergence is thus not, or at least not primarily, explained by changes in the movement's environment, such as the opening up of political opportunities; instead, movements themselves create their own (Agrikoliansky et al. 2005a, Fillieule and Sommier 2013). Movement emergence then reflects—or is the result of—reconfigurations within the social movement fields, in the course of which actors come to 'invest' in new causes (Agrikoliansky et al. 2005a), rise as a spin-off from previous movements (McAdam 1995) or get reactivated from abeyant structures (Taylor 1989). A genealogical perspective is also attentive to the different temporalities that explain the emergence of new movements.

Drawing a movement's genealogy does not consist in identifying precursor movements, but rather looking for the *roots* of the movement in question. Most definitions of social movements stress three defining elements which characterize a movement: an organizational element, the use of protest tactics, and an orientation towards social change (Fillieule 2009). The rise of these components often plays out within different temporalities and is provoked by different causal mechanisms. A genealogical approach allows the keeping together of these different temporalities, and analyzes how they are articulated. Alternately, the study will explain what accounts for the rise and the adoption of particular claims addressed to corporations, for the emergence of coalitions of different actors at particular moments in time, and for the adoption of particular tactical action repertoires used to publicly express—and sustain—such claims. Thus, in the dynamic of this process of 'emergence,' different types of theoretical insights—structures and opportunities, resources, and framing—will be necessary to explain different 'moments of emergence.' Long-term structural dynamics, mid-term dynamics of configuration of social movement fields, as well as mid- to short-term dynamics of opportunities, particular events and strategic decisions all have to be accounted for.

With regard to movement dynamics, a focus on social movement campaigns presents itself as a particularly apt strategy to capture and follow contentious interaction over time. A campaign is a "sustained, coordinated series of episodes involving similar claims on similar or identical targets" (Tilly 2008, p. 89), consisting of back-and-forth actions between a movement and its target(s). Studying campaigns provides a unit of analysis made of interactions; this unit is smaller than a movement, but more encompassing than single events and it "represents a focused cluster of interactions and interrelated collective action frames" (Della Porta and Rucht 2002, p. 3). Analyzing campaigns thus offers the opportunity to study the iterations of interactions between movement actors and their targets.[2] It allows the analysis of the articulation of the different scales and arenas where interactions take place: individual participation, grassroots groups, professionalized NGOs and their staff; local, regional, national and transnational arenas as well as political and economic spheres; and contentious, contention-connected, collective, public, or individual and private performances.

In reality, the notion of campaigns as coordinated episodes involving similar targets and goals denotes multiple phenomena. In particular, the amount of coordination and planning of campaigns differs. Some campaigns are quite spontaneous and react to imposed grievances such as the extension of airport runways (Griggs and Howarth 2002). Such campaigns are often driven by emerging

---

2   This contrasts with protest event analysis (PEA)—still probably the most popular method to study collective action. An unresolved problem with most PEA is their failure to account for the linkages between different events with one another as they belong to iterative exchanges between movement actors, targets, and other actors such as counter-movements, within specific campaigns. It is possible, however, to assign individual protest events to campaigns in quantitative databases, thus allowing the campaign to be taken as a level of analysis and to study the sequential patterning of protest events within a campaign. Rucht's databases (Rucht et al. 1999) on protest events in Germany from 1950–1997 does so. But most studies based on PEA either do not dispose of this information, or are not interested in the analytical level of the campaign.

Table 1.2   Two ideal types of campaigns

Reactive campaign	Planned campaign
Protesters, grassroots groups	Pro-active
"Outbreak", eruption	Professionals, NGOs
Polyfonia	Launched
Imposed agenda	Hierarchy
	Agenda-setting

grassroots groups. The campaigns 'erupt' when grievances appear; often, many different actors, not necessarily coordinated with one another, come to speak for the damaged population. Planned campaigns, on the other hand, are pro-active and often professionally organized: they are about putting new issues on the public agenda, for instance labor conditions in clothing production. Those campaigns do not erupt: they are the result of careful planning by professional organizations (often NGOs) with employees. Planned campaigns are often organized quite hierarchically, with a central organization or coalition in charge (see Table 1.2).

The Clean Clothes campaign belongs to this latter category. Its timing, action forms, media strategies, budget, and so on, were prepared months in advance—although unexpected events, reactions by targets, and the participation of grassroots groups sometimes interfered with this planning. Formalized structures and schedules adapted to professional workers have consequences on the outlook of campaigns (Staggenborg 1988): professionalization was thus an important driver of the dynamics of the anti-sweatshop movements in Switzerland and France. With or without the need to apply for external funding, professional structures and practices impose constraints on campaign-makers in terms of planning and evaluation of impact. The 'internal making' or 'fabrication' of campaigns in such professionalized settings has to be an integral part of the analysis. When fabricating a campaign, movement organizations bring together tactics and framing strategies to put an issue on the public agenda and pressure targets, but they also build up a collective identity. They strategize and react to external events and reactions by targets, adapting demands, tactics, and frames. It is this process of strategic actions and interactions that is at the core of the analysis of the Clean Clothes Campaigns I present.

To be sure, the focus on campaigns is also a restriction: by moving the lens to the interactions of a given campaign and its targets, we may lose sight of other actors that are not participating in the campaign as such, but who mobilize for similar issues. The field perspective—conceiving of the movement actors behind campaigns as inserted in multiple fields within which they interact with other movement actors—helps integrate the broader environment of campaigns. 'Competing' movement actors can for instance pursue less radical goals and collaborate with targets, and thus become important players within a campaign's dynamic. This leads us to the final question of movement consequences. They are understood as a result of contentious interaction in the course of which movement actors and their opponents try to shape outcomes in their favor. This calls for a processual approach to movement impact (Soule and King 2008): rather than assessing the structural conditions that favor movement outcomes, one should look at how strategic interactions shape movement effects, and how claims get transformed in this process. It involves considering the 'finish line' as moving (Meyer 2006): targets develop strategic responses, issues get displaced, new questions arise and become contested in contentious interaction.

Two Contrasting Cases: the Clean Clothes Campaign in Switzerland and France

Many core elements of the campaign had a transnational character: the CCC's scope, first and foremost; the campaign's main claims were the same everywhere and some actions were conducted simultaneously across the different countries involved. Transnational coordination was thus important, and the global reach of the movement is incontestable. Yet each CCC country coalition was different, had different corporate targets, and led to different outcomes. This makes a crossnational comparison particularly powerful: it serves to contextualize and localize—in this case, 'nationalize'—transnationally coordinated campaigns and movements. Instead of a global and unified movement, we can see the different origins and histories of the movement in different national contexts, and embed it into the dynamics of country-specific protest cycles and social movement fields.

Comparisons are useful both to show the common features of protest in markets and to investigate how and which contextual factors matter for the dynamics and outcomes of campaigns. In many ways, Switzerland and France represent very different and contrasting cases. From the point of view of individuals using the market to voice political concerns, measured by surveys on boycott and buycott, Switzerland is often referred to as one of the champions of political consumerism, and France is seen, by political commentators, as lagging behind. Switzerland is one of the overall leaders in terms of success of these action modes. In the European Social Survey 2002, 52.7% declared having boycotted and/or buycotted in the previous 12 months, compared to 35.7% in France. The most plausible factor to explain this difference is the unequal institutionalization and availability of ethical goods in both countries. Indeed, in the early 2000s, organic and fair trade food were widely distributed by Switzerland's two main retailers (controlling together more than 80% of the market), whereas such products were still largely restricted to specialized niche markets (fair trade and organic shops) in France. This difference can be illustrated by the sales figures of FLO/Max Havelaar, the most important labeling scheme in fair trade, which can serve here as a rough indicator for the differing development of political consumerism. The introduction of labeled fair trade products in Swiss supermarkets took place several years earlier than in France, and the availability and sales of such goods were much higher. The sales volume per inhabitant of Max Havelaar certified products shows that in

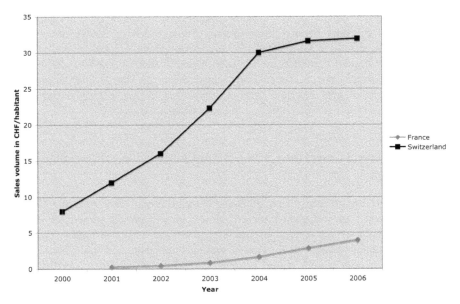

Figure 1.1   Sales volume / inhabitant of Max Havelaar labeled products in Switzerland and France (Source: Max Havelaar Switzerland and France)

France, these volumes were well below the Swiss level; in 2001, the figure is 40 times higher in Switzerland than in France, and it is still 8 times higher in 2006. The total sales in France of MH products in 2006 represents only half of the volume Switzerland already had in the year 2000. At the beginning of the 2000s, MH- labeled products in France were only available in specialized shops, not on the shelves of big retailers. This gradually changed in the course of the decade, and is reflected in the growth detectable from 2002 on.

Insights from the comparative literature on social movements also suggest that Switzerland and France constitute contrasting cases. Kriesi et al.'s study (1995) has shown that in Switzerland, around two thirds of all protest events from 1975 to 1989 originate from 'new social movements'(NSM) (environmental movement, solidarity movement, peace movement and identity movements), and one third from the labor movement (the 'old' social movement). In France, it is the opposite: around one third of protest events emanate from new social movements, and two thirds from the labor movement. A study using police rather than press records shows that the Kriesi study even largely underestimated the amount of protest by 'old' social movements in the French case (Fillieule 1997). Yet tactics such as boycotts, buycotts, the development of alternative niches or the targeting of corporations often emanate from so-called new social movements. New social movement scholars emphasized how movements turned to everyday practices as loci of change and constructed alternative spaces (Melucci 1989, 1996). Many of today's institutionalized forms of political consumption, such as fair trade or organic, have their origin within new social movements, in particular the environmental and the 'third world' movements. Kriesi et al.'s (1995) data show that precisely those two movements were more important within the new social movements in Switzerland than in France, where they were responsible for fewer protest events. In addition, Kriesi et al. (1995) argue that when compared to other European countries, France is distinct because the class cleavage there has not been pacified. In France's social movement sector, "the political organizations associated with the traditional cleavage are likely to make every attempt to mobilize their traditional potentials on all the newly emerging conflicts in movement politics; that is, they will try to absorb new issues and new collective actors into the traditional conflict" (p. 9). It is likely that this absorption also means an adoption of the traditional tactical action repertoire of these organizations, turned towards the state rather than changing individual consumer practices and constructing alternative spaces within society (see also Duyvendak 1995).

What is more, given the prevalence of traditional political actors based on the class cleavage and turned towards the state, action modes promoting individual change and bypassing the state may be less legitimate within the French social movement sector. The use of specific action repertoires depends on the perception actors have of its legitimacy (Péchu 2006). This means that to successfully link a given issue to consumption and production rather than, say, state intervention and regulation, a certain discursive repertoire (Steinberg 1999, 2002) must be available and legitimate. In France during the 1970s and 1980s, the dominance of class politics over lifestyle issues would tend to link consumption practices to politics. A repertoire targeting corporations would find less resonance among NSM groups, such as environmental and third-world SMOs. However, studies based on an analysis of protest events as reported in press sources are not best suited to research forms of political action that are not necessarily contentious but consist in the creation of counter-cultural modes of exchange, consumption, and production. In fact, this data will tend to underestimate the occurrence of such actions, for they do not constitute protest events per se. Historical studies suggest that there was definitely a counter-culture in France, nourished by the student protests of '68 and the Catholic left (Allan Michaud 1990, Berger 1985, Grignon 1977), albeit maybe not as far-reaching as its counterparts in countries like Germany or Switzerland.

Beyond movement politics, France and Switzerland also differ in terms of their political economies. The central role of the state in France is not only visible with regard to social movements, it also concerns the organization of capitalism. In the 'varieties of capitalism' literature, France has been characterized as a 'state-led' or, following market-oriented reforms in the 1980s and 1990s, at least a 'state-enhanced' type of capitalism (Schmidt 2003). The same literature portrays Switzerland as a coordinated economy, albeit with important market-based mechanisms, leading some authors to consider it a liberal coordinated economy where capital dominates state and labor interests (Afonso 2013). These divergent institutional arrangements mean that self-regulation of industries and participation of stakeholders within this process is more common in the Swiss economy than in France, where the state tends to regulate much more. The political economy context thus suggests that when movements target corporations, Swiss companies should be more inclined to opt for private regulation, quite common in Switzerland, than their counterparts in France, where state intervention is the usual mode of regulation. An example of this divergence is corporate social responsibility or 'sustainability' reporting by firms: Swiss retailers adopted this practice voluntarily in the 1990s, while French companies only started to publish such reports once the government passed a law obliging them to do so.

But also on the level of industries and corporations, the comparison can help with identifying the role structural differences of firms and industries play in explaining movement dynamics and outcomes. Of course, this depends on which companies actually get targeted in the course of the campaigns. The CCC focused on the apparel industry, but within this broad category, there exist different market segments such as high-end brands, branded retailers, no-name producers, sports clothing brands or general retailers (Aspers 2010). Each one of these potential targets has different characteristics that matter. But they could not be known in advance, for only the campaign dynamic decided which companies actually came to be the main targets. Beyond different national institutions and cultures, the comparison of two campaigns thus also serves to uncover the role of strategic interactions in movement dynamics and outcomes. In conformity with the strategic interactions approach, the comparative analysis places a particular focus on such processes and their contextualized explanation.

A Note on Data and Methods

The analytical method I use is a case-based comparison. Such comparisons analyze few cases "based on a large number of characteristics," and produce explanations that are "narrative accounts with limited interest in generalization" (Della Porta 2008, p. 207). Case-centered approaches are particularly useful for uncovering processes, paying close attention to the unfolding of events (George and Bennet 2005) and their contexts and relying on a diversity of observations. Possible data sources and observations were adapted to availability in the field. The kind of observations thus sometimes differ from one case to the other: if a type of data source was not available for one case, I used other kinds of observations that could constitute an equivalent. Table 1.3 lists the different types of observation used. Two main types of sources are the same for both cases, and used, to varying degrees, throughout the study: interviews with key informants, and the analysis of campaign material and published documents by the campaign organizations. I interviewed 37 informants—12 in France, 25 in Switzerland, using a semi-structured interview guide, the interviews lasting between 40 minutes and 3 hours, with a medium length of approximately 1½ hours. Around two thirds of the informants were current or former officials of the respective Clean Clothes Campaigns and/or the organizations behind the campaigns; the other informants

Table 1.3   Type of observations in Switzerland and France

	Switzerland	France
Origin of the campaign	Published documents from BD Interviews with campaign officials **Archival data** from the Bern Declaration Secondary sources	Published documents by Artisans du monde Interviews with campaign officials **Internal campaign documents** Secondary sources
Campaign and broader field of ethical fashion	Interviews with campaign officials and other actors in the field Published campaign documents **Participant observation** Secondary sources (press, other academic studies)	Interviews with campaign officials and other actors in the field Published campaign documents **Internal campaign documents** Secondary sources (press, other academic studies, campaign evaluations) Observation

came from other initiatives dealing with ethical fashion (such as fair trade or organic labels), government officials, and representatives of firms. Interviews were used to reconstruct the dynamic of the campaign, to get information on the main issues that rose during its duration, such as internal conflicts or strategic debates, and to learn about the rationales behind strategic decisions. The campaign documents that were analyzed consist of all the publications and documentations the respective national organizations released for their numerous campaign rounds: booklets, leaflets, petitions, rankings, etc. Basing some part of the analysis on this type of document—a kind of material that is infrequently used (or at least acknowledged, see Martin 2010) means that I use the 'raw' material of the campaign, the official communication, and not the accounts given in the press. Again, campaign material served to reconstruct the campaign dynamic, as well as to analyze the framing of the campaign and the tactics it used.

Table 1.3 also reveals important imbalances in the nature of observation between the two cases. The data types written in bold characters constitute the major differences. For the period covering the origin of political consumerism in general and the Clean Clothes Campaign specifically, I use archival data from one core organization in Switzerland, at the origin of modern campaigns of political consumerism. In France, I was not able to consult the archives of the organization at the origin of the Clean Clothes Campaign (the fair trade association Artisans du monde). Only for the specific campaign launch do I have access to internal documents from the campaign coalition (see discussion below) that allow for a fine-grained analysis of this process. However, I do retrace the campaign activity of Artisans du monde on the basis of other sources (most notably, its member publications), and I do inquire, more widely, into the origin of campaigning in general and consumer campaigns by other organizations, again using a variety of sources. Thus, the same question—the origin of the campaign—is addressed using different sources, reflecting both availability and, more importantly, the idiosyncrasies of the origins in both countries. In Switzerland, it is heavily associated with one particular organization, whereas in France, it is more the result of changes within the sector of international solidarity organizations.

For the period covering the campaign itself, the data sources are similar, but have some important differences too. Two differences are noteworthy. First, I had access to internal documents of the French campaign, but not to the Swiss one; second, I did participant observation in the Swiss case, but not the French. Both differences are linked to the moment of access to the field and to the specific histories of both campaigns. When I did my fieldwork in Paris, the French Clean Clothes Campaign was just re-emerging after a three-year-long period of inactivity. It started on a new basis, with (mostly) new staff and officials, and without the founder organization Artisans du monde. This relaunch allowed me to access the field relatively easily, and it also allowed me to gain permission to look through the (unordered) boxes of internal documents temporarily stored in the cellar of the campaign's headquarters.[3] Had there not been a change in the campaign's organization, I doubt that I would have been given access to the archives. In the Swiss case, where there has not been an organizational change, I was not granted access to internal documents.[4] For officials of the Bern Declaration, this information was too sensitive, given that they continued to target the same corporations as in the campaign's beginning and much of the internal documents concerned confidential issues.[5]

---

3   The conditions of data gathering were rather difficult, for the boxes containing the internal documents had just been moved and had never been classified according to an intelligible and visible scheme. I spent several days going through all the boxes and documents, taking pictures of all the documents I deemed important for my analysis. At home on my computer, I then classified the documents I had taken pictures of by attributing them to the different stages of the campaign. The documents in these boxes consisted of official campaign material (thus, the archives allowed me to obtain a detailed collection of all the campaign material produced by the French CCC) and of documents of internal communication for campaign preparation, as well as minutes of meetings.

4   The BD archives are publicly available at the Sozialarchiv in Zurich, but only up to 1994 and for some issues–but not the CCC–until the early 2000s.

5   Similar objections were also evoked by French campaign officials. They agreed to my consulting the archives, but some boxes concerning the communication between the campaign and corporations were kept in the administrator's office, out of my reach, and I further offered my promise not to look into confidential documents concerning specific firms. While going through the boxes I had been granted access to, I found information on corporations and their reactions to the campaign that could be perceived as 'sensitive';

The use of participant observation in my fieldwork also has to do with the timing of my empirical inquiry. Only the Swiss campaign was on-going while I was doing fieldwork, and participant observation was thus only part of the methodology mix in Switzerland. I joined a local group of volunteers affiliated to the main NGO behind the campaign and participated in their meetings and actions over a period of approximately two years. Those volunteers (at most meetings, not more than 10 people) were for the most part around my age and contributed to the actions of the Swiss campaign, even developing an innovative tactic in the form of an 'ethical shopping map.' Participant observation thus gave me a privileged insight into the inner workings of a campaign from the grassroots perspective and, by chance, also into the process of tactical innovation. In France, on the other hand, the relaunch did not coincide with a broad activation of the network of local activist groups, at least not immediately. Although the participation of grassroots groups had been crucial in the French campaign's tactical repertoire, I could not participate in them because the actions preceded my fieldwork. I could therefore only reconstruct the role and functioning of local mobilizations using other data types (interviews, archives, reports).

One last limitation of the present study needs to be pointed out: In principle, the strategic interactions approach adopted here supposes that all the actors involved in the strategic interaction studied receive equal attention—both campaign-makers and their targets should be studied with the same vigor. This study only constitutes a step in this direction, but does not yet fulfill this condition. The strategies of the movement actors are analyzed in great detail based on a variety of data, but the same could not be done for corporate actors. Access to decision makers within firms proved particularly difficult in this research field. Data gathered on firms came mostly from secondary sources—the press, different corporate reports on CSR, sustainability, or general activity, the information gathered by the campaigns themselves regarding the firms' strategic responses—and from some interviews. This methodological hiatus means that, in my analysis, decision processes within firms cannot be explained in the same empirical depth and therefore receive less attention than those on the campaign side. However, the interactionist perspective remains pertinent, and by using the information on corporate actions that were available plus drawing on secondary literature to help explain those strategies, I was able to reconstruct the corporate counter-strategies with accuracy.

---

however, in conformity with my promise, I only rely on official declarations by firms and industry organizations in my analysis, in addition to information given during interviews.

Chapter 2

The Rise of Consumer Campaigns

The 'Invention' of Consumption Campaigns in Switzerland

The Swiss CCC was officially launched in 1999 by three NGOs—the Bern Declaration (BD), Bread for All, and the Lenten Fund. Because the Swiss CCC was based on campaigns in several other European countries, all the Swiss activists had to do was adapt tactics used elsewhere to their national context. However, one of the NGOs, the BD, had been carrying out similar campaigns since the early 1970s. 'Consumption campaigns,' as the BD called them, had been an important part of their action repertoire. The BD was one of the main proponents of bringing protest to the marketplace. The analysis of the BD's history, in particular with regard to the organization's adoption of this action repertoire and its transformations over time, offers an account of the emergence of 'anti-corporate campaigns' in Switzerland on which, many years later, the CCC would build.

The roots of the BD go back to a public appeal published in 1969 in Bern by progressive theologists. It demanded that the Swiss government both change its development policy and increase public spending on it. It took the form of a petition with public (especially religious) figures as its first signatories, who encouraged ordinary citizens to sign it. In order to emphasize their commitment, the signatories committed themselves to donating a percentage of their yearly income to development projects. What began as a petition and public appeal then slowly evolved into a professional social movement organization (Holenstein 1998, Holenstein et al. 2009[1]). In order to drive the search for signatures, an organizational structure with two regional administrators was created and political claims to change development policy became central (Holenstein 1998) to their strategy.

To understand this evolution and the rise of new claims regarding development politics, it is crucial to look at the events that took place within the field of development aid in the late 1960s. Until the end of this decade, the issue of third world development was about aid projects, *not* about politics. Aid projects were

---

1   This book is actually a first-hand account of the history of the BD, written by some of its key historic protagonists (in particular, the first secretary Anne-Marie Holenstein, and Rudolf Strahm, also a secretary of the organization and very influential figure in the Swiss Third World movement), published on the occasion of the 40-year anniversary of the organization. Holenstein (1998) is the work of a historian, but this Holenstein (René) also occupied the role of secretary at the BD during the 1990s. Because his book treats Swiss development aid in general, and does not concern his period as secretary of a development aid advocacy organization, it can be considered a historical study.

conducted by six important development aid organizations, two of them secular, two Protestant, and two Catholic. The projects had mostly a technical orientation, and expertise in development stemmed from engineering and agricultural science departments. The state was only marginally engaged in development issues. Contrary to countries with a colonial history, struggles of decolonization did not occupy the internal political agenda, and development aid was therefore a mostly 'depoliticized' matter (Holenstein 1998).

These established practices, rules and cultural norms constituted a fairly stable field settlement (Fligstein and McAdam 2012). But by the time of the Bern Declaration's birth in 1969, this settlement was challenged by two distinct but complementary sources: a renewal of theological thought based on liberation theology, adopted by mostly peripheral actors within the churches, and the student and youth movement of the late 1960s. Through these two channels, ideas such as underdevelopment, dependency or center-periphery appeared, and a movement of politicization started to affect the world of development aid. Newly formed actors like the BD and student action committees pursued those new ideas using innovative action repertoires. Ultimately, those challenges provoked a reconfiguration of the field, with the rise of a new, albeit contested, understanding of development politics and the establishment of a more politicized pole within the field of development aid.

Inside the church, new voices criticized theories of modernization, stressed the need for autonomous development and accused the Western countries' economies of profiting from the global South's underdevelopment. They were under the influence of Marxist-based liberation theology of Latin American origin, but also of new economic theories on development, especially dependency theory. Such left-wing theological voices were raised internationally at the Conferences of the World Council for Churches, notably in Uppsala in 1968, where the goal of church-based development aid was described as "the establishing of economic and social justice, which has to be achieved by structural and behavioral change in the North" (Holenstein 1998, p. 28). In this context, a "movement-like uprising" (Holenstein 1998, p. 129) took place at the margins of the official church, advocating the liberation of the Third World from dependency and raising critical questions of development politics, submission and underdevelopment.

In Switzerland, these new ideas inspired the creation of many 'third world groups' in church communities. At the same time, the creation of such groups, which conceived of development issues as political questions, was also driven by the student uprisings of the late sixties. In the Third World Action Groups, which were founded at different Swiss universities at this time and were organized at the federal level in the Safep (Schweizerische Arbeitsgruppen für Entwicklungshilfe), students with religious and secular-leftist backgrounds came together. In Bern, for example, the group was created in 1968 after a rally and teach-in on the subject of the war in Biafra organized by the university's evangelical community. The newly founded group then launched a hunger strike and started planning the so-called 'Christmas action,' which was staged several times in the following years.

Using the slogan 'Denken statt Schenken' ('Think instead of making presents'), the action questioned the Christmas shopping frenzy. The group's members even participated in a Christmas sermon at Bern Cathedral (Holenstein 1998) and thus had close ties to the church. The action was, therefore, mostly situated within the religious arena, but evidence shows that it spoke both to a religious audience and the secular left: Holenstein (1998, p. 181) cites a document by a leftist organization from Zurich in which it presented the Christmas Action as part of the revolutionary struggle.

These religious youth groups also played a very important role in the process of the 'politicization' of church-based development aid organizations. One event was particularly important in this respect. In 1970, the evangelical theologians at the origin of the Bern Declaration initiated an 'Inter-confessional Conference Switzerland-Third World' hosted by the Swiss Evangelical Church, the Swiss Catholic Bishops' Conference and the Swiss Christian-Catholic Church. It united people from business, public administration and academia, political parties and unions, development aid NGOs, churches and missions, as well as representatives from the so-called 'Third World' and from religious youth groups. The youth representatives—under the leadership of the Third World Action Group Bern—had prepared an intervention concerning Swiss development aid policy. They demanded that the causes of underdevelopment be taken into account, an end to the oppression of Third World countries, and a reorganization of international trade structures. Development aid policy, they said, was not so much about giving more than it was about taking less (Holenstein et al. 2009, p. 38). In order to underline their claims, they started to actively disturb the course of the Conference, and managed to provoke a division within the Conference participants. Since the Conference did not respond to some of the youths' claims, they started a 24-hour hunger strike. The discussions during the Conference had an impact on established organizations. Notably, they influenced the church-based development aid organizations and, to a certain extent, changed their orientation: donation campaigns would start stressing the importance of awareness-raising as well as the links between Swiss development and poverty in the South (Holenstein 1998). Most visibly, in an unprecedented move, this movement led the Protestant development aid organization Brot für Brüder to controversially support a ballot initiative from the left aiming to ban weapon exports, thus opposing the traditional religious and bourgeois elite of the country.

In sum, the transformations of the late sixties and early seventies saw the rise of new actors—both religious and non-religious—who focused on development politics rather than development aid. An important aspect of this emerging solidarity movement was that it manifested itself in different arenas: it targeted the state, tried to mobilize public opinion and, even more so, tried to raise awareness of the link between Western 'over-development' and Third World 'underdevelopment' within both religious and secular audiences. At the same time, it also acted inside the religious arena. Many of its exponents—most notably the initiators of the Bern Declaration, but also delegates from the Third World Action Groups—were theologians or religiously-motivated activists; an important target of the emerging movement was the established development aid organizations, as during the Bern Conference in 1970. The transformation of the field of development aid did not, however, result in a strong polarization between secular, left-wing organizations and religious development aid NGOs. Instead, it affected all the actors of the field, albeit to different degrees. Religious organizations started to slightly change their understanding of development politics, while being aware of the fact that an important part of their traditional audience did not subscribe to the Marxist theories of Third World emancipation advocated by youth activists.

The rise of the Bern Declaration was part of this movement of reconfiguration. The organization was an expression of a new vision of development politics, and would rapidly become its most important mouthpiece. The BD represented this characteristic mix of Christianity and newly radicalized left-wing politics. While it started as an initiative of progressive Protestants, the first task of the administrator, Anne-Marie Holenstein, was to recruit Catholics. However, the influence of the Third World Action Groups and the domestic political agenda rapidly pushed the organization to take political positions on the left. The rapprochement with development organizations from the left—those united in the Safep—most clearly crystallized when Rudolf Strahm, one of the founders of the Bern Third World Action Group, was hired to become one of the BD's political secretaries. The evolution of secularization can also be seen in the BD's members. A members' survey observed that the Christian component progressively diminished towards the end of the 1970s (Passy 1998). Of course, this does not mean that the religiously-oriented adherents had left the organization, but it does point to a changing strategy and positioning of the organization itself, leading to the use of different recruitment networks which were more within the secular than the religious left.

The first political actions of the emerging BD reflected this positioning and the tensions provoked by it. In addition to supporting the initiative against weapon exports, the BD tried to involve local political institutions and civil society groups in development aid. It also supported a public campaign, orchestrated by leftist and anti-capitalist groups, against the participation of a Swiss firm in a dam construction in Mozambique. Reactions to this were revealing. Newspapers and conservative subscribers to the appeal criticized the way economic issues were thus politicized (Holenstein et al. 2009, p. 50). But this commitment towards a political approach to development politics was already part of the initial call for signatories. The declaration is a critical analysis of traditional development aid and called for a more political approach as an alternative. The BD was created to launch political actions inside Switzerland in order to change development aid (Holenstein et al. 2009). Its mandate was to fill a role that had not been assumed by the existing development aid organizations: mobilizing public opinion, carrying out consciousness-raising to show the links between economic prosperity in the developed countries and poverty in the global South, and lobbying political and economic decision makers. But, as early activists recount it, the media and many of the signatories often did not acknowledge this political orientation and instead emphasized the financial commitment of the signatories, thus presenting it as a form of charity. One of the big issues in the first years of the organization was to find ways to explicitly stress those *political* claims. Consumer actions came to play an important role in this.

The First 'Consumption Campaigns': No Claims, No Targets

In a workshop in November 1974, the newly reinforced team of the BD came together to outline ideas for future actions. Of the five options that were raised,[2] three concerned issues of consumption: an action promoting coffee from Tanzania, a campaign about the reduction of meat consumption, and the support of the banana-actions, which had already been initiated by a women's group in Frauenfeld who came to be known as the *Bananenfrauen* (banana-women). The banana-women, originating from a small women's discussion group that met regularly at a parish in a town of Eastern Switzerland, had launched a 'banana action day' with the goal of raising consumer awareness of the issue of production conditions in banana plantations after having seen a documentary on it. They were scandalized by the low price of bananas and collected signatures from consumers declaring their willingness to pay a higher price in order to contribute to improving labor standards. Initially limited to one local setting, similar groups quickly formed in many other Swiss towns. These were often the first steps to the founding of fair trade shops (Brunner 1999).

The BD actively supported the Bananenfrauens' actions, and the consumer campaigns it launched in this period shared many features with them. The first was the importation of coffee from Tanzania. For critics of traditional development politics, Tanzania had become a model of successful autonomous (i.e. not dependent) development. In the sixties and early seventies, Tanzania's President Nyerere pursued the so-called *Ujamaa* doctrine, a model of economic and social development that fostered self-reliance. In Switzerland, the third world action group in Bern had started to import Tanzanian coffee in 1973. When Rudolf Strahm went from heading this group to being the new BD political secretary, he further pursued and developed this action. Activists would sell the *Ujamaa* coffee in public squares and markets. A fifty-page document for activist instruction was produced for this occasion, containing precise descriptions of the trade relationships between the developed and developing world, addressing the problems of monocultures in development countries and the power of multinational companies. Examples and illustrations contrasted conventional views of development—based, in the eyes of its critics, on exploitation and charity—with an emancipatory view based on autonomy and fairer terms of trade.[3]

---

2   Minutes of workshop, Archives of the Bern Declaration, Ar 430.10.2, Sozialarchiv Zürich

3   Booklet of *Ujamaa* campaign, Archives of the Bern Declaration, 430.27.1, Sozialarchiv Zürich

The instructions given to activists show that in this campaign, the selling of the coffee was mostly used as a pretense (Kuhn 2005a) that actually served two other, more important goals: a) offering movement sympathizers a concrete opportunity to act—by selling coffee at stands, and b) raising awareness of the problems and the implications of the politics of development, both among those who sold the coffee and those who bought it. It was through such concrete actions that people became conscious of such issues. The success of this first 'consumer campaign' carried out by the BD encouraged the organization to launch other, similar actions. In a suggestion questionnaire sent to local action groups, the idea of a campaign with bags made of jute came out as the most popular.[4] The principle was the same: a commodity was used to raise awareness for development issues. The bags were produced by a women's cooperation in Bangladesh. Their symbolic meaning went beyond the mere question of development. The German slogan of the campaign said 'Jute instead of plastic,' stressing an environmental aspect. Moreover, through the use of a reusable shopping bag, the campaign was also able to criticize the throwaway mentality of consumer society. It thus condensed the three main sources of consumer society's criticism into one small object. The selling of the bags was once again embedded into an important information campaign, based on the premise that the goal was not to sell as many bags as possible, but to diffuse as much information and raise as much awareness as possible. Nobody should have been able to buy a jute bag without having been properly instructed on the problems of development. However, it was the success of the sale in terms of numbers that overwhelmed the organizers: the first 40,000 bags were sold (at a price of 2 Swiss Francs) in a very short time, and a year later 80,000 more bags were ordered.

The reduction of meat consumption (referred to as 'meat abdication') was the focus of the BD's third consumer campaign during the mid-1970s. Building on a theory that had become popular among third world activists in the Western world,[5] the campaigners claimed that meat consumption was responsible for hunger in developing countries. In order to produce meat for Western consumers, a tremendous amount of crops is necessary—crops coming mostly from the South. The so-called food pyramid symbolizes the way "the cattle of the rich eats the poor's crop" (Rudolf Strahm). This campaign also wanted people to reflect on their consumption habits, and as with the jute bags and coffee actions, people were given a concrete way to participate. Rather than using products to raise awareness, however, it focused on the reduction of individual meat consumption. Consumers were invited to eat less meat over a period of three months and to commit to it by signing a public declaration. This public demonstration of individual commitments was designed as

---

4   Survey on future actions, Archives of the Bern Declaration, 430.28.1, Sozialarchiv Zürich

5   Defended in particular by Frances Moore Lappé in *Diet for a Small Planet*, first published in 1971 (Ballantine Books), which advocates meatless cooking. A.M. Holenstein would translate a later book co-authored by Moore Lappé (with Joseph Collins), *Food First. Beyond the Myth of Scarcity*, 1977 (German translation 1978).

a way of documenting publicly the change of individual and private practices that would otherwise go largely unnoticed. It functioned thus as a sort of petition, but without having claims or targets: a public commitment to a private act.

The consumer campaign repertoire at this time thus consisted of *information campaigns* using particular goods (coffee, jute bags, meat) as a carrier for messages of development politics. The campaigns had no targets and no specific claims; they aimed for consciousness-raising and reflecting on the politics behind common consumption practices. Certainly, in their analysis of development and underdevelopment, they denounced the functioning of the world trade system. However, out of this general framework, no specific claims against specific actors were raised. Rather than putting pressure on specific companies, citizens and consumers should develop consciousness about development issues, and change was thought to occur through this process.

Knowledge and expertise occupied a central role. Expert knowledge drew on new economic theories of development, in particular dependence theory. The BD's professional activists were part of a transnational *tiersmondiste* network, which encompassed activist groups and scientists, mainly economists, and blurred the lines between academia and social movements. Economists were activists, and activists wrote scientific reports and books. The BD's political secretaries were themselves academics, or became experts in their respective fields of specialization through their interactions in activist networks, and translated and authored books on the subject, like Strahm's '*Überentwicklung—Unterentwicklung*' (Over-development—Underdevelopment) (1975). But knowledge was not only used to legitimize actions and advocate an alternative path to development, it was also seen as empowering. Transmitting knowledge about global interconnectedness to citizens, thereby building up awareness for development issues, was seen as a transforming force. The underlying ideology came from the critical pedagogy of Paolo Freire, whose book *Pedagogy of the Oppressed* (2000 [1968]) stressed the role of popular education for social change and was very influential in the Christian-based third world movement.

The Political Nature of Alternative Lifestyles

The broader national and international political context and the conditions at the establishment of the Bern Declaration shed some light on why such non-confrontational tactics were particularly appealing to the organization. The cold war dictated the political front lines during this era. Critical voices against economic actors and Swiss economic interests were usually countered by accusations of treason and hidden communist agendas (Kuhn 2005b). Such accusations accompanied the Bern Declaration from its very creation. Given its origins, the organization could not just dismiss them as irrelevant, or even use them for their potentially mobilizing effect. An important component of its members and sympathizers actually had rather conservative views (Wicki 1984, Kuhn 2005b). Taking political positions on the left, in this context, was always controversially discussed; consumer campaigns could be interpreted as a way of making public actions while avoiding explicitly challenging political and economic interests (see Kuhn 2005b). Undoubtedly this specific context, along with the BD's at least initially quite delicate positioning as an advocacy organization with distinctly religious origins, shaped the organization's tactical repertoire.

The use of the private sphere of consumption for political campaigns could thus be interpreted as a way of avoiding politics. But such an interpretation fails to account for the genuinely political meaning that was attributed to the changing of individual behavior at this time. The actions also need to be put into the context of *everything is political,* which characterized much of social movement activity in the 1970s. Not only everyday products such as coffee or bananas were redefined in political terms in this decade; many more social practices were part of this re-interpretation. Relationships and sexuality, housing and energy went through similar processes. In the heydays of the counter-culture, referred to as 'alternative lifestyles' in the Swiss (German) discourse, nearly every aspect of everyday life was affected by this. As in many other countries, a catalog listed information on the different aspects of alternative lifestyles.[6] The *Alternativkatalog*, published in three volumes between 1975 and 1978, contained a great variety of information on various topics, from do-it-yourself tips for the construction of environmentally friendly toilets, to information on free-range eggs, from alternative medicine to development issues. Emerging alternative market structures such as the so-called 'Lädelilade,' the 'shoppy-shop,' allowed people to produce autonomously and exchange products with others, thus escaping the confining corset of industrial work and capitalist production.

The consumer campaigns of the BD both contributed to the creation of this alternative lifestyle and built on its broad ideological premise that individual changes in everyday behavior were the key to social change. By buying *Ujamaa* coffee and labeled bananas, eating less meat, or using jute instead of plastic, everyday practices were questioned and put into a novel, political context. The books published by the organization or written by its members explained the connection between 'over-consumption' and scarcity, a situation that had to be addressed through changing consumption practices in affluent Western countries. A look at the BD's publications from this time reveals that it further developed this strand of action with courses on the topic of 'shopping—cooking—eating,' organized for teachers of housekeeping classes, still an essential part of girls' school curricula at that time. Recipes and tips for 'how to shop better' were developed, and workshops on these questions took place in many women's groups around the country.

Counter-cultural actions have been interpreted in different ways in social movement theory. Some scholars dismiss them as 'pseudo-participation' which is ultimately detrimental to movements (Donati 1989), or simply ignore them and

---

6   It was modeled on the Whole Earth Catalog, published for the first time in 1968 in the US. See Turner (2006).

only consider contentious protest events targeting states. Another interpretation acknowledges the important role of 'prefigurative spaces' (Polletta 1999) or oppositional subcultures (Johnston and Mueller 2001), "that carve out islands of freedom and resistance in the dominant society and from which social movements emerge." (Johnston 2009, p. 9) Such counter-cultural spaces both foster the establishment of collective identities and nourish and enable oppositional action. A final interpretation goes even further and insists on the political nature of changes in individual behavior and identities themselves. For Melucci, the 'challenging of codes' is the crucial way through which movements change society (Melucci 1989, 1996). He acknowledges the role of 'latent' forms of movement action, as opposed to the visible actions of confrontation with authorities such as demonstrations that are more commonly studied. Latency "allows people to experience directly new cultural models—changes in the system of meanings—which are very often opposed to the dominant social codes: (…) (it) creates new cultural codes and makes individuals practice them." (Melucci 1985, p. 800). Latency allows visibility because it feeds it with 'solidarity resources' and a cultural framework for action. But it goes beyond this role of creating collective identities: latency includes experimenting with new cultural codes, and thus the development of alternative lifestyles which have a crucial value for change *on their own*. We should analyze them not as a mere prerequisite for the 'real' contentious actions, but as constitutive parts of social movement repertoires (see also Whittier 2009).

Competing interpretations by movement scholars reflect the contested nature of such practices within movements themselves. This is certainly the case of the BD in the 1970s, where the political meaning and effects of counter-cultural tactics was contested and provoked intense debates. Internal documents and publications by core activists reveal a constant discussion around the status of consumer actions and its pitfalls. The dangers and problems these debates point out are the same many scholars have revealed: in particular, the 'depoliticizing' trends towards inward-directed actions of self-fulfillment (François and Neveu 1999, Ollitrault 2008, Donati 1989), and commodification (Frank 1997, Dubuisson-Quellier 2013a, Boltanski and Chiapello 1999, Holt 2002).

The problem of drifting towards exclusively inward-directed actions, for example, was encountered at the occasion of the meat abdication campaign, which, according to A.-M. Holenstein, appealed to people who thought that the world could be saved with personal asceticism and conversion (Holenstein et al. 2009). In 1976, the journal *Schritte ins Offene*, edited by the Evangelic and Catholic women's associations, asked A.M. Holenstein to edit a volume on the issue of alternative lifestyles. In her editorial, she quickly marked her distance with an interpretation of the counter-culture as aiming for pure self-fulfillment, by positioning it as a political issue. Against the image of the dropout and the "utopia of the selfs," she says that humans are addressed as part of a "community of destiny" on planet earth. "New lifestyle, in this context, does not mean escape or redemption for individuals, but is a process of liberation, which embraces our civilization, our relation towards property, limited resources, animals and plants, mostly however towards man himself' (Holenstein 1976). The contributions in the volume repeatedly insist on the political nature of new lifestyles, and present them as part of a collective struggle in a larger process of social transformations.

Like pure self-fulfillment, commodification was also perceived as a possible danger, albeit less directly. In a second volume of *Schritte ins Offene* edited by Holenstein in 1978, a member of the BD's executive committee gives a very critical account of the state of the counter-culture. His critical appraisal focuses on the fact that this new lifestyle was becoming commercialized, and thus losing its ability to change social life. Third World shops, organic shops, and even offers in commercial grocery stores, are taken as evidence for the increased commercial stance of the movement. The economic mechanisms, he states, are stronger than the ideas and experiments of individual groups (Braunschweig 1978). However, the appraisal of this evolution is ambiguous. In the same issue, Holenstein highlights the progress made since the publication of the 1976 volume on alternative lifestyles: the institutionalization of certain practices through commercial—albeit alternative—forms (like third world shops) or public policies (recycling by the city of Zurich) are seen as positive achievements of the movement. Market solutions to problems addressed by the BD are not unanimously dismissed as co-optation. On the contrary; sometimes, market changes were precisely what the organization wanted to achieve through its consumer actions.

Contentious Consumer Campaigns

Towards the end of the seventies, the debates around counter-cultural actions and their potential pitfalls forced the BD to rethink its strategy. The potential of consumption campaigns merely aiming at consciousness-raising was questioned. We find frequent expressions of such concerns in internal communication documents at the end of the 1970s. For example, the minutes of a meeting of the French-speaking committees (September 28/29 1979) clearly echoed the criticism of a trend to self-fulfillment:

> We need to touch people at a personal level, in their everyday lives. But beware of individual feelings of guilt, this is useless. Pay attention also not to fall into an ecological morality. It is important to reach individual actions, to be as consequent as possible, but it is even more important to look for collective solutions. It is in this desire to touch people personally, in their concrete lives, that one risks falling into escape routes as those of the ecologists or the consumers. Our project is political, we want political change. We need to be pushing for this sort of approach.[7]

---

7   Minutes from meeting of French committee, September 28–29, 1979, Archives Berne Declaration, Ar 430.30.6, Sozialarchiv Zürich (my translation)

The exact outlook of such an approach was the subject of an internal discussion paper preparing a new campaign on the 'hunger question' dating from July 1979. This paper also raised concerns against the use of tactics limited to awareness-raising and the changing of individual practices: "The action mustn't confine itself to political information and awareness-raising, but should be a political action which directly fights the origins of hunger." Such a political action can no longer "build upon the hope to 'convert the powerful' by convincing them through discussions and conferences," but "must seek the political confrontation and stand it through." This needs to be complemented by "support of the efforts of [the multinational's] enemies in the developing countries (unions, peasant organizations)," and the action should not limit itself to criticizing extant conditions, "but should show up alternatives and allow the participants to contribute to their realization. It should anticipate part of the new order."[8] In other words, the idea expressed here is one of an action that both clearly seeks confrontation with power holders, and shows up an alternative order through prefigurative tactics to which participants can contribute.

The BD had already had some (mixed) experience with more contentious campaigns against corporations. Of particular importance was the campaign against Nestlé's infant formula. This British in origin campaign was taken up in Switzerland by the Third World Action Group from Bern, which translated the brochure *The Baby Killer* into German and focused action on the Swiss multinational food corporation Nestlé. The company reacted by suing the group (as well as the editors of a student newspaper that had published an article on it) for libel. But this move turned out to be a strategic error, for it was the following court trial that allowed the issue to be publicized, which attracted the attention of the international media. The Third World Action Group had refused a settlement with Nestlé in order to lead a 'political court case' (Kalt 2010). They lost the case, but were widely perceived as the moral winners. This action thus demonstrated the potential benefits—but also the difficulties and dangers—of targeting corporations directly. The Bern Declaration was not directly part of this controversy, but it supported the accused authors/translators of the book, widely diffused information on the case, and published the French and Italian translations of the booklet (Kalt 2010). In addition, through R. Strahm, one of the defendants, there was a personal link between the Nestlé trial and the BD.

It is likely that this experience influenced the way the BD went about targeting corporations directly; confrontational tactics were always used very prudently, compared to the very strong accusation of a slogan like 'Nestlé kills babies.' The campaign 'Hunger is a Scandal' was launched in 1981. It was the result of a growing engagement of the BD in a transnational network focused on the global food system, which condemned the role of the global agricultural industry and had culminated in the organization of a counter-summit at the occasion of the

---

8   Internal discussion paper, German-speaking secretariat, July 3 1979, Archives Berne Declaration, Ar 430.30.6, Sozialarchiv Zürich (my translation)

FAO's 'World Conference on Agrarian Reform and Rural Development' in Rome in 1979. The campaign had a very broad focus: the consequences of the agricultural industry and Western lifestyles on developing countries. Particular products were chosen to illustrate the problematic consequences of global agriculture. The first one was pineapples from Del Monte and Dole, sold in the big Swiss retailer chains Coop and Migros. The BD had contacts with a NGO working on this issue in the Philippines, and canned pineapples stood for many of the problems the campaign wanted to fight: monocultures owned by multinational firms; dismal working conditions; and exotic, processed and somehow 'artificial' foodstuffs instead of natural and local products.[9]

Following a new strategic outlook, the campaign brought together confrontational action forms with others aiming at changing consumption practices. A petition addressing retailers asked consumers to sign for two things: firstly demanding that retailers reveal information on the social, environmental and health-related properties of their products, and to withdraw products that do not correspond to basic standards. And secondly, consumers could sign a statement addressed to retailers selling Del Monte and Dole pineapples. Speaking with the voice of a concerned consumer, the petition said: "I've learned that Del Monte and Dole pineapples are produced under unjust conditions in the Philippines. If the retailers do not take our demands seriously, I'm ready to support a boycott."

The use of the boycott as the ultimate weapon of consumption campaigns is very instructive. The words of the petition were chosen carefully: not a call for boycott, just the threat of one. In preparing the campaign, the issue of a boycott had been controversial, with people concerned about its legitimacy and effectiveness. The contact organization in the Philippines had conducted a survey among its members to assess the suitability of a boycott. At the same time, legal advice assessing different proposed action modes discouraged the use of a boycott, although for political than legal reasons (it stressed the difficulty of controlling boycotters).[10] Finally, the way the petition was framed also reveals that the campaigners wanted to make sure that they were strong enough for a boycott to be effective. The petition thus served as a sort of survey for the campaign organizers to see if a call for boycott could actually be successful. This interpretation is confirmed by the information in the campaign's documentation, where it said that "a boycott is a dangerous boomerang if it doesn't have the wished-for broad effect among consumers."[11] In other words, calling for a boycott without any consequences would jeopardize the campaign's position, as it risked delegitimizing it. The campaigners preferred to just brandish a potential threat while starting to negotiate with retailers in order to enhance conditions of production on pineapple plantations. This strategy

---

9   Archives of the Bern Declaration, Ar 430.30.2, Sozialarchiv Zürich

10   These documents can be found in the same archive file as the Hunger is a Scandal campaign, Archives of the Bern Declaration, Ar 430.30.2, Sozialarchiv Zürich

11   Booklet Hunger is a scandal, Archives of the Bern Declaration, Ar 430.30.8, Sozialarchiv Zürich (my translation)

actually paid off. After a first round of negative reactions, the retailer Migros and representatives from Dole agreed to negotiate with campaign-makers, and together with Brot für Brüder, it resulted in one of the first private social clauses for production conditions in the world.

Although this contentious part was an important innovation, it should not hide the fact that the non-confrontational activities actually took up much more space in the campaign's tactical action repertoire. They evolved around the slogan 'buy critically' printed on items such as tablecloths, match boxes, notepads, pins, jute bags, etc. They were sold at public venues, and particular information events were organized in women's groups, church-based groups, and so forth in order to spread awareness and to make consumers change their behavior. The goal was to raise questions regarding many aspects of consumption, recalling the variety of issues covered by the *Alternativkatalog*. This can be exemplified with the '10 rules of thumb for consumers' that were part of the campaign. These were short shopping tips, and they concerned ecology, development, health issues, a critique of the futile values of fashion, and a general critique of consumer society:[12]

Ten rules of thumb

1. Buy products that use less energy
2. Think about the environment while you shop
3. The less processed the product the better
4. Buy seasonal fruit and vegetables
5. The less meat the better
6. The less sugar the better
7. Buy coffee and tea in third world shops
8. More expensive doesn't mean more beautiful
9. Decide for yourself what is fashionable
10. Do I really need this?

The repertoire of consumption campaigns had thus undergone some transformations: the BD now directly targeted corporations and used consumer power to put pressure on them. However, raising awareness among consumers and changing their consumption habits was still a central goal of such campaigns and concerned all aspects of consumption. Raising the awareness of consumers for the global consequences of their shopping habits and changing their consumption behavior was still a privileged path to fight for environmental and social goals.

---

12   Booklet Hunger is a scandal, Archives of the Bern Declaration, Ar 430.30.8, Sozialarchiv Zürich (my translation).

Why Consumer Campaigns Were So Attractive

What explains why particular tactical action repertoires get adopted? A rapid analysis could conclude that through the rising development theories of dependency, which draw a straight line between underdevelopment in the peripheral parts of the world and 'over-development' at its center, the construction of a link to consumption is evident. In this cultural framework, changing patterns of over-development by questioning consumption in the global North seems like a natural way to act. This affinity between the dominant theory and the action mode is certainly striking, but it misrepresents the relationship between the cultural work of framing—or the construction of grievances—and movement tactics. The general theory of dependency to which the BD subscribed does not contain a blueprint for political action but must be translated into particular tactics, and such a translation can give very different results. The same 'problem' can be raised in different terms and different ways, even within the particular perspective of dependency theory. The role consumers can, should or should not play in changing patterns of development is a contested one, as shown in the discussion of how consumer campaigns work. The campaign's leaders, when talking about tactics, when writing the documentation for the campaign or when publishing books on the issue of development, contribute to the establishing of the contours of the role of consumers and consumption.

For the BD, consumer campaigns became a very attractive possibility for at least two different reasons linked to processes of distinction within the field of development politics. Firstly, it could help foster the organization's standing as a group pertaining to the 'third world movement'[13] but without conducting aid projects. Since its beginnings, the organization had been struggling to find an arena for its actions. If it was to maintain itself, it needed to figure out other ways of existing than the collecting of signatures for its call. But what could these other ways be? The organization had a hard time distinguishing itself from a charity. At the same time, in the cold war context, explicitly political actions and positions were very much criticized by some of its most fervent supporters (Kuhn 2005b). In addition, such actions were mostly driven by actors on the left of the BD, which made them less attractive to more conservative and/or religious supporters. In this context, targeting consumers and consumption allowed the organization to differentiate itself from other actors and open up its own area of activism, by discovering consumption as a new action field. Just as certain marginally-positioned actors in the fields of unionism or agricultural organizations in 1990's France started to 'occupy' the international realm (Bruneau 2004), and became

---

13   Speaking of the 'third world movement' is using the term movement actors use to refer to themselves. In most studies on the Swiss "new social movements," the third world movement is put into the category of the "solidarity movement" (Giugni and Passy 1999, Kriesi et al. 1995, Passy 1998, 2001) which consists of four main branches: development aid, human rights, asylum and immigration, and antiracism.

actors in the forefront of the global justice movement, the BD in the mid-1970s, by investing in the realm of consumption, found a way of positioning itself and popularizing its demands, and ended up being 'specialized' in consumer campaigns. The social movement field is thus crucial, and processes of specialization and distinction from other movement actors can explain the adoption of the specific tactical action repertoire.

Consumer campaigns had another advantage. They could link distant issues (Rucht 2000) in the developing world to everyday practices in the West and give people concrete perspectives of action. Scholars of action repertoires have long shown that tactics serve important movement-internal goals, in particular activating grassroots support and giving supporters something to do (Rochon 1998). To mobilize support, SMOs propose actions to their supporters (Lahusen 1996). Petitions, for instance, are often used 'for mobilization's sake': the collecting of signatures is often pursued over a long time because it allows petition entrepreneurs to mobilize members and sympathizers (Contamin 2001). Tactics thus respond to a vital condition of activist organizations: the keeping up of a certain rhythm of mobilizing actions, able to procure for activists the gratification they expect from their devotion (Gaxie 1977). Consumer campaigns for the BD fulfilled precisely this requirement. They are a way of offering concrete action perspectives to those who have joined the organization during the collection of signatures, or who sympathize with its positions. That there was such a demand for structured actions can be seen in a small study the BD's executive committee conducted in 1974, based on discussions with members of different affiliated local groups. In the report, the author enumerates a number of problems that were expressed in these interviews: the small size of the groups, the lack of gratification, the fear of autonomous actions. Launching coordinated campaigns came to be seen as a solution to these problems, by providing an action blueprint that local groups could apply.[14]

This internal dimension of the tactic was an important part of its attractiveness for the organization. But of course, consumer actions were not only about mobilization for mobilization's sake. They served both instrumental and mobilization goals. Through participation in campaigns, the abstract stake of awareness-raising could be linked to concrete issues, and thus favored the intended educational process and, ultimately, the achievement of the goals of the movement. Mobilization for action and mobilization for consensus (Klandermans 1984, 1997) went together: people became familiar with issues and learnt what they were about through the very action of participating in the campaign.

---

14   Study conducted on regional groups, Archives of the Bern Declaration, Ar 430.20.1, Sozialarchiv Zürich.

An Action Form in Conformity with its Public

While the emphasis on field dynamics and organizational needs offers an historical account of the rise of the repertoire of consumption campaigns, they also seem to be in perfect conformity with the social characteristics of the organization's members. If campaigns need to propose concrete ways of action in order to mobilize individual support, the forms these actions take must also correspond to the people who are supposed to perform them. Not every form of action is thinkable. People choose performances that correspond to their social and cultural properties, or, to put it the other way round, tactics need to be seen as legitimate, appropriate, and appealing to the audience they are intended to mobilize.

When looking at it from this angle, activism seems a delicate affair for the members and sympathizers of the Bern Declaration. The legitimacy of being an activist—of making public actions, of acting out for a cause—did not come naturally to the organization's members. The numerous traces found in the archives of the challenge—if not the fear—of becoming an activist attest to this. In the aforementioned small survey conducted among some local groups, one of the highlighted problems was the volunteers' "fear of autonomous action." Later, the BD would develop the concept of 'Mutspritzenkurse': courses aiming at encouraging its participants to become activists (literally, Mutspritze means 'injection of courage'). In a document discussing the follow-up to the first round of the Hunger is a Scandal campaign, the encouragement classes were described as "being designed to encourage (participants) to pass on their own information. This threshold from informing oneself to passing on the information to others is high, and needs time."[15]

The quite astonishing centrality of such concerns suggests that the population mobilized by the actions of the BD was not used to organizing meetings, stands, or other actions such as collecting signatures or selling jute bags. What one can read through the measures taken by the organization is that its members were often reluctant to expose themselves publicly, and did not feel competent enough to do it. Activism, even of a very moderate kind, was perceived as a risky business. This points to particular social characteristics shared by members of the BD, which made it difficult for them to become activists. A survey on BD activists in the early 1980s found that they were characterized by a high level of education and rather high-status professional positions in education, health or social services. Their income was disproportionately high; a strong minority of their members had a political identity oriented by their Christian belief, and a considerable minority identified itself with the right-wing parties (Wicki 1984). While they thus expressed the new division within the middle class highlighted by new social movement scholars (Kriesi et al. 1995), what seems to be particular about the BD's members is the importance of religion and a center-left positioning on the left-

---

15   Minutes of the colloquium "Wie weiter," October 23/24, 1981, Archives of the Bern Declaration, Ar 430.20.1, Sozialarchiv Zürich (my translation).

right scale. This could point to the fact that many of these members belonged to social groups in which activist forms of political participation were not common, and even quite illegitimate. A further indication of this is the recruitment bases for the Bern Declaration appeal, which are Protestant and Catholic parishes. One can find in the importance of this 'bourgeois' part of the BD's mobilization base yet another explanation for the adoption and mobilizing success of consumption campaigns: linking political activism to consumption facilitated the mobilization of BD's members because it allowed for different degrees of commitment—from a private commitment to change one's consumption practices to a public commitment to going onto the streets and into shops supporting the campaign, and convincing others.

Yet there is one last important aspect that the survey does not discuss at all and that seems to matter greatly: gender. Many indicators suggest that women played a crucial role in the development of the BD's consumption campaigns. One of the main inspirations for the consumption actions—the *Bananenfrauen*—was a network exclusively composed of women's groups. The 'encouragement injection classes' were directed mainly at women, as were the cooking and shopping courses. Women's groups were very visible in many activities of the consumption campaigns. Thus the consumption campaigns had a distinctively gendered aspect. For middle-class women, they became a way of raising their voices and performing actions of protest. Many studies have pointed to the leading role women played in consumer movements and in political consumerism (Chessel 2004, Cohen 2003, Forno 2006, Forno and Ceccarini 2006, Goul Andersen and Tobiasen 2004, Micheletti 2003, Stolle et al. 2005, Wiedenhoft 2008). Gender analyses of social movements have not only shown that gender differences shape the social division of activist roles and tasks within social movement groups, but also that certain causes, action repertoires and organizational repertoires, are marked by gender (for an overview of gender and activism see Fillieule 2008). Through 'gendered normative expectations' (Fillieule 2008), some causes are assigned to women (for example causes linked to health or social welfare), while others—typically the more valued and institutionalized ones—are assigned to men. The realm of consumption typically constitutes a social arena which is assigned to female gender roles.

A reading of consumer campaigns as the reflection of gendered divisions of social practices or, to put it more crudely, of men's disinterest for this practice, should not lead us to underestimate the empowering nature of such campaigns for many women participating in them. The consumer actions of the BD or the *Bananenfrauen* offered women possibilities to participate and play leading roles in political campaigns. The fact that shopping is considered a female activity opens up an arena for political action where women can exert power and build up activist careers (Micheletti 2003). But the important involvement of women in campaigns focusing on consumption practices at the same time confined them to their traditional gender role as housewives. While traditional family structures favored women's participation in the campaigns, it also epitomized and reinforced those gender roles. Campaign-makers were not unaware of this tension, but because of their political perspective on consumption, they mostly saw consumption campaigns as an emancipatory path for women. In *Schritte ins Offene*, Holenstein (1976) wrote that in the discourse on lifestyle, virtues are demanded "which were asked from the female gender for such a long time that they ended up appearing as the 'female nature': treating things carefully and softly, nursing, enabling the growth of life, caring for the health of the family." She speculated that the traditional isolation of women in the realm of the household and the family might actually be the reason why they found the courage to act. While in this traditionally private arena, many concrete ways of acting towards social and environmental change could be developed (from recycling to buying fair trade and saving energy), the men who were working in corporations as 'small cogs in a big machine' were confronted with much more constraining structures. Thus, alternative lifestyles, through their politicization of everyday lives, actually put women in a privileged position, as they had more autonomy to change their everyday practices than men.

From Fair Trade and Popular Education to Public Campaigning in France

The CCC in France was launched by Artisans du Monde (AdM), the oldest and biggest fair trade organization in France. It operates shops all over the country where it sells fair trade goods—many handicraft products, but also typical fair trade goods like coffee and tea. The shops are managed by volunteers organized in the different local sections of the association. At the national level, those local sections form the Fédération Artisans du monde, equipped with professional staff. In 2005, AdM consisted of almost 150 local groups managing 160 shops, and it had around 60 employees. Historically, the organization goes back to a public appeal by the French priest Abbé Pierre following the humanitarian crisis in Bangladesh in 1971. Committees of twinning between municipalities (called UCOJUCO; union de comités de jumelages coopération) were founded in order to commercialize products from Bangladesh, and third world fair trade shops developed to distribute them. They put into practice the maxim of *trade, not aid*, that is, developing commercial relations with third world countries in order to assist their economic development. The activists running the different local shops coordinated themselves and founded, in 1981, the national federation of AdM (Sommier and Crettiez 2006).

A few political affairs shook up the fair trade movement in its early years: notably, the boycott of South African oranges in order to protest against the apartheid regime, and the assistance to the Chilean left after the Pinochet coup in 1973, provoked a separation between the founders coming from Abbé Pierre's organization of assistance to the homeless *Emmaüs*, and the leaders of UCOJUCO, who pursued a more political approach. From the beginning, the idea of promoting development through trade led to tensions between the more or less politicized approaches, and was composed of actors who supported different political positions. This tension reflects the structure of the broader field which the organizations fighting for the development of the 'third world,' often referred to as the solidarity or *tiersmondiste* movement, are part of. It was characterized by the existence of two ideologically different traditions (Agrikolansky 2005): one tradition was comprised of Marxist and secular actors belonging to a group of anti-imperialists who, mostly in the wake of 1968, but also linked to the decolonization in Northern Africa, were fighting on issues of development and anti-imperialism. The second tradition was composed of Christian—in the French context, mostly Catholic—organizations like the CCFD (Comité catholique contre la faim et pour le développement) who pursued a development agenda. In this respect, AdM's origin actually marked an early merging of the two traditions, since organizations from both ends of the spectrum contributed to it: the Christian left around Abbé Pierre and people belonging to the anti-imperialist cause promoting fair trade. While the split of AdM from the Catholic grouping following the political debates in its early years situated it firmly within the secular and anti-imperialist group, its origin and also action form (fair trade) tended to approximate it with the Christian grouping.

As a form of political action, fair trade can be characterized as pursuing a double aim: on the one hand, it is about economic development in the global South, through paying 'fair' wages to small third world producers and by giving them access to markets in the North (Cary 2005, Diaz Pedregal 2007, Le Velly 2006, 2007, Raynolds et al. 2007, Zaccai 2007). On the other hand, fair trade organizations also seek to raise awareness of, and mobilize their audiences in the global North around, issues of development, and solidarity or what is today called 'global justice' (Clarke et al. 2007a, 2007b, Wilkinson 2007). This aspect of the movement was very important from the beginning of AdM's history. Fair trade was seen as part of a larger movement of consciousness-raising regarding issues of third world inequalities and development. AdM's official publications made this very clear. The articles of the association's bulletin, which informed the local members and volunteers of the movement, can be seen as a way of giving sense to as well as explaining the movement's actions. In a magazine feature (from August 1977) on why the organization had decided to sell handicraft, the strategy of awareness-raising was stated explicitly:

> [T]he chances of getting the public to understand our activist actions are multiplied if we can present them in a non-traditional way. First, this allows us to get in touch with people without imposing a prepared discourse on them. Thanks to the use of concrete goods that directly engage people, it is possible to treat problems like wages in underdeveloped countries, imperialism and racism.

The same article went on to express the hope that the shops could bring customers round to becoming activists themselves.[16] Throughout the articles of

---

16   The above excerpts are from the *Artisans du Monde bulletin*, 10, July and August 1977 (my translation), consulted at the Centre de documentation du tiers monde

the AdM magazine, a strongly political sense was thus given to its actions. Fair trade, it said, was not just about selling goods, it was about fighting imperialism and instituting a 'new international economic order,'[17] and should therefore help to create solidarity between the 'exploited classes' in France and in the Third World. Explicitly, selling third world goods was not about charity, but had to serve a political purpose, and therefore had both an educational and a political goal.

At the same time, the AdM publication addressed a problem the organization was facing: while these political goals may have been obvious for the movement's volunteers and activists, this might not have been the case for the customers in the shops. The publication therefore warned that selling goods contained the risk that some customers might 'misrepresent' the mechanism of action or buy fair trade for charity reasons. The necessity of a willingness to distinguish oneself from a merely charity-driven action is revealing of AdM's particular positioning in the field of the broader solidarity movement; similar to the BD in Switzerland, it wanted to set itself clearly apart from charity organizations. To pursue this strategy and its political and educational goals, AdM used the selling of goods and the direct contact between volunteers or activists and customers. Furthermore, local groups organized awareness-raising actions such as film screenings or discussions in order to inform interested audiences. Overall, its goals—and also to some extent the action forms—thus resembled the early campaigns of the BD. Products were used as a way to raise awareness for development issues, and political meaning was thus given to changing consumption and production practices. However, contrary to the BD, AdM did not mount specific campaigns but concentrated on selling fair trade goods in its shops and raising awareness this way.

The national AdM federation did not conduct any campaigns until the early 1990s. During the two previous decades, it limited itself to giving information about some of the other movements' campaigns, expressing support, and promoting them among its network of volunteers. But judging from the organization's newsletter, even this support of campaigns by other actors was very limited. In the 1980s, one finds almost no trace of such campaigns. Between 1980 and 1988, only two campaigns were mentioned: in 1982, there was an article on the Swiss 'Hunger is a Scandal' campaign, and members could order the Jute bags with the 'buy critically' slogan. And in a short feature in 1985, members could read about the boycotts organized for the 'stop apartheid' campaign. During

---

(CDTM), a documentation center affiliated to AdM and the RITIMO network, Paris, 20 rue Rochechouart.

17   The New International Economic Order (NIEO) was a resolution and an action program voted in during the United Nations' General Assembly in 1974. Advocated by the non-aligned countries in particular, it proclaimed the UN's will to work for the implementation of a new international economic order based on equity, equality, international cooperation and economic aid. It put forward a critique of global injustices and aimed at repairing them by developing the third world countries, and became a major reference for the third world solidarity movement (Rist 2007).

all this time, AdM was busy building up its network of shops and of fair trade producers and products. Rather than engaging in political campaigning, it was developing its 'commercial' infrastructure of import and distribution, in particular by creating an import center. Between the rhetoric found in the late 1970s and the practices of the next decade, one can thus identify a certain gap: although stating that fair trade should not limit itself to the commercial activities of selling products but should also give voice to the interests of third world producers in order to change the international world order, AdM nonetheless devoted itself mostly to its commercial activities.

The Renewed Politics of Development and the Rise of Public Campaigning

This situation changed towards the end of the 1980s. AdM started to propagate more campaigns and then to launch and disseminate its own centrally organized public actions. At the level of the federation, an employee was hired with the explicit goal of developing this strand of activities. The first such campaign, in the early 1990s, was the 'solidarity breakfast,' followed by a campaign on the clothing industry that would then become the French Clean Clothes campaign. These new campaigns differed from the previous efforts of awareness-raising. They deliberately aimed at touching a broader audience than traditional fair trade customers by conceiving actions with greater resonance. While the 'solidarity breakfasts' were mainly a way of promoting fair trade in France, the clothing campaign was explicitly contentious: by targeting well-known firms, they aimed at changing the rules and practices of international trade for economic actors in the mainstream market, not just by developing an alternative niche market. The goal of transforming the rules of international trade was not new for AdM, but the means to do so clearly were. In many ways, the change thus resembled the change in consumer campaigns in the Swiss case: from actions that aimed at consciousness-raising but did not raise claims against specific targets, to contentious claims directly addressed to corporations. How did AdM come to add this advocacy aspect to its line of activities?

Compared to the Swiss case of the BD, the model of consumer campaigns had become part of AdM's repertoire much later. The CCC was the first time this kind of campaign had ever been autonomously created. It had a very different origin from the Swiss consumer campaigns. To understand the adoption of this action repertoire by the French AdM, we must make a detour around other organizations from the field of 'international solidarity,' where this kind of campaign first came up. The AdM campaign built on the model of 'public campaigning,' which had recently become a central piece of the tactical action repertoire of many social movement organizations from the solidarity movement. The origin of this tactical innovation was thus not specific to AdM. Other organizations belonging to the movement of solidarity with the third world had adopted similar tactical changes during this time, and also started mobilizing their constituents through public campaigns.

According to Pascal Erard, initiator and long-time coordinator of the French Clean Clothes campaign, the reasons why AdM decided to organize its own campaign were twofold. On the one hand, it can be linked to the organization's growth over time, and thus its growing resources. But on the other hand, he also places the evolution in a bigger picture, where NGOs see political actions as increasingly important:

> there is a whole part of activities our partners push for: we have to pressure European policies, French policies, and thus we need to raise awareness among citizens to make changes ... Not everything will be resolved through money transfers, there's also a need for NGOs and for political action. There was some sort of a zeitgeist of collective reflection among NGOs of which AdM was part, and this has led the organization to launch itself on this track, too.[18]

In this interview extract, Erard refers to general *zeitgeist* where NGOs rethink their overall strategy and start making *political actions*, advocating for change. Public advocacy campaigns, most of the time with the use of petitions, was the form this change took.

Before the late 1980s, public campaigning was not part of the tactical repertoire of organizations concerned with international solidarity. Big development aid NGOs like Terre des hommes, CCFD, Frères des hommes, and others were mainly involved in development projects in third world countries and, in France, in organizing actions of 'development education.' Traditional instruments of development education included campaigns of consciousness raising by organizing local events for volunteers, developing kits for interventions in schools, in youth groups or in workplaces. While these actions were usually centered on a particular issue (such as a specific country or region, or a topic like access to water), they did not raise particular claims or target authorities, nor did they offer sympathizers specific ways to take action to pursue these goals besides a general form of awareness-raising. Petitions, which would be the main tactic used by public campaigns, did not belong to this repertoire: they "were not common practice," as one long-term activist and former head of the CCFD said in an interview.[19] The conducting of public campaigns using petitions constituted a clear change in form and scope of contentious collective actions for development aid NGOs.

This change took place in the second half of the 1980s. Why does one find tactical innovation at this point in time within development organizations, and why did it take the particular form of 'public campaigning'? The innovation is related to a major reconfiguration within the field of development politics that has its origins in the 1970s: the rise of new competitors challenged the basic terms of development aid and led to the marginalization of development-aid NGOs within the field of international solidarity. The rise of public campaigning was a reaction by

---

18   Interview with P. Erard, Paris, April 2008.
19   Interview with Jean, CCFD, Paris, April 24 2008.

the formerly incumbent organizations to maintain their position in view of the new competitors, and it was greatly facilitated by a newly created organization (Agir Ici), which developed the first public campaigning actions in France.

The late 1970s saw the rise of a new type of actor in French development politics: the 'French doctors,' that is, NGOs specialized in humanitarian interventions in crisis areas. The emergence of this new category shook up the field of development politics (Agrikolansky 2005). Suddenly, Catholic and secular development aid organizations were no longer the only actors who considered themselves advocates of the third world who promoted solidarity with the populations of developing countries. The new humanitarians equally claimed to do this, and with astonishing success challenged the established development aid actors in their own domain of expertise. The French doctors rapidly became central actors in the field, by proposing a new framework based on urgent aid, human rights, and neutrality. Médecins sans frontières was undoubtedly the emblematic organization of this new orientation. It was founded in 1971 by a group of physicians and advocated an approach radically different from both the approaches of the anti-imperialist Marxists and the Christian *tiersmondisme* dominating the field in the 1970s (Siméant and Dauvin 2004). Instead of expressing solidarity with the *wretched of the earth* (Frantz Fanon) and the 'proletarian nations,' or acting on behalf of the poor by engaging in long-term projects of development, the new players advocated an approach of urgent humanitarian aid in moments of crisis, without distinction between the parties in a conflict. In doing so, they challenged the field settlement (Fligstein and McAdam 2012) that had ruled so far. They introduced a new understanding of development aid and openly questioned the ideological partisanship of the incumbent actors. The humanitarians sharply criticized the *tiersmondiste* actors for their partiality. In a 1985 conference discussing the issue of development organized by Liberté sans frontiers, an association founded by some of the new humanitarians, the NGOs that had worked on this issue for more than 30 years and were previously regarded as development experts were not even invited (Pelletier 1996, Rist 2007). The new experts were doctors and no longer left-wing economists; development as seen by the humanitarians was no longer a question of autonomy and emancipation from dependence on the West, but an issue of human rights and democracy. They were thus part of a broader movement that would become dominant in other policy and academic fields of international development politics in the course of the 1980s. Principles based on human rights, democracy and economic liberalization were drawn up, announcing the decline of the influence of left-wing development economics and dependence theory school (Guilhot 2005, Rist 2007).

This had dramatic consequences for the existing actors in the field of development. During the 1980s, humanitarian actors achieved a dominant position in the field. They benefited from their remarkable visibility in the media thanks to spectacular missions such as the chartering of a boat to raise awareness about, and to give medical assistance to, boat people from Vietnam in 1979. Their leaders were charismatic personalities who sought out the media spotlight and quickly became well-known public figures, for example Bernard Kouchner,[20] which made them threatening competitors for the traditional actors of the field in terms of donations and recruitment, as well as of public image. The long-time *tiers-mondistes* and anti-imperialists looked somehow old-fashioned compared to the dynamic and effective French doctors.

The humanitarians' critique hit especially hard since the traditional actors of the field were confronted with other difficulties at the same time. The first left-wing government of 1981 inaugurated an era of general demobilization on the left (Sommier 2001), and the Catholic organizations were criticized from the right, too. The CCFD in particular was accused by the right-wing press of being an ally of the Marxists (Agrikoliansky 2005, p. 66), a situation that potentially affected the revenues of this Catholic organization. Thus, established development aid actors found themselves marginalized in the field they used to dominate. At the same time the two opposing poles from the seventies, anti-imperialists and religious organizations, were coming together to counter the rising humanitarian actors. This reconfiguration favored new coalitions and resulted in the creation of a new category, called 'international solidarity,' which encompassed both Catholic and Marxist actors.

The established actors also experimented with new action forms to respond to this new competition. Agrikoliansky (2005) has argued that the first anti-summit mobilization in France against the G7 in Paris held in 1988, was precisely one such common reaction. The adoption of public campaigning as a new action form was linked to this field reconfiguration, too. Organizations pursuing traditional development aid started drawing up petitions advocating specific issues linked to development politics, thereby putting pressure on the European and French political arena in the name of developing countries. In other words, during this time the development aid NGOs became more political and started to make explicit political claims instead of carrying out 'just' awareness raising actions. While public campaigning was a way of making claims in the public realm, it was *also* a (joint) strategy that the international solidarity organizations used in their field-internal competition. Petitions and other public actions were not only aimed at their explicit targets, but were also intended as a move in the field struggles to counter the rising power of humanitarians. It allowed the incumbent, formerly dominating development aid actors to become more visible and thus to respond to their humanitarian competitors, who were very present in the media. It also gave them a new means to stand their ground in the increasingly tough competition for donors' contributions and recruitment.

However, for some of these organizations, which depended heavily on church-based constituents, this also came with significant risks. Indeed, public

---

20   Who would go on to have a long-standing political career, in particular serving in different governments as State Secretary for Humanitarian Interventions, Minister of Health and Minister of Foreign Affairs.

campaigning involved taking stances on political issues, making claims and denouncing political institutions, corporations, and their practices. While this new tactical action repertoire had advantages in terms of public visibility of the organizations, and promised help in reaching new audiences, it also came at the cost of public exposure and of a potentially critical reception by the traditional constituents of the organizations. Structurally, the religious international solidarity organizations were rather reticent about the innovation. A newly-founded movement organization, Agir Ici, facilitated the adoption of public campaigning in this context. Agir Ici was created following a call for signatures (directly inspired by the call of the Bern Declaration) spread through the communication channels of the solidarity movement. Launched in 1988, the appeal had rallied 1,200 signatures of individuals and organizations by the end of the year. Agir Ici would position itself as a sort of professional campaigner (again very close to the original idea of the Bern Declaration), and thus introduced public campaigning, or advocacy campaigns (*campagnes de plaidoyer*), as they came to be called in France. The first such campaign, officially supported and disseminated by many NGOs, was launched in 1988 on the export of toxic waste to Africa. The nascent organization initially approached several NGOs but for different reasons, their leaders were very skeptical about the idea of launching public advocacy campaigns (Agir Ici 1994). They feared the reaction of their constituencies who, they supposed, did not want to launch political campaigns that made them take explicit positions on political issues. But the action model proposed by Agir Ici helped overcome this inertia because it allowed even organizations whose leaders were skeptical to experiment with the form, without fully embracing it from the start.

Agir Ici's action model was the following: to create campaigns, the activists at Agir Ici took up issues linked to questions of development, did research to gather information on it, and built up a body of arguments and a series of demands accompanied by a petition addressed to specific targets. Depending on the subject, targets could be the state, specific ministries, or corporations. This 'campaign kit' was then offered to the different organizations that were signatories of the call, who could decide to support the campaign (and buy the campaign material) and disseminate it among their networks of activists. This functioning had advantages for both sides: Agir Ici could benefit from the networks of the other organizations for mobilization and at the same time, by selling the campaign material, had a substantial source of income. For organizations like the CCFD or other development NGOs, this was a way of doing campaign work without launching their own campaigns; it gave them the possibility to experiment with a new action form and to test how their volunteers reacted to it. In its first five years of existence, Agir Ici launched 25 such campaigns. Public campaigning became a very prominent action form with development NGOs, and brought about a renewed politics of development in France. Inside the CCFD, for instance, the function of network animator—that is, the person responsible for the coordination of the numerous local volunteer groups—increasingly turned into a position of campaign coordination, which eventually became its official title.[21] Most of the campaigns were not developed by the CCFD, but by other groups, or organizations. In an interview, one of the former campaign coordinators said that there were times when the CCFD actively supported 27 campaigns in parallel.[22] It is clear that under these circumstances, not all campaigns received equal attention throughout the network; often, supporting a campaign merely meant diffusing campaign material among members, without taking any concrete action. But during this time campaigning clearly became a central component of the actions of development aid NGOs.

The founders of Agir Ici were in their late twenties and thus did not belong to the generation of *tiers-mondistes* in the traditional NGOs. As often happens, innovation was less an invention than an import and adaptation of action forms from a different context—in this case, from foreign models such as the BD, and the Dutch or Anglo-Saxon NGO campaigns. Before starting their organization and launching the first campaigns, the founders of Agir Ici studied how public campaigning worked in other places. They made trips to countries where professional 'third world lobbies,' as they were sometimes called in the French context, had existed for a long time. They traveled to the US, Canada, the UK, Belgium and Switzerland, to see what those advocacy organizations did and to figure out how they could import strategies and action repertoires in order to create a similar movement constituting a *contre-pouvoir* of NGOs in France (Agir Ici 1994).[23] Many of the connections AdM built upon had already existed beforehand, and diffusing campaigns among international solidarity organizations was not completely new. We have seen, for instance, that AdM disseminated different 'transnational' campaigns during its first years of existence. But Agir Ici went further and explicitly attempted to import, i.e. recreate on its own, public campaigns in France, rather than just report on existing transnational or foreign campaigns. On the other hand, Agir Ici also from its beginning connected the different organizations from the sector of international solidarity, both secular and religious organizations. Its creation, through a call for signatories, made it institutionally an actor linked to many organizations contributing to its financing. And through the way the campaigns worked—disseminated by a network of organizations—it spread tactical innovation through the whole sector.

It was through this organization that public campaigning became an available option; they brought the action form into the international solidarity field and conceived ready-made campaigns with petitions and tools for their dissemination. The crisis of development aid organizations, provoked by the rise of humanitarians, explains why the organizations were 'receptive' to the tactical innovation. And importantly, the organizational configuration with Agir Ici as the main campaigner, and the participating NGOs as mere 'helping hands,' facilitated its adoption. AdM,

---

21   Interview with Jean-Claude, CCFD, Paris, April 2008
22   Interview with Jean-Claude, CCFD, Paris, April 2008
23   This book is a reprint of a conference held by Agir Ici where two of its founding members discuss the organization's origin and its activities.

as part of the international solidarity field, became involved in this new kind of campaign. The campaigns it launched built on the new action form of public campaigning that had renewed development politics in France.

Field Dynamics and the Rise of New Action Repertoires

Drawing the genealogy of a movement or a campaign means tracing it back to its origins and making visible where organizations, tactics and claims come from. Starting from the organizations behind the launch of the national Clean Clothes Campaigns, one can uncover the long-term developments that constitute the basis on which the CCCs built. New repertoires emerged in long-term developments going back to the rise of new social movement actors in the 1970s. Actors like the BD or AdM linked consumption issues with the politics of development, thus finding new ways to raise awareness and mobilize citizens. In both cases, interactions within strategic action fields proved crucial to explain the rise of tactical innovations. A relational perspective that is attentive to the strategic interactions between movement actors belonging to the same movement families can thus help better understand the underpinnings of tactical innovations. New repertoires rose either as inventions by skilled new challengers who wanted to put themselves apart from the strategies used by incumbent organizations, or as reactions by incumbents to new challengers.

The Swiss BD used consumer campaigns in order to distinguish itself from traditional approaches of development politics and to mobilize a public characterized by a strong presence of religiously motivated activists. Over time, campaigns 'merely' aiming at awareness-raising evolved into campaigns raising specific claims against corporate targets. The French AdM used fair trade to raise awareness of development issues, but for a long time did not develop campaigns on its own. Instead, the tactical innovation of public campaigning was the result of the rise of new challengers within the field of development politics, the humanitarians. All incumbent actors in this field were challenged by this new approach, and new public action forms were a way of responding to this field-internal competition and threat. The introduction of public campaigning into the tactical action repertoire of organizations fighting for international solidarity would constitute a basis on which AdM could draw in the campaigns it started to conceive in the early 1990s. Comparatively, the launch of the same campaigns in two different countries was thus rooted in distinct developments in terms of tactical innovation. While in the Swiss case, the CCC was firmly incorporated into a long history of consumer campaigns, it drew on the repertoire of public campaigning in France, a repertoire which a priori had nothing to do with consumer mobilization. But the organization behind the launch of the French CCC—AdM—had been using the market for its political action since the beginning. In launching the anti-sweatshop campaign, it brought together its focus on fair global markets with the tactical innovation of public campaigning.

Chapter 3
Launching a Campaign

Public campaigning and consumption campaigns can be used to fight for many different issues, targeting any industry sector. Why make a campaign against sweatshops in the global garment industry? What explains the timing and coalition-building success of the launch of such campaigns in Switzerland and France? The tactical innovations from the seventies and eighties set the basis on which specific campaigns could build. This chapter deals with the more immediate and short-term factors that account for the launch of anti-sweatshop campaigns in both countries. It identifies the specific national and transnational opportunities and failed options, as well as the strategic adaptations that led to the rise of the Clean Clothes Campaign in Switzerland and France.

Global Supply Chains and Anti-sweatshop Campaigns

Many accounts of the rise of anti-corporate campaigns in general and anti-sweatshop movements in particular see the increasing globalization of supply chains as their main cause. Mobilizing Western consumers to fight against the exploitation of workers in production countries, anti-sweatshop movements are a reaction to the issues provoked by the off-shoring of apparel production to low-wage countries. The movements themselves put forward this explanation when they say why they target the clothing industry. A telling example can be found in a document from the French campaign's internal archives, where Artisans du monde presents its campaign project to its local chapters. The document put forward that clothing production was one of the most economically significant industrial sectors in the developing world; it stressed the numerous violations of human rights and the damaging environmental consequences of production; and it affirmed that companies, although officially condemning such practices, often benefit from them by subcontracting out to decrease their costs.[1] In other words, the globalization of supply chains creates large-scale social and environmental grievances for which Western companies are responsible; campaigns are a means to address such problems.

But this type of explanation based on the structural transformation of clothing production can hardly account for the launching of a campaign at this particular time in history. The globalization of supply chains did not start in the 1990s: it had

---

1   The other justifications pointed at AdM's offer of ethical clothes and at the appeal of such a campaign to a young audience. Undated document, internal campaign archives

already been going on for quite some time. In this respect, it is revealing that the textile branch of the labor union CFDT, which was to become a coalition partner in the French Clean Clothes campaign, had already published a book in 1978 about the phenomenon of increasingly globalized production in the textile industry (and the need to keep the industry located in France).[2] In Switzerland, the BD had published a report on clothing and fashion in 1986, addressing the issues of off-shoring and labor conditions in the developing world. Global supply chains were thus not only a reality ten or fifteen years prior to the emergence of the campaigns, but were already *perceived as a problem* at that time. It does not therefore come as a surprise to movement scholars that there is no automatic relationship between supply-chain globalization and anti-sweatshop campaigning; it only constitutes the general structural backdrop against which protestors mobilized by seizing more immediate opportunities and devising strategies to fight for their goals.

A second, more focused explanation argues that the rise of anti-sweatshop campaigns in several European countries can be explained by the fact that similar campaigns had started to appear in other countries as part of the slowly rising global justice movement against the effects of free trade and neo-liberalist policies. The growing grievances along global supply chains had provoked protests, and pioneering social movement organizations in Europe and North America had started mounting campaigns to put the issue on the public agenda. It led to the development of a transnational advocacy network (Keck and Sikkink 1998) on the issue of sweatshops and labor rights in the garment industry. The rise of this network favored the launch of campaigns in Switzerland, France, and other countries, with issues, claims and action repertoires moving across borders through processes of diffusion (Soule 2004).

The transnational networks and connections between social movement actors was undoubtedly one of the relevant contexts for the rise of new issues and claims. The fact that SMOs in other countries discussed how to make Western clothing brands take responsibility for working conditions in low-wage countries, collected information on labor abuses, and started campaigns, directed the efforts of the Swiss and French organizations behind the CCC to this particular industrial sector rather than that of any other type of product. This is particularly clear in the Swiss case: by the time the Swiss CCC was launched, the European network was already established and the Swiss coalition was simply able to adopt the general framework. For the French case, however, the situation was quite different: the French campaign launch ran parallel to the beginning of similar actions in the Netherlands and other countries. The European CCC network was still in its

---

2   Hacuitex-CFDT, "Le livre blanc pour le maintien et le développement des industries textiles, habillement et cuirs en France," October 1978, quoted by Ancelovici 2008, p. 141, note 107. Of course, the textile branch of this union was particularly concerned by this process, and animated more by maintaining production in France than by defending workers in the South. But nonetheless, the publication points out the long history of supply chain globalization.

infancy. Through personal exchanges and communication, the people at AdM were aware of these emerging struggles in other countries, but while they were influenced by them, they also contributed to their emergence.

The explanation in terms of diffusion of struggles still fails to explain the timing of campaign launches: what made this kind of campaign an attractive strategy at a particular point in time? One has to take into account the specific national conditions that led to the emergence of the two campaigns, for it is with respect to these conditions of short-term dynamics, national contexts, political opportunities and strategic decisions that the two cases differ. The same transnational campaign was thus inserted into very different national movement trajectories. In other words, for diffusion to take place there must be favorable 'conditions of reception,' with movement actors that have, or are able to acquire, the necessary resources and can seize opportunities to launch struggles. It is these local and national conditions which shape the national movements and campaigns that together constitute transnational struggles.

The Opportunities of the Promotion of a 'Third Way' in France

The immediate origins of the French CCC are twofold. Two campaigns were launched in 1995/early 1996: one by Agir Ici targeting sneaker brands and retailers called Soyez Sport (Be sports); the other one by Artisans du Monde targeting clothing retailers, called Libère tes fringues (Free Your Clothes). After this first round of parallel campaigning, they merged the next year, and together conducted the follow-up campaign 'De l'éthique sur l'étiquette' (Ethics on the Product Tag), which would lead to the establishment of the coalition called Collectif de l'éthique sur l'étiquette.

The Agir Ici campaign was part of a transnationally coordinated action marking the 1996 Olympic Games. It thus echoed the rising transnational activist networks against sweatshops. For Agir Ici, the Soyez Sport campaign was an application of the advocacy campaigns it had been running since 1988. An eight-page brochure including postcards that participants could send to sneaker brands was disseminated through a network of partner organizations, comprised exclusively of organizations belonging to the sector of international solidarity and thus very close to AdM and its partners. AdM was the leading force behind the launch of the parallel 'Libère tes fringues' campaign and the building up of the CCC coalition. It was the first time AdM had conducted its own advocacy campaign. The leaders of the organization made a strategic decision to strengthen AdM's profile in public campaigning and hired Pascal Erard, who had previously worked on campaigns for a humanitarian NGO, specifically to develop advocacy actions. In the interview I conducted in Paris, he emphasized that AdM started the 'textile project' with the idea of "developing the first real action of development and advocacy. Up to then, AdM had always been a partner in a larger coalition, mobilizing with others on collective projects. This was the first time that AdM was the pilot of its own popular education action".[3]

The people behind both campaigns perceived them as complementary, focusing on different sectors (sports footwear and clothes) and targeting different corporations with similar demands. But contrary to the AdM campaign, Soyez Sport did not have durable resources that could ensure continuity in the campaign effort; like all Agir Ici campaigns, it was a one-off that put an issue on the public agenda, but which was dependent on other movement actors to invest resources to keep up pressure in the longer run. In the anti-sweatshop struggle, this was achieved thanks to AdM's parallel campaign, which secured longer-term funding from European and French public sources. An important key to the mobilizing success of this campaign was the ability of AdM to enter into the ongoing debate on off-shoring, which allowed it to gather resources and bring together a broad coalition including unions. The launch of AdM's campaign, in other words, had an independent history that tied it closely to the specific national context of crisis in the French textile industry.

The access I was given to the campaign's internal documents allowed me to carefully retrace its immediate origins. The documents included numerous drafts of projects and comments, internal proceedings reflecting on strategies, and notes on responses by potential funders. These observations give detailed insight into the lengthy process of preparing a campaign. Overall, they clearly suggest the importance of the national and international political context for the campaign's success in securing funding, building a coalition and mobilizing the population. At the beginning of the 1990s, the structure and regulation of supply chains in the textile industry was high up on the international and French political agenda. At an international level, the multi-fiber arrangement, which had defined quotas of textile importation per country and thus protected domestic industries, was abandoned in favor of an incorporation of textile products to the general GATT (and later WTO) framework of trade relations.[4] This implied a liberalization of the textile market. In France, where the textile industry was already suffering job cuts, the threat of an ever more liberalized market for textiles and clothing provoked protests in 1993–1994. Labor unions created a 'unified front' against the massive job loss affecting the sector.[5] In one rather unusual demonstration organized by French textile companies, owners and workers marched jointly to protest against the liberalization of the textile market.[6] At the international level, the issue of off-shoring of industries to

---

3   Interview with P.Erard, Paris, April 2008.

4   The abandonment of quotas was decided in the Uruguay round that led to the establishment of the WTO, but in reality the dismantling of quotas took place gradually and was only completed by the end of 2004.

5   *Le Monde*, April 14, 1994: "La conférence ministérielle du GATT à Marrakech. Le mouvement de délocalisation dans le textile et l'habillement va se poursuivre."

6   *Le Monde*, May 14, 1993. The article adds that all major unions were opposed to this march and denounced it as a "gigantic manipulation of workers."

developing countries led to controversial discussions about the possibility of adding a social clause to global trade agreements, requiring the respect of minimum labor standards and thus combating 'social dumping.' Within France, the idea of a law against off-shoring was put on the table by the union CGT.

This political context channeled AdM's focus on the textile sector. But more importantly, AdM and the other organizations that supported the campaign were able to build on it to gain leverage when seeking funding for it. AdM had always planned to benefit from the possibility of getting public funding to finance the campaign—indeed, this was the only way to enable their proposed campaign. At least 75% of its financial resources came from public sources—the European Union and the French government.[7] Although this may seem surprising from a social movement perspective accustomed to studying movements which oppose the state, public funding was actually a common occurrence in the realm of development politics, especially with regard to development projects and public awareness campaigns (Giugni and Passy 1998; for an overview of institutionalized forms of collaboration, see Hatton 2006). Financing campaigns that raised claims about the responsibility of corporations in labor abuses, however, was something quite different. It required the possibility of a frame alignment process (Snow et al. 1986) between the interests of the campaign-makers and those of public officials: public officials had to see such campaigns as a way to pursue their own political interests.[8] At the national level, it was the debate around the issue of off-shoring that allowed for this process of frame alignment, enabling the campaign to present its goals and tactics as consistent with government preoccupations. The proposal that was designed to appeal for funding in France shows this clearly.

Under the title 'Textile solidaire,' the proposal drafted in 1993 listed a number of reasons showing that the suggested campaigns constituted an alternative approach to the crisis of the French textile industry. It mentioned the possibility that factory closures could lead to reactions such as a retreat to narrow national identities (*repli identitaire*), xenophobia, and protectionism. In the current debate, the document said, the importing of goods from developing countries was seen as creating unemployment by stealing French jobs, and industry actors were calling for protectionist measures. Against such measures and interpretations, the campaign proposed an approach of openness and fair market access. The problem of job loss in the garment sector, it argued, could be addressed by raising consumers' awareness of the issue. Furthermore, the proposal insisted that the campaign's strategy managed to pursue both the improvement of working conditions in the South *and* constituted an answer to the increased domestic political pressure for

---

7   The French Ministère des affaires étrangères co-financed the coalition between 1995 and 2002, subsidizing one fourth of the Libère tes fringues campaign and more than one third of the subsequent campaign rounds. The EU financed the coalition from the beginning (the DG VIII and the DG V) (Barraud de Lagerie 2010).

8   In the process, funders thus also channel activities of social movements by funding campaigns that are aligned to their own policy agenda (Bothwell 2001, McCarthy 2004).

tighter actions against outsourcing. The idea of a social clause in international trade agreements—later abandoned (see below)—was also advocated as an efficient tool to do so. At a time where France had a *cohabitation* government between a socialist president and a right-wing prime minister, even the French ministry of industry—hardly a traditional ally of social movements—considered financing the campaign because its approach corresponded to the ministry's position. According to an undated note from the campaign's internal documents, the sub-director responsible for the textile-clothing-leather sector was ready to grant the financing, but his superiors refused, judging that the campaign was too difficult to control.

The political context of ongoing debates on outsourcing in the clothing sector and accelerated job losses thus constituted an opportunity which the campaign-makers seized to apply for funding. The campaign's strategy of asking firms to provide information on conditions of production and to guarantee the respect of social standards constituted a middle way, not challenging market liberalization but at the same time fighting against labor abuse. The same framing and strategy of mobilizing consumers was also very much in line with the political agenda of the European Commission at this time. It favored market initiatives promoting more sustainable and ethical behavior of consumers and producers, and supported campaigns pursuing this goal. The European Union had thus funded initiatives promoting 'ethical consumption' by supporting fair trade products and campaigns aiming at raising awareness among consumers. In this framework, the Commission financed the 'solidarity breakfasts' that AdM had organized before the textile campaign. The Commission particularly sought to fund projects that promoted fair trade in France because of its weak presence in French markets compared to other European countries. According to an internal campaign document, those funders then directly encouraged AdM to design a future project that addressed itself mainly to consumers not yet conscious about the issue of fair trade, and with a European dimension.[9] The textile project was a response to this invitation. It also explicitly invited AdM to form a coalition and build up a European network.

These political opportunities, with allies in French ministries and the European Commission willing to fund market-based campaigns addressing fair trade and social standards, were thus crucial to explaining why the clothing sector became the target of the campaign. There was strong political resonance to the idea of promoting a 'third way' in dealing with the issue of off-shoring. Supporting such a campaign, policy makers at the national and European level could encourage actions by consumers to fight for better working conditions in the clothing sector, while at the same time pursuing an agenda of economic liberalization reflecting the dominant neo-liberal political climate. The goal of the campaign—raising awareness of working conditions, fighting against labor abuses but without advocating protectionist measures, was very much in line with those dominant European and national interests. In their proposals, the campaigners presented their project in this light and insisted on these commonalities. But it is important

---

9   Internal preparatory document from July 3, 1993.

to acknowledge that this was not merely a strategic move, a clever spinning of goals and tactics to please potential funders: the solution of using consumer power to improve working conditions and of fair market access was at the core of the ideology of the fair trade movement.

Clothing as an Object of Consumer Campaigns in Switzerland

How did the BD in Switzerland come to launch an anti-sweatshop campaign? The situation was quite different because the Swiss launch of the CCC came at a time when the European Clean Clothes network was already firmly established. But for the Swiss campaign, too, there was a specific national trajectory of which this launch was a part. There were quite a few antecedents to the campaign that was eventually launched in 1999, but none of them constituted a proper campaign. In the years that followed the 'Hunger is a Scandal' campaign of the early 1980s, the BD carried out a number of similar consumer campaigns. They dealt with such different products and issues as apples from South Africa, Swiss banks investing in the apartheid regime, or pesticide use in agriculture linked to the Swiss pharmaceutical industry. In this array of topics and industries, textile products also became a focus for the organization. This started in 1986, with the publication of a report on the global textile industry called 'Clothing and Fashion, Here and in the Third World.' The action was limited to the publication of a booklet and documentation in the DB magazine.[10] Many of the topics that would become crucial for the anti-sweatshop movement were mentioned here: the rise of export processing zones where national laws did not apply, outsourcing, and poor working conditions. Other issues addressed in the booklet were clothing donations for the 'Third World,' the exploitation of ethnic fabrics and exotic images by the fashion industry, and the Westernization of clothing styles in the developing countries of the South. The booklet thus criticized the social and cultural consequences of the fashion industry for the developing world. A large catalog of possible claims and actions was listed: consumers should show greater awareness when buying clothes and ask questions about origin and conditions of production, support unions and movements fighting for an improvement of working conditions, but also should be more creative by making their own clothes. The publication could very well have become a first step in a campaign, but no concerted action followed: the organization turned its attention and resources to other topics. Clothing as an object of consumer campaigns was put on ice for around 10 years.

To be sure, this absence of an organized campaign with designated action forms did not hinder certain groups or individuals from taking some kind of action. In the BD archives, one finds, for example, the personal account of a woman who, after reading the booklet, asked the manager of her local fashion store questions about the origin of the clothes. Not getting any satisfactory answers, she came

---

10   *Erklärung*, Magazine of the Bern Declaration, 1986/5.

back a second time and showed the store manager the booklet, which he then tore up in front of her. Finally, she wrote a letter to the company complaining about the incident. The official response from the company dismissed her inquiry and said that "women like you probably buy their clothes in Third World shops."[11] This suggests that at this time, clothing firms had no trouble blatantly rejecting people making such requests as Third World activists. This topic was also taken up by one of the BD's regional groups. In 1991, the group organized a series of actions on textiles. According to the DB magazine report, 18 'committed women' carried out a survey in 50 local clothing stores, asking about the origins of clothes and addressing environmental concerns. The results were published in a booklet, which also contained a list of second-hand stores and a checklist of what to look for when buying clothes. The main claim raised by these women was for a better declaration policy on countries of origin, and of the use of chemicals in production.

While these actions were isolated and did not take place inside of a more general, collective framework of campaign activity, the BD focused again on the textile industry in the mid-1990s with the publication of two booklets and a textbook for schools. The German-speaking office initiated all of these publications. At the same time—the early to mid-1990s—the French-speaking office participated in an international campaign called 'Made in Dignity' (in cooperation with the Belgian Third World shops and Oxfam Belgium) on the question of workers' exploitation in the industries of the developing world, and in particular the issue of a social clause for international trade. The more immediate origins of the Swiss campaign go back to these two initiatives.

The French-speaking office, through its participation in the Made in Dignity campaign, worked on the issue of social clauses for world trade. This question was an important issue for development aid NGOs at that time. Together with the NGO Bread for All, the BD also conducted a survey among NGOs and unions from developing countries about their position with regard to a possible social clause. This study provided arguments for a social clause by showing that this was not just a protectionist demand of the developed world, but also a preoccupation of the developing world's 'civil society'.[12] In an interview conducted in Lausanne, a long-time staff member of Bread for All, who had held core positions both in the Made in Dignity and Clean Clothes campaigns, situated the campaign thusly: "At that time there was a real movement. The CCC goes back to a dynamic that starts between 1993 and 1996, when there is a whole movement around the social clause and social standards at the WTO."[13] The struggles for a social clause were

---

11   Correspondence of BD member with Vögele, archives of the Bern Declaration, Ar 430.41.1, Sozialarchiv Zürich

12   In fact, many governments of developing countries opposed the idea of a social clause by arguing that it would slow down economic development. The Swiss study could be used to show that those governments did not reflect the position of their working citizens, and justified the fight of development aid NGOs for a social clause.

13   Interview Martin, Bread for All, Lausanne, July 2007.

an early expression of the rising global movement against neo-liberalism, and thus part of the transnational network mentioned at the beginning of this chapter. The international negotiations of the Uruguay Round on trade policy that eventually led to the establishment of the WTO opened up a forum where movement actors and NGOs could bring in their grievances. Transnationally coordinated NGOs and unions viewed the negotiation process as a chance to influence decision makers in order to implement a social clause that could improve working conditions in production countries. Like the rise of other transnational institutions, the WTO negotiations constituted a new arena where contentious actors could address their claims (Tarrow 2005).

This movement, however, did not succeed in its demands; when the WTO was established in 1995, no social clauses figured in its legal framework. In the case of the Swiss NGOs launching the CCC, this failure explains in part the turning towards alternative solutions, such as codes of conduct.

> There was no consensus [among states] on [the social clause], it was illusory. It would have been a leverage to force countries to respect working standards. There was a conscience that something needed to be done, and we saw that on the global multilateral level it wasn't possible, and thus we switched to doing something in the realm of Corporate Social Responsibility.[14]

Once the negotiation process was finished and the social clause did not gain a majority, the potential opportunities for change in the transnational arena closed down. Movement actors had to strategically adapt by looking for other options—'second-best' solutions. They found them in forms of private regulation such as codes of conduct.

These forms of private regulation, however, were not just second-best solutions for the Swiss movement actors. The strategic adaptation of the BD and its allies was no great change, since the consumer campaigns of the BD had always put consumer action and corporate responsibility at its center. This was also the case for the textile action that originated in 1994 in the BD's Zurich office with a series of publications on the textile market. This action pursued the goal of "socially and ecologically compatible and fairly traded textile products available in Switzerland." While the Made in Dignity campaign focused on an institutional solution at the transnational level and did not rely on consumer mobilization, the 'textile action' planned here focused on consumer power from the beginning. The idea to make consumers send postcards to companies figured in the project as early as 1994.[15] It was finally carried out in 1997 in a campaign called 'Let's Go Fair.' This campaign adopted the Clean Clothes framework, targeted sports companies producing shoes, and was launched in collaboration with Terre des hommes Switzerland. With the

---

14   Interview Martin, Bread for All, Lausanne, July 2007.
15   Planning documents textile action, Archives of the Bern Declaration, Ar 430.17.2, Sozialarchiv Zürich

launch of the Swiss Clean Clothes Campaign by the French-speaking office in collaboration with Bread for All and Lenten Fund two years later in 1999, the two lines of origin finally merged. The CCC was thus part of an organizational history where the topics of clothing production and working conditions in developing countries had become central. In part, it constituted a way of displacing the struggle for a social clause onto the field of corporate responsibility, strategically reacting to changing political contexts; but at the same time, as exemplified by the early consumer campaigns, the push for corporate responsibility using consumer pressure *preceded* the pursuit of international regulation. At this time, the international CCC provided a framework that merely needed to be adapted to the Swiss context, most importantly by choosing the 'right' targets.

The Logics of Coalitions

The success of the campaign launches also depended on the building of coalitions that could sustain them over time. The discussion so far has focused on the contextual conditions and strategies that made the driving organizations launch campaigns on the topic of sweatshops. But what about the other members of the coalitions—why did some organizations join the campaign and become central actors? The composition of the coalitions was in part due to strategies deployed by the campaign initiators to build up coalitions, in part the result of contextual conditions and a contingent process that made the campaign attractive to some of the organizations. Yet the composition of the coalitions had important consequences for campaign dynamics: it shaped the ideological and strategic positions that were driving the campaign-makers' tactics and strategic decisions throughout the campaign's course.

In France, the people at AdM wanted to create a national network (a *collective* as it was called) that brought together many organizations from different social movement families (Della Porta and Rucht 1995). Building a coalition for political actions was very common and meant that much previous experiences could be harnessed, but these mostly remained within the field of international solidarity, such as collaborations within the CRID (the association federating many of the organizations from international solidarity) or the campaigns proposed by Agir Ici. Coalitions allowed for more resources and the mobilization of larger audiences. But for the 'Free Your Clothes' campaign, AdM wanted to reach out to coalition partners beyond its own movement family to consumer movements, unions, human rights groups and environmental organizations. The success of this coalition-building was an important factor in the launch of the campaign: it was a condition to get funding from European sources, and it promised to have greater leverage and credibility in raising claims against clothing brands.

One of the greatest challenges in the first stage of the campaign was finding such partners. The search took place both on the national and on local levels, as the campaign was meant to copy the structure of AdM with a national coordination and actions carried out by local networks and coalitions. At the national level, AdM organized workshops to which potential ally organizations were invited in order to build up a network of supporting groups. On the basis of official statements of support that were gathered through these efforts, the local chapters were then encouraged to contact corresponding local organizations of other groups, in order to mirror, on the local level, the coalition which had been built up on the national level. Later on, this form of organization, initially termed *coordinations*, came to form the CCC coalition, which consisted of an ever-growing number of local *collectives* of locally varying coalitions. The number of organizations supporting the campaign was quite high: already by January 1996, 22 organizations were officially part of the campaign. But organizational commitments varied widely; their support ranged from mainly symbolic to an active participation in the campaign's steering committee. My main focus has been on the most involved of these organizations: next to AdM, the Catholic development aid organization CCFD and the union CFDT. Their participation in the campaign is of particular interest because of the decisive role they would come to play in it, and also because of the timing of their joining, which helped the organizational establishment of the campaign.

To persuade other organizations to join the fight for ethical fashion, AdM drafted a petition designed to appeal to a broad range of organizations from different backgrounds. It was entitled 'To Dress the North Without Undressing the South' (undated, probably circa 1994/95). While this was not the only official and public formulation of the campaign's goals and claims, it played a particular role insofar as it constituted the appeal organizations signed to officially demonstrate their support for the campaign. When drafted, it was first submitted for consultation to potential supporting groups, who could propose changes. Its final formulation thus reflected a consensus between the supporting organizations regarding the definition of the problems, the establishment of responsibilities, and the claims thus made. It therefore constituted a common master-frame of meso-mobilization (Gerhards and Rucht 1992) to which all the actors could subscribe through a process of frame alignment (Snow and Benford 1988, Snow et al. 1986)

'To dress the North without undressing the South'[16]

Many social and ecological stains can cover our clothes!

According to the United Nations, about 200 million children under 14 are working around the world. One counts also several million slaves (prisoners forced to work …). To this one must add the numerous violations of workers' rights to organize in unions (murders, imprisonment of union organizers …) and serious damage to the environment. Among the millions of persons working in such unacceptable conditions, a great number is producing clothes. Some of these clothes are sold in France.

Generally, the retailer is legally responsible for the quality of the goods he is selling, whether they are produced in France or abroad. For the time being, this responsibility only concerns the 'material' quality of clothes (type of fiber composing the cloth). We consider that it should be extended to social and ecological conditions of production.

---

16   Internal archives, French CCC, my translation.

It is in this spirit that a resolution of the European Parliament from 1994 asked 'that import corporations and the retail circuits attached to them guarantee the rigorous respect of the ILO conventions' concerning workers' human rights.

This preoccupation is also one of consumers. Since the beginning of the 1990s, surveys of the CREDOC (Centre of research for the study and observation of the conditions of life) on consumption in France show that an increasing number of French citizens wants to buy goods produced under decent conditions. But consumers don't generally have a choice because of a lack of information on the conditions of production of the goods on sale.

This is why we ask the clothing traders to provide consumers with reliable information guaranteeing that the clothes sold are produced under decent social conditions respecting workers' human rights (freedom of unionization, ban of forced labor and child labor, non-discrimination between women and men, notably) and the environment.

The appeal covers many different issues and has thus great potential mobilization capacity (Gerhards and Rucht 1992, p. 580). In the first sentence, ecological *and* social problems are linked to the issue of clothes. Later on, it lists child labor, slavery, union rights and environmental damage as problems raised by clothing production. Finally, it suggests a parallel between its claims and the methods employed by consumer organizations—that is, the extension of legal responsibility beyond quality towards the social and ecological conditions of production. Thus the frames used were likely to appeal to a variety of movement actors from environmental, human rights, and consumer movements as well as from unions. And indeed, this was the appeal's explicit goal.

However, although ecological concerns were expressed quite prominently, no environmental organizations eventually joined the coalition. The same was true of human rights organizations. Despite the framing and direct invitations to organizations from the human rights sector to join the campaign[17], none of them took part in the coalition. The problem was hardly a lack of 'connectedness' of the different frames, nor of structural connections between those different movement families (Gerhards and Rucht 1992). If it were a question of structural ties, then why did unions and consumer organizations join the campaign? If anything, evidence suggests that organizational ties were weaker between the field of international solidarity, unions and consumer organizations, than with environmental and human rights groups. An indication of this lies in the very fact that AdM saw a need to produce a list with contact information of consumer organizations and unions for their local chapters. These lists, together with instructions on how to 'sell' the campaign to those actors (see below), suggest that they evolved in very different social universes. Ties were thus created by the campaign in the course of its elaboration and its actions.

---

17   I found, for example, a letter addressed to Amnesty International inviting them to participate in a meeting and to join the campaign.

Internal documents show that it was a strategic choice of the campaigners to seek out unions and consumer associations as potential allies. There were strategic reasons behind the choice of bringing together these three movement families, which outweighed the greater obstacles of coalition formation. AdM estimated that allying consumers and unions to the struggle was a good strategy when applying for funding. In projects, these two categories of organizations were regularly mentioned as potential partners in the campaign, alongside the traditional international solidarity network. Those three groups together were also thought to have the greatest legitimacy to influence corporations. The way the campaign presented itself is an indicator of the importance the campaigners gave to the presence of these three groups. In all official documents, the participating organizations were always classified into three groups and presented as such, rather than, for example, in an alphabetical listing of organizations. Even more so, the organizations of international solidarity would always be listed third, despite the fact that they were at the origin of the campaign and had fought for this kind of issue for decades; consumer organizations were listed first and unions second, although there were far fewer of them.

Thus consumer organizations and unions became target organizations for the campaign, and special efforts were made to find such partners. Their preoccupations were very prominently addressed in the different formulations of the issues and the claims, as for example in the appeal discussed above. But even more so, they were contacted and invited to participate in meetings and workshops and a significant effort was made in order to present the campaign to them and show why they should be interested in supporting it. Judging from the list of supporting organizations, these efforts paid off. Indeed, various consumer organizations and unions were ready to support the campaign. However, for most of these organizations the commitment did not go much beyond symbolic support. This was particularly the case for most consumer organizations who supported the campaign. Of all the organizations from the group of consumer associations and labor unions, the only one that became a major player was the union CFDT, first through its clothing, leather and textile federation (HACUITEX), then rapidly through other branches and its national federation.

Framing alone was not enough to persuade the CFDT to actively participate in the campaign, nor was it the special efforts AdM made to persuade the union. Instead, my analysis suggests that it was vested interest that counted much more: the union could use its participation in the campaign as a way of differentiating itself from its main competitor within the movement field, the CGT. Again, this had to do with the debates regarding off-shoring that characterized France in the early 1990s. From early on, the 'moderate' position of the CFDT within this debate made it appear a natural ally of the campaign. Rather than condemning off-shoring, the CFDT insisted on its benefits for developing countries, and put its role in job losses in France into perspective. This moderate stance reflected the transformations the union had gone through in the 1980s and early 1990s in the course of a reconfiguration of the French labor union field. Responding to declining membership and political changes, the CFDT had abandoned references to class struggle in favor of discourse based on negotiations, institutionalization, and Europeanization (Ancelovici 2008, Béroud and Mouriaux 1998).[18] This ideological and strategic turn, which was not achieved without internal disagreement, led the union to stress the benefits of international trade, both for developing nations and for French workers.

Thus the framework of the Libère tes fringues campaign fitted in with the position defended by the CFDT. An early formulation of AdM's textile project, dating from the beginning of the year 1994, cited an article by Yvonne Delmotte, then general secretary of HACUITEX and later of the national federation. In this article, she stated that countries from the developing world served as scapegoats in outsourcing discussions, and that it was necessary to alert consumers to the consequences of ever-lower prices. There was thus a similarity in the analysis of the issue of off-shoring, development, and the roles consumers can play, between the two organizations, which brought AdM to approach the CFDT very early on.

But the shared analysis of the situation or the aligned frame alone does not sufficiently explain why the CFDT actively joined the campaign. What was primarily important in this process was the fact that the CFDT could and did 'translate' the campaign into the issues at stake in the field of trade unions at that time. This struggle was defined by the competition between unions, in particular between the CFDT and its main competitor, the CGT. By supporting the campaign, the CFDT was also making a move in this field: confronting the CGT. To fight outsourcing, the CGT's textile federation advocated a law punishing it. This law, proposed for the first time in 1993, would severely reduce off-shoring practices and thus protect jobs in the French textile industry and would implement quotas in the retail sector to limit the share given to imported goods. The CFDT strongly rejected such a law, dismissing it as a protectionist measure. But the more moderate union was also under pressure to show that it was acting against off-shoring, which it could do by supporting the anti-sweatshop campaign. It could not only reject the CGT's proposition, but at the same time promote an alternative solution and action mode to its members. In the CFDT textile federation's journal, it said that

> this campaign responds positively and concretely to the problems of off-shoring, and it is a real social and political response to the North/South divide. It counterbalances the CGT's campaign that promotes a demagogic, unrealistic and protectionist law against off-shoring. This law is a bad answer to a real problem.[19]

---

18   There is some debate on the interpretation of this change, some authors claiming that it is actually the continuing influence of the catholic origins of the union which account for its position in the 1990s, and the reference to class struggle was merely a parenthesis, while others observe a series of ruptures after 1978 (Béroud and Mouriaux 1998).

19   HA.CUI.TEX n°505, May 1997, p. 12

The campaign was thus used in a different arena—the field of trade unions—with its own logic and issues of struggle. For the CFDT, joining the coalition meant shifting the campaign's goals towards objectives it was pursuing within the field of trade unions. Using the anti-sweatshop campaign, CFDT members were asked to organize debates with their colleagues, with members of other unions, with the population in general, and in firms where the CFDT was not yet represented. Thus, the campaign became an element in the power struggle with the other unions, and also a potential tool for the recruitment of new members.

To be sure, this shift of meaning did not imply a change in the campaign's claims or of the way it was framed, nor did it shift the overall goals of the campaign—the adoption and independent control of codes of conduct by retailers. It was just a matter of different organizational *uses* of the same campaign. The use of the campaign as a means to adopt a visible alternative position to the CGT was driven by the CFDT's leaders, notably from the textile-clothes-leather and the service federation, and also from the ASSEDOC, the unions' consumer branch.[20] These branches officially joined the campaign from its first phase, but didn't actively promote it to their members initially. Promotion only began in the second phase—one year later—when the supporting federations published an appeal in their magazines and asked local sections to participate in the campaign's actions. However, this appeal did not seem to have had a lot of success; in May 1997, HACUITEX magazine complained that very few sections had ordered the campaign material. One could thus conclude that the CFDT's use of the campaign, at least at the beginning, was mostly a political and symbolic one. The debate about off-shoring had made AdM's campaign an attractive option for the union leaders to display their willingness to fight for better social standards in global supply chains.

The path which the Comité catholique contre la faim et pour le développement (CCFD) took to join the campaign was very different. The CCFD is the Catholic bishop conference's development aid organization. It has no direct individual members; its organizational members are 28 different Catholic movements and services, that is, the Catholic associational network composed of associations for youth, workers, the elderly, etc. These associations have mostly recreational purposes. But thanks to this network, the organization can count on a very large number of potential participants for its actions. As an NGO specialized in development aid, it was part of the sector of international solidarity. The shared goals and claims between AdM and the CCFD meant that the campaign did not need any significant transfer work. Although a letter presenting the project that AdM sent to the CCFD in mid-1995 stated that the document, being a presentation for internal purposes, was "still very 'boutique'" (that is, rooted in AdM's culture), the fact that the document was nevertheless sent in this form indicates that mutual

---

20 A particularity of the French consumer movement is that it is composed of three kinds of organizations: specific consumer organizations like UFC Que choisir, organizations having emerged out of associations for the defense of families, and consumer organizations which are branches of the major unions.

comprehension did not constitute a major problem. And whereas, in order to form local coalitions mirroring the national one, explicit guidelines for AdM volunteers were produced describing how to speak to consumer organizations and unions (where to find them, what kind of specific arguments to use), no such thing seemed to be necessary for fellow international solidarity organizations.

The CCFD, like many other organizations from the international solidarity sector, began supporting campaigns and mobilizing its members in petition campaigns often launched by Agir Ici. The CCFD thus also officially supported Agir Ici's campaign Soyez Sport, by buying the campaign material and encouraging its members to collect signatures. The nascent Libère tes fringues campaign was not officially joined in its first stage, but the campaign material was also distributed among its members.[21] Only after the first round, in 1996, would the organization start to take an active part in the campaign. This decision was driven by the success the campaign had (together with the parallel Soyez Sport actions launched by Agir Ici) in mobilizing the CCFD's members, in particular those belonging to its youth organizations. It turned out that youth organizations belonging to the CCFD—notably, the young Christian workers (JOC) and the young Christian students (JEC)—took up the campaign very enthusiastically, which led the CCFD to start supporting it more actively.

> Among the CCFD's members, there was one actor, one movement, the JOC, which mobilized other youth movements (…), they decided to participate directly in the campaign and to become actors in the campaign. And they led the CCFD in this campaign.[22]

At first, those consumer campaigns were not met with particular interest by the organization—no more interest than other campaigns that were regularly supported. What provoked the CCFD to get interested in it was the way the campaign resonated with its youth organizations. The preoccupation with youth organizations had been on the agenda of the CCFD for a little while; Jean-Claude, the person I interviewed, was initially hired to organize the space dedicated to young people in an event on development called 'Terres d'avenir,' and was then offered a permanent contract in order to further develop actions targeting a young audience. During the interview he explained how he and another representative from the CCFD attended the evaluation of the campaign's first round:

> At this evaluation, it was said that there should really be a follow-up: it has mobilized a lot of people, it appeals to the youth, there should be a second campaign. That's what became 'Libère tes fringues,' which was born with a second campaign the year after, and this time we contributed directly, the

---

21   Interview with Jean-Claude, CCFD, Paris, April 2008.
22   Interview with Jean-Claude, CCFD, Paris, April 2008.

director of the 'campaigns department' decided that the CCFD would get active in the campaign, and so we started participating in this emerging group.[23]

What is revealing in this passage is that Jean-Claude makes it sound as if the main reason why the CCFD started supporting the campaign—namely, its mobilizing effect and in particular its appeal to a young public—explains why a second phase of the campaign was staged. But this is not the case: the initial project always contained two campaigning stages. The mobilizing effect explains why the CCFD got actively involved. It thus reveals the rationale behind the CCFD's interest in the campaign: its potential for mobilizing the youth associations affiliated with the development aid organization. At the same time, as another CCFD official put it, the participation by the CCFD was of great value for the other members of the coalition, since its broad network of supporters promised to greatly increase the number of signatures collected.[24]

In the case of the CCFD, the process of 'interest alignment' (Mathieu 2012) therefore ran through channels other than those identified for the CFDT. The CCFD started investing organizational resources into the campaign as a reaction to the success the campaign had had with its young members. This is what persuaded the CCFD of the value of this campaign: it was not only consistent with the organization's goals, but appealed particularly to a public the organization was nurturing at the time. In opposition to the CFDT, where this path was guided by strategic considerations of union leaders, a bottom-up process took place in the CCFD. The practical, action dimension of the coalition setup triggered the participation of the CCFD in the campaign Libère tes fringues.

Compared to the French campaign, the coalition that was built up in Switzerland was much less ambitious. It consisted of three organizations: BD, Lenten Fund and Bread for All, all of them belonging to the field of development aid politics. Consumer organizations and unions did support the campaign from time to time, but they were only occasional partners, never integrated into the campaign's organizing structure. The analysis of coalition-formation is therefore less intriguing than in the French case—in many ways, it seemed to be a 'natural' coalition. Nonetheless, for the two development aid NGOs, actively pursuing a campaign that explicitly singled out and blamed big Swiss corporations for working conditions at their subcontractors' factories, was qualitatively quite different from what they had done before. While they had been associated with many initiatives aiming at improving working conditions in global supply chains, they had been working on developing solutions for this, not on putting new issues on the agendas of corporations. The partners were very close in their policy goals and approaches, and had collaborated in the past. Lenten Fund and Bread for All had both been associated with different initiatives of 'political consumption' in Switzerland. Together with the other big development aid organizations, they were

---

23 Interview with Jean-Claude, CCFD, Paris, April 2008.
24 Interview with Xavier, CCFD, Paris, April 2008.

also founding members of Max Havelaar Switzerland, the fair trade label. Bread for All had already been involved in the negotiation of the Del Monte social clause in the follow-up to the 'Hunger is a Scandal' campaign. Often, the two NGOs conducted such initiatives in collaboration with the BD—as for example in the case of the label STEP in the sector of oriental rugs. There was thus a strong proximity between the actors of the Swiss CCC.

Bread for All and Lenten Fund had experiences in campaigning, but the campaigns had traditionally been of a different kind. They were the clerical organizations that carried out the yearly ecumenical campaign, which had been established in 1969 aimed at raising awareness of development issues and raising money for the Christian development organizations. However, these campaigns did not make claims against specific targets; they focused on non-controversial and rather general issues, such as poverty or access to water, in order to raise as much money as possible. The participation in the CCC constituted an important innovation in this respect. Although this campaign targeted Swiss corporations, shaming their practices and raising specific claims, it became the 1999 ecumenical campaign, i.e. the two organizations used it for their yearly request for donations. Neither organization had the strong activist and volunteer networks of the French CCFD (which is the French equivalent of Lenten Fund). The ecumenical campaign was disseminated in Catholic and Protestant churches and church groups, but only very rarely did it lead to specific actions. This means that there was certainly no particular grassroots 'demand' for campaigns or ways to act, in contrast to the CCFD. A political campaign as mounted by the CCC—targeting important and powerful Swiss firms like Migros, the major retailer—was actually a rather risky business for the two organizations, since it could scare off certain conservative donors, following the same pattern that made the church-based organizations refrain from politically 'sensitive' objectives in the 1970s.

Interviews point to a strategic renewal observed in both organizations towards more direct attempts at shaping the political agenda and changing the global economy. This change was under way at the end of the 1990s, partly also responding to the need to appeal to a broader and younger audience[25] through catchier campaigns. Lenten Fund was reinforcing its development politics actions, and Bread for All, which had been more involved in issues of development consequences of global supply chains and for whom it was a direct continuation of its participation in the previous Made in Dignity campaign, wanted to continue its commitment to social clauses using codes of conduct as a new instrument. The active role these two organizations played in the launch of the Swiss CCC came out of this general analysis of the role of global markets in development politics, and the goal of holding corporations accountable for working conditions in the developing world. As a novel way of pursuing these policy goals, the CCC fit very

25   Bread for All and Lenten Fund suffer, like all church-based institutions, from a lack of generational renewal of their aging members and supporters (interview with Robert, Lenten Fund,Lucerne, July 2007).

well into the political agenda of the NGOs. If we broaden the perspective, the end of the decade corresponds to a moment of growing political mobilization with regard to topics of global justice. Towards the mid-1980s, participative actions of the BD declined as the organization chose to focus more on lobbying and other activities that did not require broad popular mobilization. The late 1990s, coinciding with the launch of the CCC, partly corresponded with a return to the mobilizing actions that had characterized its beginnings. This was also true for the two other organizations involved, Bread for All and Lenten Fund. In the course of the early 2000s, public campaigning was increasingly adopted by both of the organizations, supporting campaigns for debt relief, a petition on Swiss development aid, or launching their own campaign on workers' rights in the computer industry. In Switzerland, the global justice movement was particularly characterized by the strong participation and influence of big NGOs from the development aid and environmental movements (Giugni and Eggert 2006).

Explaining the Rise of Anti-Sweatshop Campaigns

Using a genealogical approach, this and the previous chapter have analyzed the different developments that led to the rise of anti-sweatshop campaigns in Switzerland and France. Although part of a transnational network responding to global issues and raising the same claims in many countries, the emergence of the Swiss and French campaigns owed much to specific national conditions. In the rise of the campaigns, the analysis has separated different 'time lines.' Some developments are long term and have deep historical origins: this is the case of the rise of the action repertoires on which the campaigns built. Field realignments were particularly important in these processes of tactical innovation. Challenger actors developed new tactics to position themselves vis-à-vis incumbent field actors (as was the case for the Swiss BD and its use of 'consumption campaigns'), or incumbent actors adopted new tactics to respond to the rise of new challengers (the case of France with the rise of 'public campaigning'). The launch of campaigns targeting corporations of the clothing sector built on these developments.

From a more short-term angle, the rise of anti-sweatshop campaigns needs to be put in the context of the increasingly globalized clothing production and more particularly, the rise of a transnational network fighting against Western clothing brands. This channeled the attention of French and Swiss actors towards the clothing industry and the multiple grievances in its supply chains. However, the timing of the campaigns' launches and their success in building up coalitions was dictated by developments that took place in the more immediate environment of the organizations. Political opportunities, failed options and strategic decisions constituted important steps. In France, what stood at the beginning was AdM's strategic decision to strengthen its profile in public campaigning and it was the debate about the off-shoring of the national textile industry that proved to be the decisive context. This meant that the global scope of the textile industry was present in the public debate and was portrayed as threatening French workers' livelihoods. Campaign-makers astutely framed their actions as a response to this crisis when applying for funding. They gave the issue a different meaning, focusing on the threats to workers in the global South rather than those of French workers. When building a coalition, this link between issues could bridge the distance between international solidarity organizations and unions by constituting a common theme. For the CFDT, joining the campaign was also a strategic move in the field of trade unions: it could position itself in this debate against its main competitor, the CGT.

In Switzerland, the focus was first on advocating a social clause in the GATT framework, a goal that was high on the agenda of the growing movement against neo-liberal free trade. The on-going negotiations constituted an opportunity to bring in such demands. Strictly speaking, the actions of the BD's French-speaking office in this regard were not restricted to the global garment industry, but concerned trade in general. When the prospects for a social clause in international trade agreements evaporated, the activists had to find another way to fight for the respect of social standards in the factories of developing countries, and decided to join the European Clean Clothes Campaign that had already attracted the attention of their colleagues from the German-speaking office. The latter had conducted various public awareness campaigns that pointed to labor abuses and other problems related to this industry consistent with the firmly established repertoire of consumption campaigns. As early as the mid-1990s, they had envisioned a campaign directly targeting corporations, and in 1997 they had taken up the CCC framework directed against brands of sports footwear. The activists from the French part of Switzerland then took this over and finally launched the Swiss CCC in 1999, together with partner NGOs that used the campaign as an effort of strategic renewal. Failing strategies and strategic adaptations together with new resource allocations thus guided the launch and timing of the CCC in Switzerland.

The comparison of the emergence of these campaigns shows how the same transnational campaign is inserted into different national contexts and dynamics. Different paths led to the rise of this campaign, explain its timing, and affected the coalition-formation process. That the short-term factors explaining the timing of campaign launches have to do with campaigners making use of opportunities (by linking the issue to the public debate on off-shoring in France) or reacting to failures through strategic adaptation (by switching arenas from international regulation to directly targeting corporations in Switzerland) is in line with the theoretical expectations of strategic approaches to movement studies (Goodwin and Jasper 2011). The analysis developed in this and the previous chapter adds to this the theoretical importance of field configurations and struggles that can help in understanding the strategies pursued by movement organizations. In Switzerland, field struggles had led to the rise of a movement organization specialized in campaigns on the politics of consumption, which used its growing expertise to challenge many different industries over time, be it directly or through national or transnational regulation. In France, the rise of new competitors had pushed international solidarity organizations to develop public campaigning. In the launch of the Libère tes fringues campaign, in addition, the CFDT could use the issue to score points against its main competitor in the field of French unions.

The nationally specific conditions of campaign launches and coalition-building also had consequences for the further campaign dynamics. For strategic choices, tactics, and interactions with targets, it mattered when and how the campaigns were launched. A later launch—as in Switzerland—meant that the issue of corporate social responsibility was already more widely recognized than at the time the French campaign began, which might have favored positive outcomes. It also mattered a lot who the coalition partners were: they could bring in crucial resources and skills that might help campaigners to achieve their goals. But they could also shape campaign dynamics through the conflicts around strategic orientations that broke up in the course of interactions with firms.

Chapter 4
Building a Campaign

Petitions, company evaluations, press conferences, street actions, meetings with local store managers; inventing slogans and printing brochures, postcards, reports or newsletters; planning campaign launches, advising grassroots groups, evaluating actions … The list of what the campaigns did and said in order to mobilize and persuade companies to yield to their demands is long. This chapter and the following one delve into campaign-building—firstly from the point of view of tactics, and secondly looking into the cultural aspects of campaign-making. How did the campaigns voice their demands? Building a campaign starts with the professional planning of campaign rounds, the preparation of tactics and the organization of participation. The campaigns' professional structures were central to the outlook of the campaigns in both countries: a commonly accepted blueprint of campaign-making guided what campaigners did. There was a central tactic at the core of each round of campaigning. Around it, campaigners used a variety of other actions to put forward their demands. I start by looking at the process of professionalized campaign-making before analyzing the campaigns' different use of tactical action repertoire and the resulting 'campaign styles.'

Professionalized Campaign-Making

The Clean Clothes Campaign was a professionalized campaign. Conceived and carried out by hired staff working for social movement organizations, its actions were launched after long phases of preparation, including strategic planning and careful scheduling of events. Campaign organizers developed graphics and visuals, designed booklets and other publications, thought up events and actions to publicize the campaign and attract media attention. In short, the campaign-makers had the professional know-how necessary to apply an established blueprint of 'public campaigning' (Lahusen 1996). This decisively shaped the outlook of the campaigns.

The established blueprint of public campaigns had different origins. In France, it was introduced by Agir Ici, which brought in more professional approaches towards campaigning. From the beginning, Agir Ici saw itself as a professional campaigner, meaning an advocacy organization whose 'product' was campaigns. These campaigns always followed the same model: a petition putting forward a claim addressed to one or several targets, a booklet (a so-called '*quatre-pages*'), and a precisely defined schedule. Campaigns were financed by selling campaign material—i.e., petition postcards, pamphlets—to the organizations supporting and disseminating campaigns. Thus, the campaigns devised and planned by Agir Ici were based on a commercial relationship between social movement organizations. At the same time, this served to build up broad ad hoc coalitions.

When launching its first clothing campaign, AdM, was not used to the professional approach introduced by Agir Ici. In fact, the idea of fair trade had developed as a niche market based on voluntary work. Professional structures first emerged with the development of a central import agency, and then, during the growth of the 1990s, through the (controversial) use of more professionalized techniques of sales management and marketing as a way to deal with the growth in the number of AdM shops (Le Velly 2007). The launch of the French CCC was concomitant with this movement of professionalization within AdM. It meant that AdM used tactics that could be controlled and planned in advance, professionalization leading to the development of campaigns that were compatible with formalized structures and schedules of professional workers, as in many other cases (Staggenborg 1988).

In addition to professionalization, the campaign's outlook was also channeled by its external funding. Many studies have shown that funding institutions shape the organizational structure of movements and channel their tactics, usually favoring moderate and professional SMOs over more radical, informal and grassroots organizations (Bartley 2007a, Bothwell 2001, McCarthy 2004). Funders 'cherry-pick' such organizations when providing money and create pressure for the developments of professional structures, especially by preferring project-specific funding, which goes along with a shift towards more moderate and 'measurable' goals and strategies. The French CCC depended heavily on external funding coming from public institutions: the European Commission and different French ministries. Applying for this funding required a high formalization of the campaign's actions: for example, it required a detailed advance planning of campaign activities over the funding period (which could last up to three years), the formulation of precise goals, as well as an external evaluation of the campaign's success. This created a strong institutional pressure on the campaign organization. A professional approach was a basic requirement in order to obtain funding.[1]

The Swiss campaign did not rely on specific external funding, but was also characterized by a similarly professionalized approach. The three organizations behind the Swiss CCC were all professionalized NGOs. Bread for All and Lenten Fund both specialized in development aid projects and fundraising, and relied almost exclusively on paid staff members. When the campaign was launched, both were about to develop their domestic advocacy activities in development policy; and both had 30 years of experience in joint public campaigning for fundraising.

---

1   As Staggenborg (1988) notes, the relationship between professionalization and funding is a two-way street, since it already takes a certain amount of professional skills on the part of an organization in order to apply for funding (i.e. the skills of how to write an application and how to design a 'fundable' campaign). In turn, public and private funding further push towards professionalization.

The BD, in turn, had also become a professionalized social movement organization, and had increased its paid staff over the years, leading to a growing specialization. This specialization was topic-related, but also included specialists in public relations and communication. Thus, while the Swiss campaign was not bound by external requirements towards formalization and rationalization, the professional structures of the organizations made up for this. Resource management required careful planning of campaign timing, and the internal competition between different campaigns meant that the attention and resources the organizations could give to each one of them was limited.

The professional nature of the campaigns is evident in the social organization of the campaign and the characteristics of the campaign-makers. Structurally, the French coalition was an ad hoc organization lacking the formal status of an association; the employees were thus formally hired by AdM, but in practice worked for the campaign coalition and were paid for by the public funding that financed the campaign. These professionals created the campaign and developed its strategy and tools under the strategic lead and overview of a 'steering committee' (and, in a later stage, a number of commissions on different specific topics) made up of representatives from the main organizations involved in the coalition. Depending on their personal interest and investment, these representatives were more or less equally involved in the development of the campaign. In the first few years, only one employee worked for the campaign, effectively creating and coordinating it; toward the end of the 1990s, a second position was created, in charge of communication and coordination of the increasingly numerous local coalitions. Finally, two more positions were added in the early 2000s, separating the position of 'local network support' from the one of communication, and adding a specific position for the relationship with targeted companies. Including an administrative assistant, the team eventually consisted of five employees. It was at this time, with one employee exclusively dedicated to animating the network (that is, as one interviewee put it, essentially 'vulgarizing' the campaign for the local coalitions, giving them things to do and making sure that actions were spread out over the whole French territory), that the campaign was the most active in terms of actions and production and dissemination of different campaign tools.

The staff members who filled these positions were experts in professional campaigning and NGO work. The long-time coordinator was a law school graduate specialized in international and development law who had worked for two different NGOs before being hired by AdM, both times running public campaigns. The others had similar professional profiles: the campaign's communications officer had previously worked for the CCFD for more than a decade, where he had been in charge of youth networks and campaigns. Before occupying the operating position in the CCC coalition, he had participated in the campaign's steering committee. The campaign's network animator had studied information and communications with a specialization in multimedia. She was hired by the campaign coalition in 2001 as an intern, primarily because of her multimedia skills, since the campaign was developing internet tools for internal communication at this time; her internship was then transformed into a full position, when the former network animator left. The person responsible for negotiations with firms was an engineer who had previously worked in the private sector. The other employees shared similar professional features. With one exception, they were not activists originally working within one of the coalition organizations. Rather, they oriented their professional ambitions toward the NGO sector and were recruited for their professional skills.

This trait was similar in Switzerland: the professionals constructing the campaign were certainly convinced of the cause, and some of them had been activists in the past, but not necessarily for the same movement. But they were all in their respective positions because they pursued a career in the NGO sector and had been hired by organizations. Those in charge of the campaign at the Bern Declaration had university degrees in the social sciences and were relatively young when they started working there. In the other two organizations, those working for the campaign were specialized, within their NGO, in questions of political campaigning, for which they had developed a particular expertise.

Campaign Blueprint

The professional approach had important consequences for what the campaigns looked like. What I call campaigns here—the Clean Clothes Campaigns in Switzerland and France—actually consisted of regular, time-limited and sequential 'sub-campaigns' or 'campaign rounds' which together constitute the CCC. Tables 4.1 and 4.2 list the different campaign rounds in Switzerland and France. Each of these campaign rounds was centrally planned and implemented by the campaign organizations in a top-down manner. When doing so, organizers followed a campaign blueprint, meaning that each and every campaign consisted of the same main features. Such campaign 'packages' were usually designated by a name, and consisted of particular claims, performances, and targets.

In France, every campaign round was given what marketing professionals would call a claim, that is, a sort of campaign slogan that served as the campaign round's official designation. 'Free Your Clothes,' 'Play the Game,' 'Ethics on Tags,' or 'Exploiting is not Playing' are catch-phrases around which campaign rounds are built. Switzerland's campaign did not always use explicit names for the different rounds, but also evolved around such subsequent packages of claims, action forms, and targets. For each round, a central action mode was chosen: mostly petitions and rankings, i.e. evaluations of the firms' 'social records.' While participation options were more diverse than that, each round nonetheless evolved around such a main 'contentious performance' (Tilly 2008). Finally, specific targets were picked for each round. These could be specific firms, firms belonging to a specific category, business associations, or political players and institutions. In other words, while there was great variety as to the *content* of these different components, the components themselves were all present in every campaign.

Table 4.1   Campaign rounds in Switzerland, 1997–2008

Targets	Sneaker brands		Clothing retailers	Uefa	Triumph	Fifa		IOC	Clothing retailers	Clothing retailers	none	Clothing retailers
Main performance(s)	Postcard petition		Postcard petition	Petition	Boycott Postcard petition	Petition		Petition	Ranking	Ranking	buycott	Petition ranking
Campaign name	Let's go fair		Clean clothes campaign	Play fair	Triumph	Play Fair		Play Fair	Prêt-à-partager	Prêt-à-partager	Shopping Guide	Revolution
Switzerland	1997	1998	1999	2000	2001	2002	2003	2004	2005	2006	2007	2008

Table 4.2   Campaign rounds in France, 1995–2005

Targets	Clothing retailers	Clothing retailers	Retailers (sports)		Local public authorities	Local public authorities	Retailers (toys)	Retailers (toys)	Retailers (sports)	Retailers (sports)
Main performance(s)	Postcard petition	Postcard petition	Postcard petition	Label social	Ranking	Ranking	Ranking petition	Meeting managers	Petition	Postcard petition / Meeting managers
Campaign name	Libère tes fringues	De l'éthique sur l'étiquette	Jouez le jeu		Pour l'école, consommons éthique	Achats publics, achats éthiques?	Exploiter n'est pas jouer	Exploiter n'est pas jouer II	Jouez le jeu JO	Jouez le jeu II
France	1995	1996, 1997, 1998		1999	2000	2001	2002	2003	2004	2005

Devising a campaign round is strategic work: tactics are associated with targets to achieve maximum effect. However, this general view of the main actions used in each campaign round is only a rough picture of the complexities of campaign-building. Documents accessed in the campaign's internal archives allow us to obtain a more detailed picture of this strategic process. One typical example is the preparation of the strategy for the campaign round '*pour l'école, consommons éthique.*' Document 1 is a partial reproduction of an internal document from November 16 1999 detailing the strategy devised for this round. In the first column, the table distinguishes the different targets of the campaign. Some are explicit targets, such as city councils, which are challenged to take action in favor of social standards in public procurement policies, in particular school equipment. Other targets are called 'secondary': audiences whose support campaign-makers seek in order to gain leverage for their demands. Teacher and parent associations, producers of school equipment, political actors, and the general public are listed as secondary targets. Each one of them was to play a particular role within the campaign economy. The other columns define the goals for each target, the actors who carry out this part of the campaign (who?), the action forms (how?) and the tools. On this strategic micro level, too, one thus finds the triptych of targets, claims (objectives) and action forms. Their articulation is pursued with great accuracy, especially with increasing (financial and human) resources and professional knowledge.

At the height of the French campaign, increasingly complex strategies were put in place, where different actors put pressure on targets through different sources, creating direct and indirect influence chains (Zietsma and Winn 2008). The campaign differentiated targets according to their priority, and chose different action forms to reach each one of them. Thus the last campaign brought together a variety of actions: individual pressure on targets through letter-writing to local managers of shops hoping that this would lead to bottom-up pressure within the companies, and releasing media-centered information and thus targeting corporation headquarters directly. The whole strategy was explained thoroughly to the local coalitions in a campaign manual, and summed up by a synthetic scheme (Document 2). The language and illustrations used in internal brochures of training and campaign presentation show the absolute control in such campaign designs. It is as if nothing was left to coincidence; campaigns developed fully planned collective actions assembling different strategies concomitantly.

Such tables and illustrations also reveal the crucial importance of campaign *tools*, i.e. the tangible materials produced in order to make campaigns. For each campaign round, a number of tools were elaborated in order to transmit and support the campaign message. Tools are the materialization of movement campaigns and contain, but are not limited to, the specific devices and materials of the main performance (such as petitions or rankings). The CCC of each country produced an impressive number of such tools. They are of both internal and external use and are linked to the claims-making process in more or less direct ways. When paying closer attention to these tools, one realizes that campaigns do not limit themselves

Document 4.1   Campaign fabrication, internal document campaign coalition France, November 16 1999

Targets	Goals	Who?	How?	Which tools?
Main target City council	Obtain commitments (to be specified) ethical consumption social label Education	Local coalitions	Letters Meetings	Pre-written letter Information file (to be photocopied locally)
Secondary target Teachers	Obtain commitments for school purchases Support local coalitions against city council Educating students	Teacher unions	Letters Meetings Internal publications Memorandums	Pre-written letter Information file Different publications
Secondary target Parents' associations	Obtain commitments for school purchases Support local coalitions against city council	National organisations with support of teachers, local coalitions	Letters Meetings Internal publications	Pre-written letter Information file Different publications

to the rhythm of claims-making rounds, but evolve equally around continuing efforts of information and consciousness-raising.

We can get an appreciation of the variety of tools in France thanks to a listing that figured in the campaign material distributed to the local coalitions in 2005. On this list there are more than 20 different tools that deploy the campaign's message in different forms: posters, stickers, pamphlets, brochures, etc. All those tools had a price and could be ordered at the campaign office. Specific audiences could be reached with specific tools: there were tools for young people, for use in school, for the general public, for the media, etc. In a 'campaign kit,' the main tools were combined. It consisted of 120 pamphlets, 120 petition-postcards, 60 stickers, 1 quiz, and posters on different themes (5 directly linked to the campaign, 2 on the theme 'made in human rights' (and also 30 postcards using this theme), and 1 poster with the name of the campaign, '*de l'éthique sur l'étiquette*'). This kit was the basic material of the campaign and was therefore offered as a feature with a special price. Every local coalition should purchase at a minimum this material to carry out the campaign. Additional tools could be used according to particular

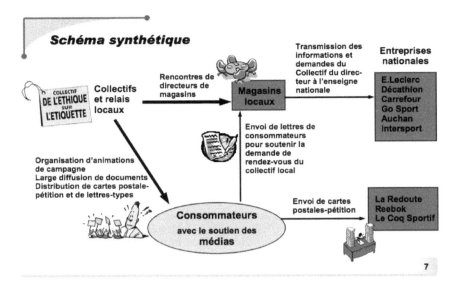

Document 4.2   Strategic deployment of the 2005 campaign round "Jouez le jeu II", from campaign manual, p. 7

interests and needs. These included a small book, a file with the profiles of the different corporations and their ratings, videos on working conditions in China or Thailand, and a slide show. While most tools were designed by the campaign-makers themselves, some came from international campaign coordination or had other origins. The economic exchange that was going on between the national campaign organizers and the local grassroots coalitions is reminiscent of the way Agir Ici sold its campaign packages to NGOs. This exchange was beneficial to both sides. For the campaign-makers, selling this material to local coalitions helped the campaign finance its activities. Many of the organizations in the local coalitions disposed of small funds so from their perspective these tools constituted a service that helped them stage public actions and fill them with content.

The creation and dissemination of a variety of such tools characterized the French campaign from the beginning. But unquestionably, the 2005 round constitutes a kind of climax in the development of this: the number of local coalitions was at its highest, the campaign-makers had a maximum of resources and past experience, and had brought the number and diversity of tools to a level that surpassed previous campaign rounds. Tools not only characterized the French campaign, but were a defining feature of all national CCC's, including the Swiss one. Sometimes, tools would travel from one country to the other. The European secretariat produced a great number of booklets, pamphlets, etc. used by national campaigns. But there was also bi-national exchange, with tools developed in one country traveling to campaigns in other national contexts. The Swiss campaign, for instance, produced an exhibition of drawings by a famous cartoonist on the issue of sweatshops, which was also later used in France. Just like its French counterpart, the Swiss CCC thus used and produced a variety of tools. Besides the classic postcards and this exhibition of drawings, tools produced by the Swiss campaign included a short film on the production of clothes, a map and a 'fair' t-shirt. But the use of tools differed between Switzerland and France mainly due to the different organizational structure of the campaigns, which I will discuss more closely in the next section of this chapter. In France, where the campaign relied on the participation of local coalitions of activists, a whole series of tools was developed in view of this 'intermediate' collective actor, which would then build on it in order to disseminate the campaign. Internal newsletters and, most importantly, a 'campaign manual' produced for each campaign round, explained the campaign to these local activists. In the run-up to a campaign round, training sessions were held for local activists. With the increasing professionalization and standardization of campaign making, the training session and the campaign manual became the center-pieces of each campaign round. The Swiss campaign was much less inclined towards such collective participation; the dissemination of the campaign was less participatory and often simply relied on mailings.

Besides very careful and long-term strategic planning and the production of tools, a final, defining characteristic of the campaign blueprint is the importance of evaluation. External or self-imposed constraints mean that campaigners often need to be able to evaluate their campaigns. Funding agencies require intermediate and final reports in which the beneficiaries of the funding account for their use. Campaign impact, then, needs to become measurable in one way or another. This has consequences for the outlook of those campaigns. In particular, campaign goals were deliberately kept low and achievable, or broken down into a series of intermediate goals. Through such strategies, campaign-makers tried to make sure of achieving some tangible results. Almost everything could become a measure of campaign impact: the number of signatures on a petition, but also the number of postcards and brochures distributed, the attendance at a particular event, or the number of protests staged for a given campaign round. Of particular importance were media appearances, which were fervently followed and accounted for (thanks to specialized press review services, this task could be outsourced). Thus campaigners themselves (and not just social movement analysts) are the first ones to try to measure their own influence. Evaluation is a requirement by funders, but it was also used strategically, as an argument in the ongoing struggle. Successes were put forward but sometimes also minimized, in order to enhance mobilization.

These observations on the existence of a campaign blueprint as the result of a professional approach to campaigning reveal a practice that is extremely relevant to understanding the functioning of the campaigns. It means that in both countries the Clean Clothes Campaigns were highly centralized, top-down campaigns and followed a standard model of campaigning. This blueprint, as well as the main claims and indeed the general CCC framework, were the same in Switzerland and France. But with regard to the tactics the campaigns used within this blueprint, and to an even greater extent the forms of participation they encouraged, the campaigns differed.

Giving People 'Something To Do': the Campaigns' Tactical Action Repertoires

Reflecting on the reasons for the French campaign's success in its first round, its long time coordinator considered that it "raised the public's awareness by proposing concrete actions".[2] One of the keys to the campaign's mobilizing power would thus be that awareness-raising—a process identified with meaning, frames, 'cognitive liberation'—was associated with practices: through 'concrete actions' like signing petitions or attending events, people become aware of new issues. This points to the central role of such practices—commonly referred to as 'action repertoires' in the sociology of collective action (Tilly 20080, Taylor and Van Dyke 2004)—in movements and campaigns. Actions are a paramount part of movement activity. Campaigns put in place a number of mobilization options through which people can take part in the campaign: they organize rallies, internet petitions, or sit-ins; they stage street theaters people can watch, show films, invite speakers. Campaigns conceive actions for various reasons: to put pressure on their targets, to attract media attention, or to give activists and sympathizers a way to signal their commitment to the campaign's cause; hence, tactical repertoires play a role for both external and internal goals.

I first discuss and compare the tactical action repertoires of both campaigns, that is, all the 'performances' they stage in order to promote their cause. Table 4.3 lists all action forms mentioned as having been conducted in any of the Swiss and French campaigns' publications or in any other report on the campaigns. Action forms that were merely thought of at a planning stage but that were not actually carried out are not included. Some action forms were directly deployed by the campaign coalitions, while others were staged by the numerous local groups that participated in the campaign. It is impossible for the listing to keep track of all these grassroots actions, because this information is not systematically available. For example, in an edition of the BD magazine it says that during the year 2004, more than 10 CCC actions were held in 7 Swiss cities. But it does not specify what some of them consisted of, and I could not identify these through other sources. Even more local actions were held in France: for example, for the 1996 campaign launch, local activities were held in more than 60 cities, according to a publication by the campaign. Again, I do not have records of all of these actions. Of course, this limits the systematic analysis of the tactical repertoires, especially if one wants to draw conclusions about the relative occurrences of specific pieces of the repertoire. The analysis developed here is therefore qualitative and allows the identification of the variety of action forms, but not their systematic investigation.

---

2   Interview P. Erard, Paris, April 2008.

Table 4.3   Action forms employed by the Swiss and French campaigns

France	Switzerland
Individualized participation Postcard petition Petition Letter-writing Contacting deputies and candidates Contacting mayors	*Individualized participation* Postcard petition Petition Letter writing Protest emails
Protest Action days Solidarity breakfast Stands, gatherings March Pamphleting Meeting local store managers Symbolic actions Press conferences	*Protest* Stands, gatherings Pamphleting Action days Conferences Participation in town runs wearing ccc tshirts Symbolic actions Press conferences
Awareness-raising Exhibition School intervention Fashion show Conference Contacting corporations Movie screening Theater Tours of conferences with third world unionists Writing and publishing documents	*Awareness-raising* Exhibition School intervention Creation of textbook/method Tours of conferences with third world unionists Movie screenings Fashion show Writing and publication of documents, reports
Consumer Giving grades to retailers (rating)	*Consumer* Selling a "clean" t-shirt Boycott Evaluating and rating corporations Producing and publishing an ethical shopping map Tips for consumption behavior
Lobbying/institutional Meeting corporate executives Participation in and organization of conferences Training workshops for retailer buyer personnel	*Lobbying/institutional* Meeting corporate executives Participation in conferences Building of multistakeholder monitoring project Monitoring of code implementation

But from the records that were analyzed, and from the general functioning of the campaigns, it is also clear that the local actions were channeled by the campaign and served to disseminate the campaign's message, documents, and actions such as petitions. Thus, a plausible point can be made that the vast majority of them consisted of variations of the actions listed in the official documents.

The listing reveals the variety of action forms and their limits, similarities and important differences between both countries. The length of the list shows that the campaigns were characterized by a wide range of actions staged in order to promote their cause. While there were central, characteristic action forms such as the petitions and ratings, campaigns cannot be reduced to this: a whole tissue of actions was built around them. Yet it also appears that there are clear boundaries. Many known and possible actions do not appear, like the smashing of store windows. Thus, there is a clearly delimited tactical action repertoire, which appears to be fairly similar in both countries. But there are also notable differences, in particular with regard to the development of consumer action forms.

Using the underlying dimensions of public/private, contentious/contention-connected, and collective/individual, the tactics can be classified into five categories: protest, individualized participation, awareness-raising, consumer, and lobbying/institutional. All of them characterize both the Swiss and French campaign. Some actions constitute what can be termed *protest* tactics: gatherings, stands, distributing leaflets on the streets. Individualized participation designates the actions where individuals are called on to sign, or write letters or contact their deputies. Consumer actions consist in the use of consumer power—buying or not buying given products—in order to advance a cause. All three of these categories are thus contentious actions: they are used to raise and enforce claims on targets, be it publicly or privately (such as through private consumption choices). Awareness-raising actions are designed to appeal to an audience in order to put forward a broader message of awareness to a particular issue. They are not contentious, but belong to what Tilly calls contentious-connected activities (Tilly 2008). Finally, the lobbying/institutional category is comprised of actions carried out by the campaigns' professional staff. This latter category consists of actions that are not contentious either, but in addition, they are not directed at a public audience, but stay confined to an institutional context. They include forms of negotiation—and even collaboration with—the campaigns' targets, rather than opposition. Together, these tactics constitute the circle of the campaigns' tactical action repertoire (see Figure 4.1). The circle points to the importance within the tactical action repertoires of private rather than public, individual rather than collective, and also non-contentious performances.

Another dimension this typology reveals is the existence of both participatory and non-participatory tactics. Part of the tactical repertoire consists of professionalized practices—lobbying efforts and even policy-making practices that do not involve mobilization and are carried out by paid staff of the campaigners. When the campaign-makers stage a press conference or release a statement, write letters to corporations and meet their managers, participate in conferences

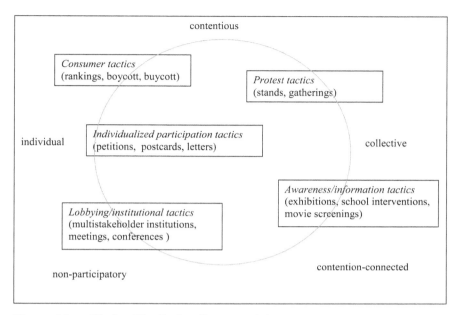

Figure 4.1 **Circle of tactical action repertoire**

or publish expert reports, organize a training session on codes of conduct or negotiate and put into place, with corporations, a system of code monitoring, they act without mobilizing their members or broader audiences. All this belongs to a professionalized repertoire of NGOs or professional SMOs, and the observation of an ever increasing reliance on such practices—to the detriment, supposedly, of participatory action modes—has led a number of authors to deplore the increasing 'NGOization' of civil society (Fisher 2007, Jordan and Maloney 2007, Skocpol 1999, 2003, Skocpol and Fiorina 1999) and the preponderance of 'advocates without members' (Skocpol 1999).

However, in contrast to this critique, my analysis of these professionalized campaigns' tactical repertoire also shows that these lobbying and institutionalized actions are actually combined with tactics based on popular mobilization, albeit in different ways and to different degrees. They put in place a number of *mobilization options* which allow people to participate in the campaign, both individually and collectively. The tactical repertoire both consists of and creates the offer of participation. When campaigns launch a petition, this gives people the opportunity to become a petitioner. But the relationship is not always so clear and uni-directional: campaigns also rely on grassroots groups to disseminate their message and petitions. In this case, they are dependent on the existence of such 'intermediary' groups and their willingness to disseminate the campaign, but they can also activate such groups, by giving them an opportunity and content to mobilize around. Furthermore, participatory tactics appeal to audiences in different roles; they can call for more or less strong participation. Between participating in a local group and staging several events a year, merely attending a movie projection, and reading in the press about a ranking of firms' social performances and then becoming a political consumer, there are different levels of commitment the campaign calls upon. This means that the distinction between participatory and non-participatory tactics is not the same as the difference between individual and collective forms of participation: participatory tactics may appeal to individualized forms of participation—what Micheletti (2003) calls 'individualized collective action'—or to collective forms, like the organization of events, gathering of signatures, etc.

The different pieces of the tactical action repertoire are thus complementary. They are associated in a variety of manners, with some typical pairings. Most notably, protest forms go together with individualized participation. Here, the articulation is simultaneous: The staging of protest actions is a means to achieve public visibility for a campaign, but it is also a way to incite audiences to sign petitions or send postcards. Lobbying and institutional tactics are associated with all the other forms of protest in a temporal order: it is the accumulated and diverse pressure from the other tactics (individualized participation, consumer forms, protest, awareness-raising) that should enable campaigners to enter into contact with corporations, thus making possible the use of these tactics; in turn, once such direct access is open, campaigners may want to refrain from participatory tactics, or use them only to make occasional pressure on specific aspects. While these forms of articulation are typical and characterize both campaigns studied, a close comparative look reveals that the links between action forms, as well as the respective weight and role of the different types of tactics, are very different in both countries. There are, in other words, different participation styles to be found, based on a different use of this common tactical action repertoire.

Switzerland: A Campaign Without Activists

"The goal of the campaign is not to bring as many people onto the streets as possible. Change can be brought about with direct contact. Our main goal is to have influence there, this was the idea from the beginning. Mobilization isn't all that important."[3] This statement by the campaign's principal coordinator sets clear priorities on lobbying and institutional tactics rather than mobilization. A large part of the Swiss campaign's activity goes towards (direct) contact with corporations, collecting information about their practices, or urging them to join multi-stakeholder initiatives. The interview excerpt says something about the general economy of the Swiss campaign's tactics: it privileges lobbying tactics, carried out by the professional staff of the NGO working on the CCC. During my fieldwork, I had to learn this 'the hard way.' I had planned to do participant observation in order to study the functioning of protest against corporations, but as I started my fieldwork on the Swiss CCC, I quickly realized that there was, finally, not a lot to participate in. Most of what the campaign did—evaluating

---

3   Interview with campaign coordinator, Zurich, January 2007.

companies and publishing these evaluations, launching petitions, making public statements—was done by the campaign staff, during office hours, as part of their job. It consisted of activities that are "monotonous, isolated, and difficult to access" for participant observers (Hannerz 2003, p. 211). Without getting hired as an intern, it is difficult to observe this. Protest activities by activist groups, which lend themselves particularly well to participant observation, were marginal in the campaign setup, but this does not mean that they were absent.

Participation mostly occurred in two forms: conventional and consumer tactics. This means that the campaign incited sympathizers to participate *individually*, without forming groups and being physically co-present in actions. Through individualized participation, people could become campaign actors by signing petitions and sending postcards, letters, or emails to companies or sports associations. From the 'Let's Go Fair' (1997) to the 'Revolution in the Fashion Industry' (2008) rounds, 7 petitions were launched. The first was a postcard petition: the campaign printed postcards that people could send directly to corporations. This form of petition allows the creation of a direct link between a corporation and its customers, signaling to corporations that their costumers care about conditions of production. Participation in this kind of action is 'pre-shaped.' It depends very heavily on the political offer. Petitions are launched, protest letters and emails are prepared, etc. These activities typically occur at the CCC headquarters[4], but they can also be undertaken by grass-roots groups, which adds an additional layer of mediation. These types of actions directly target companies and try to mobilize the highest possible number of participants. Besides these 'pre-shaped' action forms, campaign booklets and the Swiss CCC website specifically invited people to participate through other actions, such as speaking with store managers, asking for information about working conditions, writing original letters, and more—in sum, performing individual contentious practices inspired by the campaign, but not pre-shaped by it.

Through *consumer* tactics, the campaign gave people the opportunity to participate in the campaign through their consumer behavior. The campaign published information about companies' negative or positive practices. Consumer forms of action used by the campaign are the evaluations and ratings of corporate social performances, negative publicity for companies by specific campaigns, and a map of ethical shopping sites. The first postcard campaign specifically contained information on firms' practices with regard to conditions of production, and this information was regularly updated. Different criteria were taken into account in order to reflect the changing environment and the reactions of the targets. The evaluations were at first published in the campaign's newsletter. Later, in 2004 and 2006, a joint publication with Switzerland's biggest consumer organizations was released, thus reaching a much wider public. In these publications, a consumer

---

4   They either originate at the national level, as with the postcard petitions, or in the case of the so-called urgent appeals (calls for action on particular cases of labor abuse to support local workers in their struggle) at the level of the International Secretariat.

vocabulary was adopted, with companies classified into three categories (avant-garde, followers, and 'ignorants'), and some certification systems and labels were explicitly recommended. The campaign adapted the typical action repertoire of consumer organizations, consisting of comparative tests of different products or brands (Aldridge 1994). With the publication of an 'ethical shopping map' in 2007, political consumers were given a tool that showed them where to buy 'ethical' clothing. The consumer action forms thus contained implicit or explicit buycott recommendations and boycott threats. It gave consumers orientation as to where (not) to shop. Although the campaign generally did not call for boycotts, its evaluations were destined to use consumer power to target corporations.

What these tactics have in common is that while they offer sympathizers ways to participate in the campaign, the participation mostly remains individual, quick, occasional, and not very committed. Undertakings such as signing a petition, asking questions when buying clothes or not buying a particular brand, are part of a broader collective action, but they are also carried out individually. Compared to this, the role and importance of protest tactics—collective actions like gatherings, events, stands, etc., was relatively minor. When the campaign was launched at the end of the 1990s, the BD had lost all but one of its regional groups. The two other organizations in the coalition had networks of volunteers in the parishes, but these volunteers did not actively participate in campaigns. This means that there was no activist base that could be mobilized for protest actions such as manning stands or gatherings to promote the campaign. But even within the professionalized approach, a campaign usually needs at least some public protest events, to publicize the claims and to provide pictures for the media. Sometimes—underlining the lack of an activist network—it was the staff members of the campaign organizations themselves that were present at such events. The absence of an activist network meant that in the campaign strategy, protest mobilization was not really counted upon. The dissemination of petitions, ratings, and other campaign material did not rely on intermediaries like local groups or mobilization events, but was supposed to reach its public directly (notably by mailing them to the organization's members).

However, in spite of the absence of grassroots groups, the campaign did sometimes actively encourage a more activist and collective involvement in protest actions. In the campaign's brochures and newsletters, readers were not only invited to sign the petitions and change their consumer behavior, but also to talk about it with their friends, families, and colleagues. For example, the campaign's web site provided ideas, including information stands, street theater, and sports events; people were asked to organize information events or stands in their parish, youth group or just with friends in order to promote the campaign. For specific actions, particular audiences were targeted. For example, for a campaign round targeting the International Olympic Committee, the campaign tried to convince local sports associations to jointly sign the petition and become 'sweat-free' sporting associations.

Many of these calls had limited success—there never was a movement of 'sweat-free' sports associations, for instance, but some sports groups did support the campaign nonetheless. The appeals thus did attract some protest. Members of the BD, for example, might get more involved than simply reading the magazine and signing the petition. One of the members of the BD regional group I participated in, for example, said that before joining the volunteer group, when she was only a simple member of the organization, she used to order campaign pamphlets and distribute them at the university to other students; other such examples of occasional protest participation can be found in various instances. For example, in 2004 a section of the Association for the Taxation of Financial Transactions for the Aid of Citizens (ATTAC) campaigned for the CCC by participating in a 12km run while wearing CCC t-shirts.

In some cases the campaign also provoked more long-lasting forms of collective activism. In a town in the east of Switzerland, a group of volunteers formed an association and started conducting public actions in order to diffuse the campaign in the early 2000s. This group, named Globalance, formed from a Parish in a traditionally left-leaning neighborhood of the city[5]. The Pastor of the church was also a member of the BD steering committee, i.e. the overseeing board of the organization. The group was composed of approximately 15 people, mostly young high school students, living in the same neighborhood and, for some of them, frequenting the church. It first organized a fashion show for 'fair' clothes at a local music festival in 2001. More such actions were subsequently organized—a stand and fashion show at the 'church days' of a neighboring town, public podiums and workshops. They wrote letters to shop keepers and organized a local 'referendum,' asking consumers to cast a ballot for clothes produced under better social conditions. Once established, the group became quite an important player in the local social movement field; it started getting involved in protest events that were not linked to the CCC, such as demonstrations against the war in Iraq and protests against the World Economic Forum in Davos, and ended up organizing the first social forum of Eastern Switzerland. In this case, the CCC, with the help of a promoter institutionally linked to the BD and with close contact to young people in a local parish, served as a trigger to mobilize a group who subsequently extended its movement activities to connected issues such as protest against globalization and war.

My fieldwork also led me to another group that formed through the indirect impulse of the CCC. The coordinator of the Swiss campaign had told me about the group and gave me their contact information. I attended some of the group's monthly meetings. The group had no institutional link to the BD at all, nor to any other NGO associated with the campaign; indeed, the members of the group were outsiders to any kind of political action. They were a group of friends—all of them in their late teens and early twenties, who knew each other from school and who were still students. Having read about labor abuses at an Adidas subcontractor (a case publicized by the CCC network and reported in the media), they decided to

---

5   The following account is based on an interview with a former member of the group, and on accounts of its actions in the media.

do something and launched a petition against the German corporation. In order to get help in formulating the petition, they turned to the Swiss CCC. The group collected around 1,000 signatures at different events; it also staged an action in front of the Zurich Adidas store and talked with its manager. However, it turned out to be very difficult for the members of the group to sustain their actions, and the reaction from Adidas—a polite but impersonal letter pointing out the company's CSR policies—was very disappointing to them. Eventually, they turned to the regional group of the BD in which some of them became involved[6]. The disintegration of this (highly informal) group based on a network of friends is linked to their lack of resources, organizational difficulties and a lack of activist skills. The fate of the group shows how the CCC was able to motivate and nurture collective action, but also that the campaign had come to 'own' this issue (Gusfield 1981); new rising actors had to refer to it, and targets would interact with the CCC on this issue, and not with other groups.

In addition to these two cases of groups that had formed, the campaign also constituted a decisive input to the few remaining regional groups of the BD, notably the newly formed regional group in Zurich which became very much involved in the Clean Clothes Campaign. The group consisted of a small number of volunteers, the majority in their twenties or early thirties, students or graduate students, who had grown up and socialized in families politicized to the left and were often already close to the BD. After its creation in 2004, the group first participated in a protest action in front of a store classified as 'ignorant' in the CCC's 2004 ranking. After that, the group members produced an ethical shopping map of a big Swiss city, thus adding a new tool of consumer action to the campaign's tactical repertoire. In a short time, the regional group thus established itself as a force the campaign could count on. This led the campaign coordinator to conceive of a campaign which relied more heavily on local groups running it, in particular creating a stand and a short film to show while collecting signatures and selling a 'clean' t-shirt.

In sum, the Swiss CCC relied on protest tactics on different occasions, but they did not play a significant role in the overall tactical repertoire. Activist participation was rarely explicitly orchestrated by the campaigners but it was certainly encouraged by their communication tools. However, for these actions to take place, the campaign could only count on a very limited network of activist groups. Therefore, much more than actively using protest tactics, the campaign provided contents which activist groups belonging to the wider network of the development politics and global justice movement could adopt, apply, and disseminate. This contrasts with the functioning of the BD's campaigns in the 1970s, where local activists were the major carriers; and it contrasts significantly with the French campaign's characteristic mix of tactical action repertoires.

---

6   Actually, I put them in contact with the BD group and thus created a link between two groups that had not existed previously. They had turned to me for help, perceiving me as an expert and consultant and putting me in a dilemma with regard to my role as a participant observer (Balsiger and Lambelet 2014).

France: Orchestrating Massive Grassroots Mobilization

What distinguished the French campaign from its Swiss counterpart, and indeed from all the other national Clean Clothes Campaigns—and a fact the participants in the French campaign took much pride in—was the strong involvement of a network of grassroots groups staging protest actions. At the height of the campaign, in the early 2000s, there were more than 120 local coalitions (so-called *collectifs locaux*) who covered nearly every French *département*. The formation of local *collectifs* was actively encouraged and played a central role in the campaign; when the national coalition hired a second staff member it was mainly to encourage the network of local groups, and when the campaign finally numbered four employees, one of them was fully dedicated to the support of the network of local groups. These grassroots groups were a vital part of the campaign's tactical repertoire, contributing to the campaign by carrying out numerous local actions. The exceptional character of this tactical repertoire can be seen in the number of events organized for a given campaign round. A document of the French coalition evaluating the 2004 Jouez le Jeu campaign states that for this round (which was integrated into a worldwide anti-sweatshop campaign related to the Olympics in Athens), 500 events were organized in 35 countries, and 335 of these events took place in France (in 89 different *départements*). Of course such self-declarations cannot be taken at face-value. But it is certainly true that within the European context, the French campaign was exceptional in its mobilizing strength.

The French campaign was thus very much the opposite of the Swiss one. The campaign rounds were designed around the existing network of grassroots groups and activists; indeed, they became the very engine of the campaign. It is as if the campaign served foremost to feed the local groups with new content and tools to disseminate and mobilize. The strong integration of protest was set up from the beginning, with the Libère tes fringues campaign. The local AdM groups were collecting signatures and disseminating the campaign material. But it really took off with the 1998 campaign round. The structure around local *collectifs*—built on the model of the national *collectif*—was possible because most big organizational members of the campaign (such as AdM, CCFD, CFDT) had a substantial network of local groups. These different organizations encouraged their local groups not only to disseminate the campaign, but to reproduce the coalition structure at the local level. In the run-up to the 1998 campaign, the main organizations brought together their address files and communicated them to the local ADM (or other) groups that had been active in previous campaigns, asking them to form local coalitions to launch the 1998 campaign locally. A document gave them detailed and valuable advice as to how to proceed: it told them to first make a list of possible groups and persons to contact, and then send a letter of invitation for a meeting. For the meeting, the national campaign-makers had already thought of the list of points that had to be discussed in order to organize the coalition. Thus, the formation of local coalitions was something the national campaign-makers did not leave to chance, contrasting with the Swiss campaign which contented itself with vague encouragement.

As a result, the creation of the grassroots movement followed institutional ties. The great majority of the local coalitions were driven by local groups belonging to one of the three main organizations, and most of the members of the coalitions were groups whose 'mother-organization' was a member of the national coalition. But occasionally one also finds similar dynamics to those observed in the Swiss case: new groups formed to promote the campaign, or groups that did not belong to the broader network of campaign organizations, joined it. This was the case, for example, with student groups and also local ATTAC groups that joined the campaign's grassroots network. The difference from the Swiss campaign is that there was a highly developed and institutionalized structure to accommodate these groups. While such grassroots mobilization was very loosely tied to the campaign activities in Switzerland, they were structurally integrated into the campaign in France. A newsletter was dedicated to the communication between the campaign's headquarters and the local *collectifs*. With technological progress, a protected member space on the campaign's website was created to facilitate this communication. Campaigns were planned and launched by making the actions of grassroots groups an essential part of them. This means also that the whole grassroots mobilization was in fact a highly orchestrated, top-down endeavor. From the impulse to local coalition creation to the timing, content, and tactics of the campaign, everything was planned in the central campaign office.

The campaign templates were created in the coalition's national office and campaign manuals destined for the local *collectifs* were produced for each round. These kits presented the campaign, its claims and its tools to the local activists; they contained many practical tips for the organization of local protest events, and encouraged groups to evaluate their actions and give feedback to the national campaign. With the campaign's local network growing, so-called local correspondents, representing different territorial regions, were designated in order to facilitate the campaign's communication and diffusion. Training sessions were held to explain the campaign; national training days assembled the local correspondents, who would, in turn, organize regional sessions for the different local *collectifs*. The orchestration of the grassroots mobilization was thus overwhelming. The most important tactics were created and 'fixed' by the campaign; this was notably the case with petitions and rankings, but the campaign tried to 'control' other tactics, too. An interesting example is the local meetings with store managers. While this tactic was decentralized, the campaign put into place an impressive control effort around it. Local groups were meticulously instructed on how to proceed, and were to report to headquarters on the procedures of the meetings and their results, which were summarized in a detailed 28-page synthesis of the interviews that had taken place. Thus, there were some tactics—the campaign's main performances—which were implemented as uniformly as possible while nevertheless counting on the local grass-roots groups to carry them out.

But in spite of this orchestration and attempts to supervise local actions, this by no means led to uniform action throughout the French territory. As the coordinator put it: "politically, it was channeled, but pedagogically, it was very open".[7] What he meant by this is that the campaign provided the political content and tools: claims, argumentation, booklets, flyers etc. Within this framework and outside of these core actions, the local *collectifs* were strongly encouraged to organize their own activities for the campaign launches and, more generally, for an ongoing promotion of the campaign. The campaign manual of the 1998 round, for instance, stated a goal of action in 60 *départements* (stating such numerical goals was always a way of making an evaluation of the campaign's success possible). Actions should, it said, symbolize the campaign, allow the involvement of the public beyond the signature of the petition, allow all the local organizations to participate depending on their experiences, require neither a big budget nor long preparation.

The campaign manual then goes on to suggest an example of an action day that could be organized, including a stand in the city center, a meeting with store managers to which local journalists are invited, an exhibit, and a walk from one shop to the other. The campaign uses the French term *animations*, which designates a series of linked performances (Tilly 2008) to promote the campaign. With growing resources dedicated to the local *collectifs*, the campaign ended up by almost inviting local coalitions to conduct their own 'micro-campaigns,' using the same template for their actions as the one applied by the national campaign. In a document created for the 2004 campaign, named Feuille de route (roadmap), a three-step model was suggested: preparation, communication, and evaluation of the action. The *collectifs* were asked to define their goals (general and specific), and to list their actions by determining their public, the partners for the action, place and date, and the tools and resources required. The campaign coordinators provided an example for a press announcement and a form for the evaluation.

The actions always followed a similar pattern, consisting of a public action where information on the campaign was distributed and signature collection took place. These actions were occasions for protest tactics (by the members of the local *collectifs*), individualized participation tactics (the collecting and signing of petitions or the meeting of managers) and awareness-raising tactics (giving away general information on the topic of ethical consumption). But in spite of their similarity, a closer look also reveals how the composition of local coalitions colored the actions that were organized to promote the campaign. Depending on the characteristics of the local groups involved in the campaign, the local mobilization tactics took different forms. The diversity of these appropriations can be illustrated thanks to 'experience files' that the campaign-makers collected. These were short reports written by local coalitions to describe their actions in order to share their experiences with other local *collectifs*. The reports were collected on a dedicated website for international solidarity groups to share their experiences[8]. The 'experience files' illustrate how

---

7   Interview P. Erard, Paris, April 2008.

8   www.educasol.org.

the campaign's local tactics were embedded in other activities of the groups and how the actions continued beyond the schedule of the national campaign, although they cannot be said to be representative of all actions. Written for the use of other local *collectifs,* and thus dealing with the details of the actions and the problems they posed, they constitute very rich material concerning the functioning of local *collectifs* and their actions, and the forms of appropriation of the campaign's tactical repertoire at the grassroots level.

One experience file comes from a local union of the CFDT reporting on its awareness-raising activities among the *comités d'entreprises.* This local CFDT group—composed of three retirees, one of them having been involved in the Libère tes fringues campaign—formed in the spring of 2001 in light of the campaign to be launched at the end of the year. In September, the local Third World shop sent invitations to a number of groups to set up a local *collectif,* possibly following the instructions in the campaign manual, and the CFDT group responded to it. An action day was organized on November 20th, with stands in the city center and at the local Carrefour store, where signatures were collected and information and documents (the rankings and postcards) given to the interested public. After this action day, the experience file says, "a debriefing meeting was organized and one could feel if not a loss of interest, then a difficulty to find persons to take care of the continuity of the *collectif.*" It was decided that each organization would turn towards its traditional audience in order to further promote the campaign and collect signatures. The CFDT group started to contact different local and regional organs of the union, in order to find people inside the union structures and corporation committees to disseminate the campaign. Eventually, this led the group to find another way of disseminating the campaign, by trying to influence the purchase policies of corporation committees for Christmas presents.

Another example is the *collectif* from a city in Brittany, animated by a local international solidarity group. This coalition organized an action called 'Santa Claus is on Strike,' taking up the theme set by the national campaign launch, where a symbolic demonstration of Santa Clauses had been held. The action had its own budget which was financed partly by contributions of the involved groups, partly by the city. Three types of action were carried out: the *collectif* sent out a press release to the local press, three school interventions were held featuring the use of pedagogical tools from the campaign, and a small march was organized with members of the *collectif*'s organizations as well as some interested students who followed the school intervention. The march, in which according to the file around 100 participants took part, included several stops to distribute pamphlets, letters and ratings.

Finally, in one city in Eastern France, the city council voted in a motion favoring ethical purchases as a result of the Achats publics, achats éthiques campaign; the city government then wanted to expand this commitment with the help of educational programs, and contacted AdM for this purpose. Together with another association—the Ligue de l'Enseignement—school interventions were planned and conducted, using the solidarity breakfast as an intervention tool. Two employees of the education service of the local government attended a training session run by the national campaign coalition. The local actions here were thus actions of awareness-raising, taking place within an institutionalized context.

The experience files illustrate how at the grassroots level participating organizations shaped the actions according to their particular interests and preoccupations. Development education groups linked the campaigns to development education programs, while the CFDT section tried to mobilize corporation committees. The reports further show how the campaign's actions were often inserted into a series of other actions undertaken by local organizations. Actions of development education and school intervention were conceived as extensions of the CCC, and the issues of fair trade, development, and ethical consumption were treated at the same time. Through these popular education actions there was an ongoing thread of activities linked to the campaign, independent of its specific schedule. But it is also clear that it was the campaign framework, with its launching days and collective tools such as petitions, which facilitated the local functioning as coalitions. The action days—filled with protest events and signature collecting—were moments for cross-organizational mobilization; outside of this framework—at least this is what the experience files suggest—actions were often limited to one single organization working in the area in which it was specialized.

Who Participates, and How Much?

Who were the participants of the campaigns, and how many of them were there? According to an independent evaluation of the French campaign carried out to fulfill a requirement of EU funding, its petitions obtained 20,000 signatures in 1996, 80,000 in 1997, 140,000 in 1998, and 180,000 in 2002. The mobilizing force of the campaign thus steadily increased, following the growth of the local networks. The Swiss campaign had the same postcard campaign running over several years. According to indications one finds in campaign newsletters and in the magazine of the Bern Declaration, 48,000 postcards were sent in the campaign's first year (1999), and a total of 70,000 until 2003. The French campaign mobilized more citizens, yet if one accounts for the population difference (France having almost 10 times more inhabitants than Switzerland), the Swiss campaign appears to have been the more successful. But the number of participants in the Swiss case cannot actually be directly calculated from the number of postcards sent, since one and the same person is likely to send more than one postcard. Accordingly, it is difficult, from these numbers, to draw any conclusion as to the relevance of the movement with regard to the country's total population. Consumerist participation is also very difficult to measure. Firstly, the campaigns only give implicit recommendations and because their strategy is mostly one of 'discursive political consumerism,' and not an explicit boycott or buycott, its message is rather ambiguous. But even if they called for boycotts, measuring participation in boycotts is notoriously difficult (Friedman 1997).

There is more reliable data on the activists participating collectively in the campaign. In Switzerland, this concerned few people. Many of those participating offered only ad hoc support; just two groups that got involved over a long period of time were identified: the Globalance group, and the BD regional group. Overall, this makes for not more than two handfuls of activists. A quick assessment of their social properties, based on interviews and (in the case of the regional group) participant observation, shows that they were mainly young (that is, in their early to late twenties) and mostly students. Interviews with a number of volunteers from the BD regional group showed that while they all had different trajectories, they were all already characterized by various ties to NGOs, social movements or Parish associations in their childhood and adolescence, before they joined the group. In France, I can draw some conclusions on participants from the organizational data. It suggests that the social basis was both much broader and more diverse than in the Swiss case. From the beginning, the French campaign built on local activists of the different coalition organizations. An inventory dated August 8 2005 lists 114 such local coalitions. No data is available for the number of participants in each of them, but a reasonable estimation based on the experience files and indications I was given in interviews would say that they numbered somewhere between 5 and 15 members, whose degree of commitment in terms of time investment and participation certainly varied greatly. This would lead to a protest basis of somewhere around 500 and 1,500 volunteers, spread all over the country. More reliable information is available on the organizational composition of the local coalitions. The inventory lists 64 groups coordinated by AdM, 8 by the CFDT, 7 by CCFD, 4 by Peuples solidaires, and 28 by other organizations, most of them from the sector of international solidarity. Some of these local groups only consisted of one organization, but the majority were indeed coalitions.

The 2005 listing features the names of the organizations present in each local coalition. Overall, more than 60 organizations are mentioned; the organizational population on which the campaign drew was thus very broad. However, many of them were not present in more than one or two local coalitions, while others were present in most of them. Table 4.4 lists the most frequent organizations. Not surprisingly, AdM is the most represented organization, participating in 82 local coalitions; it is followed by the CCFD (68) and the CFDT (62). Associations of international solidarity follow.

The composition thus reveals which organizations weighed the most within the coalition. But it also reflects the diversity of the landscape of associations in France. Regarding this, the analysis shows that of the three groups of organizations that the campaign put forward to claim representativeness (international solidarity, unions, consumers), the sector of international solidarity is by far the most represented (AdM, CCFD, Peuples solidaires, etc.). The CFDT is also fairly present, but few other unions (the CGT being part of 12 coalitions). Finally, consumer associations are decidedly less important: the CLVC (19) is the organization that is most involved. The analysis also reveals some surprises: organizations defending human rights are present in many local coalitions, but do not play an important role at the national level (LDH, Amnesty, FDH); also, the parents' association FCPE is involved in many local coalitions.

Table 4.4   Composition of local coalitions: organizations present in 5 or more local coalitions

Organization	Number of local ESE coalitions of which it is part (in 2005)	Organization	Number of local ESE coalitions of which it is part (in 2005)
Artisans du monde	82	Agir Ici	12
CCFD	68	CGT	12
CFDT	62	Francas (popular education)	10
International solidarity (Ritimo, Cimade)	50	Fédération syndicale unitaire	10
ATTAC	26	Amnesty	9
CLCV (consumer association)	19	CSF (family association)	9
FCPE (parents' association)	19	Jeunes ouvriers chrétiens (JOC)	6
Peuples solidaires	17	Confédération paysanne	5
Ligue des droits de l'homme (LDH)	15	Fédération des droits de l'homme (FDH)	5

This analysis thus reveals the great diversity of associations involved in the campaign, but also, at the same time, its boundaries. The great majority of organizations belong to international solidarity, family and consumer organizations (but to a much lesser extent), unions (but in great majority the CFDT), and human rights groups. What is absent is revealing: in particular, there are no organizations belonging to the social movements on the far left, with the exception of ATTAC and the Confédération paysanne, both of which came to play a crucial role in the French global justice movement (Sommier et al., 2007, Agrikoliansky et al., 2005b). The fact that ATTAC originates within the *tiersmondistes* networks and that AdM is a founding member of it, probably explains its presence within certain coalitions; a lot of co-membership is likely to occur between these organizations. The next chapter continues the analysis of what the campaigns did and said; in particular, it will take a closer look at the collective action frames the campaigns used and at their collective identities, which sheds additional light on the boundaries of these coalitions.

Chapter 5
Campaign Styles and Protest in the Marketplace

This chapter continues the exploration of campaign building in Switzerland and France by focusing on cultural aspects. Campaigns are not only about tactics and participation, they are also about meaning. It appears that throughout the course of the campaigns, campaign makers were careful to communicate a message that was not perceived as radical, yet remained assertive enough to provoke changes, thus developing a balanced approach. What frames did they use and how did they present themselves to the public in order to broadcast this message? Which collective identities did they put forward? In the second part of this chapter, I add this analysis of campaign styles through frames and collective identities to the insights from the previous chapter on tactical action repertoires, in order to discuss the specificities of protest 'in the marketplace.' I show how both campaigns adapted their tactical and cultural repertoire to the particular institutional context of markets, and discuss the most important cross-country differences.

Collective Action Frames

In their booklets, petitions, or press releases, campaigns make public their demands and justify their claims, whether they are directed towards a general audience or towards members and sympathizers. They say what the problem addressed is about and thus engage in framing efforts (Snow 2004, Snow and Benford 1988, Snow et al. 1986). Collective action frames are properties of social movement organizations, "located in their records, brochures, fliers, and placards rather than merely in the heads of individuals" (Snow 2004, p. 387). To identify the collective action frames the campaigns used, I base my analysis on such primary sources: I gathered campaign publications such as booklets, pamphlets, petitions, and so forth.

The Swiss and French campaigns used a similar collective action frame, which characterized the whole internationally coordinated Clean Clothes Campaign. It built on opposing the 'dirty' clothing industry, characterized by social and environmental exploitation, to a market where clothes are produced in a 'clean' way. The basic structure of the information booklets produced in Switzerland and France was very similar. A substantial part of them was dedicated to the documentation of exploitation and worker abuse in factories in the developing world. Working conditions were described in much detail, sometimes illustrated with pictures. Corporations were characterized not only as responsible for this

Table 5.1   Frames addressed at potential campaign participants in France and Switzerland

Exploitation frame	Consumer frames		
	Consumer protection	*Consumer responsibility*	*Consumer power*
Documenting labor abuse cases: child labor, slavery, low wages, very long work hours, insalubrious conditions, union-bashing (F/CH) Personalization of exploited workers (F/CH) Responsibility of retailers in deterioration of labor conditions (F/CH) Profits of multinational companies (F/CH)	Lack of information: Consumers as ignorant victims (F) Right to be informed; transparency (F/CH)	Change consumption habits to change corporate practices (CH)	Consumer mobilization can make a difference (F/CH)

evolution—they were said to control the commodity chain and to push for ever cheaper prices and shorter production delays—but also as its main beneficiary. Against this improper functioning of markets, a counter-model was suggested, in which market functioning would be fair. The main solution advocated for reform of the market and improvement in working conditions would be the adoption of a code of conduct and its independent control. Using illustrations of cost distribution for a given product—shoes or a T-shirt—the campaigns moreover argued that such changes would not make clothes more expensive; they would simply lead to a fairer distribution of the benefits along the supply chain.

A closer analysis of the campaign documents suggests that the campaign makers used two main frames to mobilize activists, sympathizers, and, more generally, consumers: an exploitation frame, and a consumer frame which can be declined into several sub-frames. Table 5.1 presents the components of these different frames, and mentions in parenthesis their occurrence in the two countries studied.

Representing Exploitation

A lot of space is dedicated to documenting instances of labor rights abuse. The first French campaign ran under the slogan '*Are our clothes clean?*,' and gave a clear answer by stating '*100% child labor, 100% slavery, 0% unions.*' These three main issues were carried through the whole duration of the campaign, although the symbols were reversed in order to stress a positive message (that is, fighting for clothes with 0% child labor, 0% slavery, and 100% free unions). The exploitation frame puts forward documented cases of labor abuses such as child labor, slavery, forced and unpaid overtime, insalubrious conditions, or low wages. At the other end of the chain, retailers and brands had come to rule the market, pushing for ever lower production costs. They were represented as responsible for this development, while at the same time being its main beneficiary. This way of putting things was also crucial in the Swiss campaign. The first Swiss CCC booklet portrayed working conditions in production countries as 'unworthy,' 'nightmarish' and 'exploitative.' Using a representative example of those conditions, it described a Chinese production plant with 'XXL working time' and 'XXS wages,' with factory workers who work 'on average' 93 hours per week, seven days a week, sometimes up to 24 hours in a row. Of the 32 page booklet, 10 pages were used to illustrate these conditions, addressing the exploitation of female workers, child labor, union bashing, unsanitary conditions, subcontracting, and free export zones. On the following seven pages, companies were presented as beneficiaries of these conditions, using data on the rising benefits gained through moving production to lower wage countries. Thus, exploitative working conditions were directly linked to, and contrasted with, the ever growing benefits of Western multinational brands.

The depiction of labor abuses, both in general and by using concrete examples, was often done in fact-driven ways: calculating working hours, insalubrious conditions, low wages, and so on. But the campaigners also used forms of personalization in picture and text, which allowed for a more emotional appeal to consumers. Thus, beyond the cognitive framing of exploitation and its beneficiaries, the campaigns also used more emotional strategies to mobilize. An example of this personalization can be found in a documentation of the Swiss CCC from 2002, where one reads the description of the working life of Yetti, a 21 years old seamstress in a factory in Indonesia.

> I had hoped to be able to support my family through my work in the factory. But it turned out differently. Although I work every day from morning to late at night, I earn so little that I cannot send any money home. Sometimes I work 80 hours a week and earn no more than 4 francs a day. Recently our supervisor said that each one of us had to sew 350 pieces a day before we're allowed to go home. When some of us protested, they were threatened and some of them even beaten. That way we work until late at night and are completely exhausted. […] 1700 people work here, most of them young women like me. We work for Adidas, Germany. That's where the things we produce are sent to and sold at very expensive prices—a shirt for 80 francs, as I've heard. For this amount I have to work 20 days!

In a French publication accompanying the exposition for the Libère tes fringues campaign, one can find the portrait of a worker from Guatemala, a member of a union, who was beaten to death—presumably by armed men trying to intimidate workers. There are other such depictions of suffering in the campaigns, appealing, it seems, to the pity of Western consumers, and thus using the same emotional strategies that are often applied by humanitarian organizations (Boltanski 1993). Workers' misery is prominently put forward through portrayals and pictures, and contrasted with the luxury choices of Western consumers, as exemplified by the story of Yetti. Personalization and identification with workers and unionists from the South was also one of the aims of the conference tours by unionists and NGOs; they delivered first-hand accounts of cases of abuse, but also of collective struggle. Such tours were organized by the international office of the CCC; the invited workers traveled around different CCC countries and spoke in various venues. First-hand accounts could also be used for campaign launches, directed at the media. Thus, for the re-launch of the French campaign in 2008, a Chinese worker was invited to speak at the Press conference, and interviews were arranged with radio and newspaper journalists.

However, personalization and depictions of suffering are only one part of the story, and it is necessary to nuance the place appeals to feelings of pity occupied in the framing of the campaigns. The language was more often factual than emotional. More importantly, appeals to emotional reactions contained another aspect which did not put forward the exploitation and individual suffering of workers, but aimed at creating solidarity with workers struggling collectively to improve their working conditions. In this respect, the campaigns clearly differed from those humanitarian appeals that mostly rely on appeals to pity and compassion with the main goal of collecting money for immediate relief (Boltanski 1993) and without politicizing questions at all. In the framing of the CCC, it was always made clear that the actions were part of a collective struggle. Consumer power in the West was complementary to workers' fights in the South; through their participation in the campaigns, consumers could contribute to improving working conditions. For instance, in the booklet for the French 1998 campaign, it says "Because they refuse to be mistreated, workers from production countries DO NOT JUST WAIT FOR US TO GET MOBILIZED. But their action is often doomed to failure. We can help them by becoming consumer-citizens" (capitals in the original). The campaigns underlined the solidarity dimension by insisting on episodes of collective struggle by workers in the South.

Consumer Protection, Consumer Responsibility, and Consumer Power

Consumption frames were declined in various forms. First, there was a consumer or 'consumer protection' frame. This was especially developed in the French campaign. From the first campaign round, the image of product tags was used, and the product tag became the official emblem and name of the campaign ('Ethics on the Product Tag'). The consumer argument develops around two core aspects. On the one hand, consumers were presented as victims of the carelessness of corporations regarding conditions of production. They might buy clothes produced under inhumane circumstances—that is, by children or slaves—without knowing it. A document from the 1998 campaign 'Jouez le jeu' round stated: "we can be led to buying clothes and sports shoes produced under intolerable conditions. For now, consumers have absolutely no guarantee that would allow them to buy products of good 'social quality.'" A similar point was made in a brochure from the 1996 round:

> Clothes and shoes produced under such (intolerable) conditions are sold in France. However, for now the clothing and shoe shops do not give any reliable information on the conditions of production of the articles they sell. It is thus impossible to give preference to corporations that effectively respect fundamental social and environmental rights.

Thus, the campaign unveils to consumers that they might buy clothes made by children or slaves without knowing it. The campaign lifts their ignorance, and asks them to mobilize in order to make corporations tell the truth on these issues in the future, allowing for a truly informed purchase.

In Switzerland, the use of this kind of consumer frame was less explicit in the first campaign documents. It would become central, however, at a later stage, when the first company rankings were published together with consumer associations. These rankings evaluated the 'social records' of companies with regard to their respect for labor standards. In these rankings, the targeted retailers' transparency was one of the criteria: "Customers have a right to transparency," the booklet stated, and corporations should inform them about their social records. More characteristic of the Swiss campaign was another kind of consumption frame, related to the political consumerism tradition. Rather than being about consumers' rights to accurate product information, it adopts a rhetoric of consumers' *responsibilities*. It is about how they should behave as consumers, and how changes in purchasing behavior may change corporate practices and even transform society at large. This type of framing was implicit in the rankings published after 2004; it can be found more explicitly in 'consumer tips' given by the campaign in some of its publications. In a documentation dating from 2002 called *Textilkodex—Das Schnittmuster für gerecht produzierte Kleider* (Textile code: the pattern for fair clothes), one page was dedicated to such consumer advice. Some of those tips could very well have figured in a publication of a consumer protection organization, too. It was suggested, for example, that effects on clothes like oil finish, 'worn look' or 'wash and wear' may hint at the use of environmentally harmful products. But other tips were about how readers *should* consume: "Developing your own style of clothes will be cheaper in the long run than following every short-term fashion […] The clothes collection bin is not a storage place for wrong purchases." In another publication from 2008, consumers were asked to privilege fair trade and organic clothes, to think twice about the 'throw-away mentality' and to privilege better quality instead. Finally, in a supplement to the BD magazine speaking to a young audience (Fair Future 01/2006), the organization told its readers: "don't buy cheap clothes, you know they won't last long," and "don't buy cheap sales offers, they contribute to our wasting of clothes."

This consumer responsibility frame from the Swiss campaign was much less present in France. Here, the campaign used this frame in the beginning, when the campaign was also a means of promoting AdM shops. But subsequently, such rhetoric was mostly absent. In particular, the ratings published by the French campaign, which imitated the template of school grades, had a distinctively less consumer frame; they were not accompanied, as were some Swiss publications, by recommendations of particular labels or brands. Particularly telling, in this regard, is the '*mémo du consom'acteur*' (a 'guideline for consumer-activists') published by the French campaign. For the major part of it, this guideline was not about how political consumers should consume, but what they should do *outside* of their everyday consumption to protest against corporations and thus make them change practices (things like signing petitions, joining a local *collectif*, etc.). The consumer-activist was thus much more an activist than a consumer orienting her purchases by political goals.

The final consumption frame that was widely used was a 'consumer power' frame. Campaigners maintained that consumer power—collective action by consumers—could push corporations to change their behavior and to assume responsibility. This frame thus had a performative character: it tried to produce a bandwagon effect. By saying that consumer power can make a difference—and by using historic examples for this—consumers are mobilized and the prophecy thus fulfilled. This motivational frame is supposed to convince audiences that they are not alone in their concerns. Taking action is worthwhile and protesting can make a difference because many other consumers have the same concerns and are willing to act accordingly. Different means were used to support this belief. The French campaign repeatedly quoted polls carried out by the research agency Credoc showing a growing social awareness among consumers. It also referred to past consumer campaigns that worked. Both campaigns also regularly mentioned the number of postcards sent and signatures collected. Such displays of the importance of the movement or its potential were not only addressed to the campaigns' targets (corporations), but were also intended to mobilize internally—in order to counter skeptical observers maintaining that such campaigns are useless and do not change anything at all. The brochure of the French 'Jouez le jeu' campaign round, for example, addressed the skeptics directly:

> If you, consumers, demand the adoption of a code of conduct […], you have a chance to be listened to. And the more you are, the more you'll be credible. […] Naïve? No. The leaders of sports retailing are keen on conserving their positive image: it's the very essence of their marketing strategy.

A Reform-Oriented Ideology

The French and Swiss campaigns' collective action frames do not contain any references to dependency theories of development. They concern the issue of working conditions in sites of production for textile products, and do not address the question of development. The scope of the campaigns is limited. In the 1970s and early 1980s, the dependency theory frame helped to construct the role of consumption, consumers, and multinational corporations in the process of development of third world countries, and in particular to build up a direct link between consumption practices in the North and development in the South. Now, given the absence of any reference to this theory in the Clean Clothes Campaign, the different frames together still make sense in an overarching narrative, but it is a different one. In this view, the presence of multinational corporations in developing countries is no longer pictured as having disastrous consequences per se. On the contrary: if firms respect minimal social standards and thus adopt an ethical approach to their business, they can be an important force of development. The development of a textile production sector is seen in a positive light, as a sign of growing economic development—but it must go together with the respect of labor standards. Advocating codes of conduct to improve working conditions, the Clean Clothes Campaign wants firms to become allies in the pursuit of a more ethical development. Through codes of conduct, they should promote workers' rights at their subcontractors' factories in countries like Bangladesh, China, or Honduras. Dependency theory and the quest for an alternative market has thus given way to the moral responsibility of global corporations. Multinational corporations are no longer depicted as responsible for underdevelopment in general, but only for certain, particular abuses and thus only guilty of specific misdemeanors, not systemic ones—problems that could be fixed through a better legal framework, whether it be public or private. The master frame or the basic ideology of the campaign, one could say, was reformative and social-democratic, rather than anti-capitalist and revolutionary.

The organizations participating in the coalitions in Switzerland and France mostly shared this common ideology. The core organizations belonged to the moderate, reform-oriented left, and not to the radical, anti-capitalist one. When the founding organization behind the French campaign, Artisans du monde, moved more to the left in its political stance in the course of the global justice movement, it became increasingly difficult for the fair trade organization to continue being a driving force in the campaign, as it disagreed fundamentally with some of the campaign's core strategies but failed to impose its views. I will discuss this process in more detail in the following chapter, but it hints at the importance of a certain ideological cohesion within coalitions. However, while this seems to be important for core actors in the coalition, on the margins—that is, mostly on the local level and without an important political commitment and responsibility in the campaign—some organizations with more radical ideological worldviews did participate in campaign actions. Specific action frames, in these instances, mobilized groups in spite of diverse ideological backgrounds. Rather than pointing to the capacity of such frames to mobilize consensus and action (Klandermans 1984, 1997), it might hint at the observation that it is the very fact of performing (contentious) actions—organizing a rally, signing a petition, collecting signatures—that allows those involved to overcome differences with regard to framing, and thus enables the participation of individuals and groups that do not share the same worldviews.

Who We Are: Campaign Styles and Collective Identity

Meaning is not only attached to frames, it is also more deeply anchored in how a campaign presents itself through its actions. Tactics 'talk,' too. Which tactics and frames are used and which ones are dismissed, and *how* tactics are used, says something about how campaign makers want to be perceived by others (Jasper 1997). Campaigns construct a recognizable collective and public actor. They give a message about who they are—they build up a collective identity. They do this by enacting a certain culture of protest or, in analogy to Eliasoph and Lichterman's concept of 'group style' (Eliasoph and Lichterman 2003), a 'campaign style,' which corresponds to a (disputed) understanding of what form collective action should take and what image should be given to the outside. Collective identities are thus also strategically created and publicly displayed (Bernstein 1997).

In accordance with their reform-oriented ideology, the Swiss and French campaigns both aimed at producing a self-image of the campaign as a strong, yet reasonable actor and potential partner for corporations in collaborative initiatives on code monitoring. The campaigns did not want to appear as radicals raising impossible demands; they did not want their targets to be able to dismiss them as idealists disconnected from the realities of market competition and supply chain management. Instead, with their broad reliance on conventional action forms and reformist framing of demands, the campaign coalitions in both countries wanted to appear as reasonable and respectable actors with whom corporations could dialogue and negotiate. Whether this strategy worked or not is another question that will be discussed in the next chapter, but interviews, participant observation, and document analysis all suggest that this self-representation was the campaign makers' intention. Three observations from my fieldwork can illustrate the strategies of the two campaigns' self-representation: the controversies around some issues and tactics considered as too 'emotional' or radical, the meticulous justification of the objective validity of the rankings they published, and more generally the way tactics were chosen, justified, and carried out.

Controversies around tactics or frames can help show the implicit boundaries of collective identities and reveal the strategies of self-representation (Ghaziani 2008). In France, this can be seen in the discussions on the issue of child labor and the use of strategies using child labor to mobilize support. While local *collectifs* were sometimes in favor of this kind of strategy, the campaign makers dismissed it as excessively emotional, therefore irrational and possibly even self-defeating, because it was calling for the wrong type of adherence to the campaign. Child labor worked extremely well as a mobilizing theme. Reports of child labor for popular brands had repeatedly provoked media scandals, damaging public images of brands and compelling them to apologize and take measures. Of all the issues addressed by the campaign—wages, overtime, security, right of association, etc.—child labor was the one companies most easily embraced and were willing to fight against, presumably because of the high negative publicity that goes along with publicly revealed cases. But despite this strong potential to mobilize the media and consumers and provoke reactions from firms, the campaign's attitude towards child labor was ambivalent and its use of the child labor argument cautious. While almost every publication featured child labor as an issue—it was, for example, one of the three claims made in the French campaign's slogan, along with freedom of association and slavery—it was also always accompanied by qualifying remarks. Child labor, it said, was not the main problem—it was but a symptom of the larger problem of poverty. A ban on child labor might often have dramatic consequences, not least on the children themselves. Because their families cannot afford to send them to school but on the contrary depend on their financial contribution, children might be driven into activities that are hardly preferable, like crime or prostitution. According to the campaigns, a focus on child labor alone was therefore not sufficient, and campaigns and boycotts focusing on child labor could have consequences worse than child labor itself. The official campaign therefore sometimes found itself going against the demands of its audience and local groups, for the issue of child labor was a popular one.

There were sound arguments for the adoption of a nuanced position on the issue of child labor, but the campaign-makers rejected a simplistic answer to this problem not just because of the questionable consequences of such policies; they also wanted to avoid being perceived as adopting an excessively emotional posture. In an interview, the person in charge of the local network in the French campaign addressed the problems that the popularity of the issue of child labor raised. After evoking the complexity of the problem, she states:

> On this subject, we tried to explain things in a more nuanced and realistic way, also because we didn't want to fall into something too dogmatic, merely pointing at human misery, because that's the risk when one speaks of children: a depoliticization of the question.[1]

This statement points to the specific positioning of the campaign, built on an opposition between a rational and an emotional approach. On the 'rational' side, one finds a nuanced and realistic vision. On the emotional side, the position is dogmatic, depoliticizing, and voyeuristic in pointing at human misery. These qualifications contain two stances against which the campaign makers define

---

1 Interview with Nadia, French CCC, Paris, April 2008.

themselves: one that isn't realist because it is too dogmatic and radical, and one that isn't realist because it is depoliticizing. The campaign's stance is defined in negative against both of them: the campaigners do not want to appear as radicals claiming unrealistic demands nor as excessively compassionate. A further observation confirms this observation. In one of a number of files destined for the campaigns' local correspondents—the one about 'awareness-raising'—the activists are warned of pitfalls. Concerning child labor, it says

> the public will be more receptive to the problem of child labor (than to that of
> social rights of adults). It can thus become a trigger for an intervention, before
> extending the debate to the exploitation of adults. But it is important to show that
> if child exploitation needs to be banned, it also needs to be put into an economic,
> social and cultural context which excludes all radicalism.

The preoccupation with 'too' emotional and all-or-nothing stances similarly characterized the Swiss campaign. Its position on child labor was the same—it never put forward child labor as the main issue.

The campaigns constantly oscillated between the requirement to produce strong and widely appealing messages in order to mobilize the public and get media attention, and their willingness to present a nuanced picture and appear as a potential negotiating partner to the firms they targeted. The rankings can show this dilemma, too. Rankings were strong messages; they evaluated well-known companies, gave them mostly bad grades, and put them in an order and thus in direct competition with each other. Especially in France, rankings were quite radical: they contained explicit judgments about companies' policies that left no room for interpretation, and were written in a tone indicating a morally superior perspective. But at the same time (and because of this strong message), the campaign makers dedicated great efforts to making these rankings 'objective' by using fact-driven knowledge and expertise and serious methods of inquiry. To assess their 'empirical credibility' (Jenness 1999, p. 556), the campaigns relied on reports on labor abuses coming from different sources within the transnational network of the anti-sweatshop movement. The international coordination of the CCC was the most important source of this kind of research and coordinated investigations on different subjects—the documentation of labor abuses but also, in the course of the unfolding of the campaign and of corporations' counter-strategies, the effects of the wide use of social audits. Examples and reports coming from the North American anti-sweatshop movement were also often referred to. But 'scientific' methodology was not only important in order to prove the validity of the claims. A meticulous methodology was also applied for the evaluation and ranking of the corporations. Different criteria like CSR policies and transparency were defined and points were given for each one of them, with the points total forming the ranking. The information given on each corporation—based on questionnaires sent to the firms, and on research based on their published documents and web pages—was very detailed. These investigations were very time-consuming and were taken extremely seriously. The French campaign, in addition to an employee specifically dealing with this task, employed interns to assist him in the collection of this information.

The published evaluations and rankings thus took great care to be transparent, objectify the criteria used, and justify the methodology. The Swiss rankings gave detailed evaluations on different aspects—quality of codes of conduct, implementation, transparency of the firms. The French 'barometer of social quality'—the last ranking the campaign published—went the furthest in its methodology. Precisely because firms had reacted very strongly to previous rankings and perceived them as a very radical tactic, the campaign-makers developed an extremely complex and carefully thought through methodology to evaluate each firm's performance in order to appear as objective and 'scientific' as possible. The methodology consisted of measuring the performance on two issues—the management of social responsibility and the information the company gave out, measured by commitments, practices, and (for the second issue) transparency, weighting them respectively 20%, 50%, and 30%. In the calculation each criterion featured several sub-criteria, each one being measured by several indicators (indicators of process and indicators of accomplished efforts). It is true that this last ranking pushed the complexity of the methodology rather far, but the rankings produced previously had already relied on elaborate calculations. This use of 'scientific' methodology was meant to provide the campaign with legitimacy as an objective evaluator of the corporations, rather than politically motivated.

Finally, the wish to portray themselves as reasonable and serious players can be seen in many other examples. It is visible when analyzing what campaigns say and do, but also in *how* they do it. For instance, when at the launch of the French Exploiter n'est pas jouer campaign a demonstration of Santa Clauses was organized in order to attract media attention, this action was doubled by a 'serious' press conference where a spokesperson for the campaign—not dressed as Santa Claus—explained the claims. Public appearance was also of great concern in the street actions of the regional Swiss group I had joined. An episode from my fieldwork illustrates this. A few weeks before Christmas, I was one in a group of three activists distributing pamphlets about labor conditions in the toy industry[2] in a busy shopping street. On the first Saturday we positioned ourselves directly in front of a famous toy store. When the store manager found out, he was not pleased about our presence and ended up calling the police. The most experienced member of our small group discussed the situation with the store manager and the policemen, who strongly encouraged us to move our action further away from the store. We finally retreated to a café and ended up distributing the rest of our pamphlets somewhere else. When more pamphleting took place on the following weekend, we got clear instructions: despite the fact that none of our behavior had

---

2   *Stricto sensu*, this was thus not the CCC but a very similar campaign on codes of conduct in the toy industry. But the same regional group would stage actions for both campaigns, which were carried out by the same NGO and had a very similar outlook.

been illegal or required prior authorization, the person in charge of the campaign told us not to place ourselves in front of the same store but to carry out our action in more neutral spaces like bus stops. Direct confrontation or even provocation should be avoided.

The professional nature of the campaigns means that the campaign-makers have to control everything that takes place under its label. They need to monitor grassroots participation and make sure that they do not trespass on the campaigns' collective identity. This is why the coordinator instructed us on how to behave when pamphleting. In the case of the French campaign, the unity of this style required a great effort of supervision of the grassroots movement. The contribution of grassroots groups was highly encouraged, but also had to take place within the boundaries set by the national coalition. In the documents serving the internal communication between the national headquarters and the local chapters, one finds countless examples of how local actions were channeled. The material, tools, and training the French campaign put into place to coordinate the more than 100 local groups was designed to give them information and sustain the mobilization, but also to shape and, ultimately, control the self-presentation of the local coalitions who represented the national *collectif*. There were certain rules and certain boundaries about what local chapters should and should not do, and how they should appear. To some extent, such rules were implicit and taken for granted. Thus, it was clear that local groups would not organize protest forms that went beyond the tactical repertoire of the campaign as, for example, violent tactics to keep customers from purchasing in a given store. But in the campaign material, one can find some explicit calls to advocate a moderate approach and use a nuanced argumentation. In the *guide du correspondant local* from 2005, a document produced by the campaign headquarters and directed at the local groups, the campaign calls for caution with regard to boycotts and arguments on outsourcing. Regarding boycotts, it says

> Even if the *collectif* denounces explicitly the companies it targets, it does not call for boycotts, but only publicly addresses them. Be careful not to radicalize the accusation by indirectly inferring the shortcut pressure = boycott.

And on outsourcing,

> even though the topic of the collectif and outsourcing are both consequences of the ultra-free market globalization, one cannot systematically deduce a causal relation between them. The collectif does not take a position on this.

Both these 'pitfalls' point to a positioning of the campaign coalition as a moderate actor, which explicitly wants to avoid both tactics and discourses that would put it closer to the far left. The *mot d'ordre* of professionalism and respectability thus extends to the use of contentious action modes. When protesting, the campaign continues to defend its identity as a professional and reasonable player. Protest is activated in a strategic way and carried out in a contained manner.

When do we find an avoidance of 'passionate' approaches in favor of a sober, nuanced one, and when are emotional and more radical strategies admitted? The strategies need to be related to the social properties of the campaign-makers and the field positioning of the organizations behind the campaigns. The controversies on the use of certain tactics and frames are embedded in the position the campaign and the organizations behind it take in the broader field of social movement organizations. Using more or less radical and emotional strategies serves to distinguish oneself from other approaches, and to achieve a certain credibility in the face of targets, if sometimes to the detriment of a more popular public appeal. In both countries, the campaigns saw themselves as holding a position in the center, between two opposing strategies: a humanitarian, charitable approach, and the radical, uncompromising approach of the anti-capitalist left. Between these two poles, the campaigns traced a middle way and deployed a style of balanced protest. That there was not always a consensus on what this meant, and that strategic disputes increasingly came to characterize the campaigns will be the subject of the next chapter. But also from a comparative perspective, what is striking is that this balanced approach did not translate into the same tactical action repertoires.

What is the 'Middle Way'? Cultural Contexts of Campaign Repertoires

Generally speaking, campaign tactics and framing were very similar across both countries. Core tactics were the same—petitions and rankings. Frames were mostly similar, and both campaigns aimed at presenting themselves as a reasonable protest actor pursuing a balanced approach. This similarity is not surprising, given that the campaigns were part of a European network of coordinated campaigns. The national members of the Clean Clothes network shared the same campaign framework; claims and goals (in particular the Clean Clothes code of conduct) were identical, and campaigns were often launched on the same theme at more or less the same time, in particular on the occasion of transnational sports events. Claims and action forms thus circulated. Furthermore, the main national organizations that carried out the campaigns came from the same movement families, shared the same reformist ideology, and had many other characteristics in common, not least their strong professionalism. But in spite of this similarity and the shared goal of casting a balanced message, the tactics campaign makers in both countries employed were quite different. In particular, the use of grassroots participation and collective protest was much higher in France, while in Switzerland, consumer tactics were more developed.

The French campaign's establishing of a broad coalition and its wide use of grassroots groups results from the desire to show the extensive involvement of consumers and citizens in the issues raised by the campaign throughout the French territory. It also reflects the organizational patterns that are different in Switzerland

and France, with French organizations building on the large network of local activist groups, and Swiss organizations lacking them. Behind organizational variation, the analysis of the campaigns' self-presentation suggests an additional interpretation of this difference. Both campaigns were trying to put pressure on the retailers they targeted, yet they also wanted to appear as reasonable potential partners and therefore sought to deploy a moderate form of protest. It seems that this balance was attained at different points of equilibrium in the two countries: what a campaign has to do in order to be perceived as legitimate was not the same. What was seen as a necessary and legitimate strategy in France was perceived as too radical in Switzerland: the building up of an impressive network of local coalitions staging regular protest actions was looked at with some bewilderment by the Swiss campaign coordinator. In an interview, he told me that his goal was not to mobilize as many people as possible in the streets, in an obvious nod to the French case to which I had referred. Instead, he said, he wanted to lead an efficient campaign, even if it consisted mostly in lobbying and mobilized many fewer activists.[3] On the flipside, it meant that what was perceived as perfectly legitimate in Switzerland was seen as insufficient in France: the Swiss campaign style, characterized by the individualized and merely occasional participation of citizens and consumers, could not count as serious campaigning in the French context.

There are thus differences in the shared meanings of what constitutes a legitimate form of campaigning even for actors belonging to very similar ideological backgrounds and pursuing the same goals. It points to nationally differentiated patterns of participation. These patterns are not immutable 'civic cultures' (Almond and Verba 1963): the study of the campaign's origin shows that the Swiss Bern Declaration used very participative forms of campaigning in the 1970s and early eighties. But since then, the organization seems to have succeeded in imposing itself as an advocacy group whose voice can count without a need to broadly mobilize its public. In France, on the other hand, not having grassroots support for the campaign was portrayed as stigmatizing; for French activists, it stood for 'Anglo-Saxon styles' of political campaigning[4] that were less preoccupied with raising consciousness among the public than by achieving short-term goals. In this respect, rallying broad grassroots support was a message just as much directed at a campaign's targets as at its social movement sector audience. And it had a self-reinforcing tendency, too. When the French campaign decided to make the ranking its main action form in the early 2000s, local coalitions complained of lacking a 'hook' for public actions. They demanded more participatory tools such as petitions or letter-writing, to provide some form of action at their gatherings. In Switzerland, such a dynamic could not take place since there were no established activist networks to disseminate the campaign. The less mediated way of the Swiss campaign, with the campaign organizers directly communicating with individual

---

3   Interview with campaign coordinator, Zurich, January 2007.
4   Interview with Jean-Claude, CCFD, Paris, April 2008.

sympathizers in their role as petition signatories or political consumers, was a much better match for the consumer tactics of the repertoire.

Tactics and Frames in the Marketplace

The analysis of the tactics, frames and collective identities of the campaigns reveals some of the specific forms that protest takes in the market place. The case studies suggest that the tactics and the logics (Della Porta and Diani 2004) movements use when targeting corporations instead of state authorities, have certain distinct features. To voice their claims and put pressure on their targets, the campaign-makers adapted their tactics to the institutional setting in which they took place. They devised tactics and framing strategies that used market competition, firms' reputations, and consumer power in innovative ways in order to create 'assertive' action forms (Amenta 2006) with regard to corporate actors.

Rather than relying on collective marches or demonstrations, the movements deployed their force in an individualized form through postcards and letter campaigns. Petitions bring signatures together, aligning them on sheets of paper, and thus show the numerical strength of the movement. Classic petitions are used by both campaigns, but they actually relied much more on postcard petitions. In a way, the postcard petition can be seen as an adaptation of the petition to a context where there is more than one target—in this case, several companies are targeted at the same time. Postcards allow the division of the petition among those targets, and can be used in both an individual and a collective way. On the one hand, the campaigns asked participants who sent postcards to the targets to notify the campaign, in order to obtain an overall number. This success in terms of numbers is important, especially with regard to media reports. It gives the campaign something to communicate to the media, just as the localized collection of signatures constitute occasions for media reports. Furthermore, it shows the strength of the movement and thus its importance and representativeness. But on the other hand, the campaign organizers encouraged the individual sending of postcards to targets. The effect, it is presumed, will be greater if a company receives, say, 1,000 postcards sent individually to them by consumers than one package containing those 1,000 postcards sent by the campaign organization.

Scandal also served to build up threat (Offerlé 1998), through damaging the public reputations of corporations. Firms that have managed to build up recognizable brands are particularly sensitive to their public image and reputation; scandal can be a very efficient way to make them yield to demands (Bartley and Child 2011, Soule 2009). The campaigns themselves reveal scandals such as particular cases of labor abuses, often through the transnational network of the CCC. But many such scandals are also revealed by other actors, in particular the media, and the campaigns can use them to pressure companies. But while information on labor abuses was widely used by both Clean Clothes Campaigns, they were most of the time of a general nature and not linked to a particular firm, with only a few exceptions. The specific 'urgent appeals' in support of a particular labor conflict were not at the center of the campaigns, and the organizations only invested limited resources to disseminate and publicize them. Only twice—once in each country—did a specific corporation become the target of a bigger campaign effort (through an urgent appeal): Carrefour's implication in an accident at a factory in Bangladesh, and the Swiss underwear producer Triumph's production in Burma. In these cases, the weapon of scandal was used specifically; but usually shaming was done in a general manner, which gives it less leverage. This, of course, had to do with the campaign organizations' reluctance in the use of strategies deemed too radical.

Framing firms as responsible for working conditions in general and particular cases of labor scandals were part of the campaigns' framing strategies directed against firms. But this was complemented by a frame that pointed at potential benefits that firms could obtain by changing their practices: firms should change because there was a consumer demand for it, because 'there was something in it' for them. This 'profit' frame was used explicitly in the Swiss campaign to encourage firms to adopt codes of conduct: "By demanding 'clean' clothes, we tell the companies that the sense of justice is also a way of distinguishing oneself from one's competitors."[5] The French campaign's use of this frame was less explicit, but nevertheless evident. The repeated reference to the growing numbers of consumers caring about social issues showed that there was a potential market for socially responsible corporations. And the campaign used the competition between retailers to heighten the pressure on them through its rankings. An internal document clearly reveals that rankings were designed to take advantage of market competitiveness:

> This comparative table puts companies in competition, and those that are not yet committed will be the bad pupils regarding human rights at the workplace, which will lead them to react. It's a question of (public) image and one knows that corporations care more and more about this.[6]

The collective action frames the Swiss and French CCC used to address firms thus relied on what Raeburn (2004) calls frame blending, i.e. a 'dualistic rhetorical strategy.' The CCC, like the LGBT groups studied by Raeburn, "combin[ed] an ideology of ethics with an ideology of profits [and] argue[d] that doing the right thing is good for the bottom line" (Raeburn 2004, p. 218). It was a stick-and-carrot strategy: putting pressure on companies by publicly denouncing them, but also promising potential benefits if companies yielded to demands and thus moved out of the spotlight. Thus, the framing strategies, too, were adapted to the marketplace: they used competition between firms and emphasized the profit that could be made from selling 'ethical' fashion.

---

5   CCC booklet in Switzerland, 1999.
6   Internal document, (undated, probably circa 1999), campaign archives

The profit frame derived its credibility in great part by the brandishing of the rising force of political consumers, which campaigns used both as a threat and a promise. But actually, this rise in 'ethical' consumers was, to a significant degree, a result of the campaigns. The campaigns put forward the growing power of political consumers, but they also strongly contributed to the creation of this very social figure. In the campaigns, a narrative was constructed around the idea that there are more and more concerned consumers who raise questions about conditions of production. These consumers address 'their' clothing store directly, by sending them postcards and letters with questions regarding their social record. On the postcards of the French Libère tes fringues campaign, the style suggested that an individual consumer was speaking directly to the corporation: "Since your firm is one of the leaders of the clothing industry, I'm addressing you in order to know if you have social and environmental criteria regarding the selection of your subcontractors." The Swiss campaign used the same rhetorical 'trick' and encouraged consumers to send letters asking ever more precise questions.

These postcards convey the idea that a consumer addresses her clothing store purely out of personal concern. In some cases, this is probably true. But it is difficult to determine to what extent such preoccupations actually *already* exist within the activists and petitioners that support a campaign before the campaign puts in place the tools (public framing and postcard petitions) that allow consumers to express them. Quite clearly, however, it is only *because of* the collective *mise en forme* by the campaign that they come to be voiced. Thus the campaign, while saying that it is the expression of such rising concerns among consumers, and that it speaks in the name of political consumers, in fact very much contributes to create them. It does not just give voice to a latent concern, but it (partly) constructs this concern and creates the tools that help to disseminate and express it. This performative aspect of a campaign's activities is common to all politics of representation (Bourdieu 1991, Offerlé 1988, 1998).

The existence of such political consumers is crucial to the stick-and-carrot strategy of a campaign. It is not only because campaigns build up a threat and publicly attack corporations, that the latter should yield to demands, it is because consumers care about issues of labor conditions and want to buy ethical or 'clean' clothes. The existence of such concerned consumers shows the 'pragmatic legitimacy' or viability of ethical practices (den Hond and de Bakker 2007, p. 907). The French campaign does this explicitly by repeatedly quoting polls showing a growing preoccupation of consumers with social and environmental issues. A study conducted by the Credoc in 1993 entitled *Vers une consommation engagée* (Towards a political consumption) showing that about half of French consumers choose products because the producer has a humanitarian or ecological commitment, is cited repeatedly in campaign materials. But perhaps more importantly, the campaigns gave consumers the possibility to act as political consumers when purchasing clothes (Balsiger 2010). Consciousness-raising and educational tactics is thus aimed at informing and educating specific audiences to the implications of consumption and the functioning of global markets. The educative tactics of the campaigns—their reliance on non-contentious tactics like school interventions or other actions of consciousness-raising such as film screenings or conferences—thus played an important role in this process. They were designed to make consumers more conscious. This is actually also what firms thought the campaigns should do: produce this awareness. Once consumers integrate this into their practices and become willing to pay more for cleaner clothes, firms said, it will be possible to implement better working conditions.[7]

Finally, the ranking of companies according to their 'social records,' played another role besides putting pressure on firms: this consumer tactic also gives potential political consumers guidance in their purchases. Ratings and recommendations thus equip political consumers with choice to facilitate their purchases as political consumers. While this aspect remains mostly implicit, it is nonetheless clear that firms are put into competition with regard as to where consumers should shop. In France, explicit buying recommendations were not given, mostly because none of the targeted firms fulfilled the campaign's demands. But in Switzerland, the campaign ended up embracing the buycott as an explicit tactic: it recommended specific labels and published an 'ethical shopping map' of the stores that sold ethical fashion.

Consumption was thus an important aspect of the campaigns' tactics and framings. They put forward the rising force of 'political consumers' while at the same time contributing to changing consumer preferences through their tactics of awareness-raising and orientation tools. The role of consumption—not as an individual act, but as a practice that is shaped by different collective actors—must be incorporated when we study how movements challenge markets. More generally speaking, the analysis of the campaign building has shown how tactics and framings use the marketplace setting in many ways: in addition to promoting political consumer behavior, they directly compare firms' 'social records' and thus use market competition to make firms react to demands; they argue with the potential profits as an incentive to action; they try to take advantage of the importance of reputation to threaten firms; and they individualize petitions to reach different targets simultaneously.

---

7   This position was expressed, for example, at a round table on the guarantee of social quality in supply chains, organized by the French CCC together with representatives from companies and political actors in Lille, June 2 2005.

Chapter 6
Campaigning Over Time

Strategic Dilemmas, Interactions, and Field Dynamics

Campaigns deploy tactics and frames over time. They interact with their targets and adapt their strategies to changing environments. The 'campaign styles' identified so far were not universally applied throughout the duration of the respective CCCs. Campaign-makers innovated, reacted to the firms' actions, and debated strategic issues all along. This chapter focuses on the campaigns' strategic actions. It gives a dynamic account of what the campaigns did over time and sheds light on strategic disputes and decisions. What strategies did the campaigns use? How and why were strategies made and unmade? And what drove strategic disputes?

The campaigns' activities were characterized by great regularity, but this apparent regular dynamic hides a back-and-forth between campaign-makers and their targets and important strategic disputes on further courses of action. The main question was always the same: how could companies be made to yield to campaign demands, meaning the adoption of a code of conduct and, more importantly, be made to submit to independent controls? The answers to this question varied: should campaigners put more emphasis on opposing companies or on proposing solutions for collaboration? Should they publicly shame those firms who did not comply with demands or rather reward those who did? In general, campaign-makers wanted to do both at the same time, and often that is what they did. The two strategic options were complementary, two sides of the same coin. But they were also in conflict. Prioritizing one over the other was a strategic dilemma (Jasper 2006): no one knew with certainty which option would yield greater results.

The coalition members' preferences varied and depended on personal and organizational characteristics. But more importantly, the positions and strategic decisions were shaped by two other factors. I will first look at the reactions of the firms targeted. The counter-strategies they put in place to react to campaign pressures changed the environment in which the campaigns took place. Strategies needed to be re-evaluated, but this sometimes proved difficult. Second, campaign-makers themselves were part of a dynamic environment. The multiple fields within which they were inserted—the field of unions, international solidarity, or social movements more generally—experienced changes that affected the strategic options of the campaigns. Together the strategies of targets and the dynamics affecting the fields of which coalition partners were part, shed light on the strategic disputes and decisions that characterized the campaigns.

Keeping Up the Rhythm

If one looks at the global picture of campaign activity over the years, its regularity is extremely striking. Tables 4.1 and 4.2 of Chapter 4 illustrate this. The campaigns appear to have been structured into regular campaign rounds that followed each other in a steady rhythm. In France, a campaign round was launched almost every year. The first campaign round, which began in late 1995, was followed by a second, beginning in late 1996, and a third taking place in the spring of 1998. After that, the yearly rhythm was followed precisely. In Switzerland, a similar picture emerges, although the rhythm was less sustained, with two two-year breaks from 2002 to 2004 and 2004 to 2006. In fact, had it not been for an action driven by a grassroots group, there would have been another two-year break from 2006 to 2008.

Looked at it from this angle—which is the perspective campaign organizers themselves have on their campaign—it is as if external opportunities and events did not influence the campaigns' course at all. In view of existing theories of movement dynamics, this is quite surprising. Such theories would predict that one sees increased mobilization and campaign actions when external opportunities constitute a favorable climate for contentious action (Della Porta and Diani 2004, Tarrow 1998). But if the campaigns reacted to what could be considered opportunities, it was by integrating them into its regular action agenda. Thus, big sports events such as the World Cup and the Olympics were used in order to have a platform for claims; but their foreseeability made it easy to incorporate these opportunities. The only instances which disturbed this regularity were suddenly-imposed grievances (Walsh 1981), in particular cases of workers' protests and strikes that were disseminated in the so-called 'urgent appeals.' If the analysis were to focus on those appeals, we would have a different picture. Most of these appeals, however, were marginal with regard to the overall campaign activity, and did not take up many resources. For most of the time, the campaigns followed their own rhythm. Campaign launches were planned far in advance and were programmed by taking into account a variety of other agendas; their timing was never spontaneous, but carefully chosen in order to maximize each campaign's impact. The day of the launch was scheduled months in advance; press releases were prepared, campaign material created, printed, and distributed to the different participating groups. Campaign launches, in this respect, have more in common with the launching of corporate advertisement campaigns than with the gradual or sudden emergence of protest waves.

However, much as campaign organizers attempted to autonomously decide the timing, the rhythm was also constrained. With regard to distance from the previous campaign, although keeping up a regular rhythm maintains the pressure on targets through regular actions and reporting in the media, there's a balance to be found between keeping up the pressure without overdoing it, and handling scarce resources with parsimony. The regularity also points to the fact that the agendas of most participating NGOs are filled with many recurrent and routine events, constituting regular gatherings for the social movement communities (Staggenborg and Lecomte 2009). Every organization tends to have its own calendar with recurring dates and events: labor day, European fair trade day, fortnight of fair trade, week of international solidarity, annual kermess donation, 'Public Eye on Davos,' and so on. While some of these events have existed for a very long time, many are new and have emerged only recently. The field of international solidarity, perhaps more than others, is full of them. The relationship between a campaign like the CCC and these recurring events is one of both competition and mutual nourishing. On the one hand, when a campaign is launched, the organizers need to take into account these various calendars in order to make sure that there is space for their message to pass through—given the media's limited reporting capacities (Hilgartner and Bosk 1988); but on the other hand, many of these regular events are open in scope and constitute perfect occasions to advocate a specific campaign. For instance, activists of the BD would organize a stand for Labor Day and, on this occasion, also collect signatures for a CCC petition.

What further shapes the timing and intensity of campaigns is the great number of campaigns that are sometimes taking place at the same time. The network character of the dissemination of campaigns means that the same organizations are often campaigning for different issues originating in different coalitions and organizations. The person who had been responsible for campaigning at the CCFD for a long time and then worked for the CCC coalition observed a change in the number of campaigns and thus an increasing problem of 'rhythm':

> Before, we had the Lent campaign for the Catholics and the annual food day for the general public—one in March/April, and the other one in October—two moments of the year; there were the holidays in between where one could rest, a time for training, well-established rhythms. Now with the campaigns, it's the whole year. You can never rest.[1]

Those internal constraints strongly restrict a campaign's rhythm. A campaign relying on wide participation has to take into account the activists' schedule and their capacity to mobilize.

Finally, events of different kinds may be exploited for the campaign and thus shape the campaign's dynamic. Both the international CCC and the national campaigns made conscious use of such events. Campaigns were launched on the occasion of the Soccer World Cup in France, the Olympic Games, the annual start of the school year, or Christmas. Christmas becomes an opportunity for a campaign on the conditions of production of toys because it is a time when people shop a lot for toys. But in this case again, the line between an opportunity to advocate a campaign and the risks associated with it is tenuous. People might be occupied with other things during the Christmas period, and there's big competition between charity organizations for peoples' attention during this time; in the example of the

---

1   Interview with Jean-Claude, CCFD, Paris, April 2008.

Olympics, media attention is likely to give massive cover to the athletic aspects, but might neglect other questions related to it.

The professional organizing of campaigns thus requires a constant balancing between different constraints. In addition to the constraints linked to different agendas, tactical decisions were first and foremost a question of resources. Striking though the regularity of campaign actions may be, their constant renewal from one campaign round to another is just as great. Such renewal, of course, requires a great deal of resources. In France, almost every year, new campaign material was created: new visuals, petitions, and so forth. A more sustained rhythm could hardly be followed, given the limited human and financial resources available. The fact that the Swiss campaign had a less sustained rhythm was also a consequence of its more limited resources. In other words, it is not only because grassroots groups are sometimes flooded with different campaigns that activity is limited. At the level of campaign entrepreneurs, a more sustained rhythm does not seem to be possible either.

Constant Renewal

Regularity does not mean redundancy. In fact, the observed regularity hides a diversity of action modes, targets, and claims. While the overall framework stayed the same—applying the campaign blueprint over and over again—every specific campaign had a different focus and was a new variation of the framework. This variation took different forms. Specific targets were varied. The Swiss campaign first targeted producers of sneakers and then clothing retailers. In subsequent years, sports federations (UEFA and Fifa) and the firm Triumph became explicit targets, the latter as a result of an 'urgent appeal' by the international network. From 2004 on, the clothing retailers that had been initially targeted came back into the spotlight. There was also variation concerning action modes. (Postcard) petitions were used in the first campaigns, then, between 2004 and 2008, the campaign relied solely on rankings, and launched another petition in 2008. The French campaign, too, changed targets and action modes in its course. Emphases were set on different targets: clothing retailers, big general retailers (*grande distribution*), sports retailers, local authorities. After an initial targeting of specialized clothing brands, the French campaign focused on retailers in 1998. From then on, the targeted firms were mostly the same, but they were targeted using different products: clothes in general, sports gear, and toys. In between, the French campaign also targeted local political institutions. There was also variation with regard to action forms: the first three campaigns were characterized by petitions, the campaign then turned to the use of rankings, and came back to petitions in 2002, together with a big operation of meetings with the managers of local shops.

Thus, beneath the impressive temporal regularity, there is a corresponding variation in action forms and targets. The changing of targets and content avoids serving up the same story year after year. Claims stay the same, but are dressed up differently. Sustaining the mobilization and securing media attention requires a variation in forms and targets from one campaign round to the next. But of course, the mere chronological listing of campaign rounds does not exhaust the question of campaign dynamics. In the following, I take a closer look at the strategic disputes and suggest explanations for the making and unmaking of campaign strategies over time.

Showdown in France: The Clash between Campaigners and Retailers

A central strategy of the French campaign was to advocate a 'culture of results,' as its coordinator put it in an interview. This means that the campaign did not raise maximalist demands, but pursued a series of small-scale goals which the campaign-makers thought were achievable. Incidentally, this also broadly corresponded to their ideology, one of market reform and not radical change. But it was most of all a strategic choice. Breaking down the long-term goal of global respect of labor standards in the garment industry into many small steps of partial improvements, served to keep the mobilization alive. Building a series of intermediate goals was largely a matter of the framing of movement achievements, an essential tool of campaign dynamics (Gupta 2009, Meyer 2006, Suh 2004). A balance between achievements and not-yet-achieved goals had to be found for every campaign round. While being used as a motivational tool for mobilization, this strategy also had effects on the course the interaction with targets took, and became progressively more difficult to maintain as the targeted companies started to develop their counter-strategies.

The campaign started with fairly clear-cut claims: companies should adopt the code of conduct developed by the CCC,[2] based on the respect of the International Labor Organization's core convention;[3] this code should be controlled by an independent organism, and consumers should be provided with information on the social conditions of production. At the same time, however, the first French campaign round did not directly raise these claims, but rather asked three selected companies the following three questions: do you have any social and environmental criteria to select your subcontractors? What are these criteria and how do you control them? And if not, what measures do you intend to undertake? In addition to kicking off the narrative of the 'concerned consumer,' this questioning also

---

2   The choice of codes of conduct as the main instrument was the result of discussions within the European network of anti-sweatshop campaigns The pioneering Dutch campaign had developed the *Fair Wear Charter for Clothing and accompanying documents*, published in 1994, a document that was at the origin of the Clean Clothes code of conduct.

3   The prohibition of forced labor, the freedom of association, protection of the right to organize and collective bargaining, equal remuneration, prohibition of discrimination, minimum age, and elimination of the worst forms of child labor. One of the more controversial issues with regard to the content of the code was the question of minimum vs. living wage. I do not enter this debate, because it was never central to the campaign dynamics in Switzerland and France, contrary to the question of code monitoring.

resulted in breaking the demands down into smaller steps, and left the field of potentially positive responses open. More than making claims, it was about raising an issue on both the public and corporate agenda. In the second round one year later, the fact that some corporations had reacted to the first round by contacting the campaign coalition, was presented as a success. The second round needed to keep the pressure up so that corporations showing an interest would start a dialogue with the campaign-makers and adopt a code of conduct. This time, the claim was more explicit, but still very modest: the leaders of the targeted companies were to 'open up discussions' which should lead to the adoption of a code of conduct based on fundamental social rights of workers, accept an independent and transparent control thereof, and inform consumers. The petition targeted the Conseil national du commerce (the association which organizes the principal French retailers), and more particularly three companies chosen both because they had shown some signs of interest and were the leaders of their respective branches. The first round had not provided such an objective justification for the choice—something the campaign-makers came to see as a blunder, since they couldn't explain why they were explicitly targeting those three companies.[4] Subsequently, this led the campaign to a strategy that focused on targeting the whole industry, rather than individual companies.

First Promising Reactions

This second campaign round brought about a number of results, highlighted by the campaign organizers in a booklet accompanying the third round. Some companies started discussions with the campaign coalitions. Those were not the ones targeted by the two previous rounds, but retailers that had been addressed by the campaign launched in parallel by Agir Ici (see Chapter 3 on the campaign launch). At the end of 1997, Auchan—one of the biggest general retailers in France—had adopted a code of conduct and was willing to participate in an experimental project with the campaign coalition regarding the controlling of the code. Carrefour and Camaïeu, two other retailers, were said to be in advanced negotiations with the *collectif*; the sports retailer Décathlon was reported to be working on the elaboration of a social chart, and the campaign coalition had opened up discussions with the Conseil national du commerce.

Jouez le Jeu, the third campaign round, stated as its ultimate goal the creation of a social label. Again, it asked companies to adopt a code of conduct and accept independent control. This time, the targets were the National Federation of Sports Retailers (Fédération nationale du commerce des articles de sport et de loisir), as well as the main sports retailers individually. Benefiting from the soccer World Cup held in France, the petition and the postcards raised unprecedented support, and protest and consciousness-raising events were held all over France. At this point, in the late 1990s, most of the firms the campaign had targeted had adopted codes of

---

4	Interview with P. Erard, Paris, April 2008.

conduct as a reaction to the campaign. These codes were not complete in the eyes of the coalition: most of the time, they were explicit about the banning of child labor but 'forgot' union rights. Nevertheless, they were seen as a campaign achievement, progress, and first step in the right direction. Some firms went further than mere code adoption. Carrefour started a partnership on the supervision of the social audits with the Fédération internationale des droits de l'homme (FIDH), an NGO that was not part of the campaign coalition. At the same time, Carrefour also signaled to the campaign coalition that they might be ready to collaborate. The same was also true for another clothing firm, Promodes, and for Auchan. And things were also moving at the level of industry and business associations. After the Jouez le Jeu campaign, the sports retailer federation issued a code of conduct, which its members could adopt. And the Fédération des entreprises du commerce et de la distribution (FCD; the business association of trade and retailing of which most big retailers were members) created an entity called Initiative Clause Sociale (ICS). This entity was founded with the goal of conducting and coordinating social audits among its members. It constituted thus an industry-wide initiative in response to the campaign's claims, a joint strategy by the main targets. It focused on social audits as a way of dealing with the issue of code monitoring. But the FCD also signaled that the campaign coalition might become associated with the development of this new initiative. In sum, after three campaign rounds by the end of the decade, there were several promising signs that suggested progress could be made.

In this context, the campaign coalition decided to interrupt public campaigning for a year in order to expand negotiations with firms, develop models for code monitoring and work on what was called the 'social label' project, i.e. the development of a label attesting to the respect of social standards in clothing production. There were other strategic reasons for this interruption, too, which are suggested by internal documents from the campaign archives. For one thing, it seemed difficult to launch another similar campaign relying on petitions without giving the impression that the actions did not have any effect, thus risking demobilization. Campaign-makers expressed the fear of demoralizing local coalitions if it were to repeat the same actions again (see discussion below). Also, the repeated launching of petitions meant that the campaign had to be capable of mobilizing increasing numbers of people; otherwise, it took the risk of being perceived as in decline and being taken less seriously by the clothing retailers. And finally, the pause was a sign of the campaign's changing environment. The fact that many companies had adopted codes of conduct and showed—to varying degrees—a willingness to take action displaced the focus of the struggle towards the second part of the campaign's claims: the question of code implementation and monitoring. In other words, the first rounds of campaign action and targets' reactions—the first movement *outcomes*—had changed the context in which the campaign took place. While the first stage was characterized by the placing of a new issue on the agenda, the second stage was about the *shaping of institutions* that would deal with this problem. Institution-building became the major contentious issue.

Finding Ways to Monitor Codes

The modalities of code monitoring and implementation were still very uncertain at this time. Most of the different European campaigns (including the Swiss one) were confronted with the issue. They demanded that companies accept independent control, but no institution or model existed for this process. The campaigns wanted something that was still to be created, and they did not come up with a ready solution. Campaign-makers themselves did not know exactly what form 'independent control' should take. The French coalition's goal was the creation of a *social label*, a label that would give consumers information about the social quality of the clothes they buy and allow the control and monitoring of the implementation of codes of conduct. But the definition of a social label remained very vague. The booklet of the 1998 campaign round stated that the adoption of a code of conduct together with the acceptance of an independent control constituted a first step toward the creation of a social label. This would be a guarantee of 'good social quality' for consumers. A note in the booklet specified that

> there is no model on which one could build to create a valid mechanism of independent control. This is why, in a first step, the *collectif* and interested corporations will experiment with different systems which, after evaluation, will be the basis for the independent control we want to put into place. We also take inspiration from similar experiences conducted in other countries.

The firms, too, had become active in experimenting with monitoring systems. Companies organized in the FCD turned to a known template in order to deal with this new issue: auditing. Auditing was usually used for quality control, but could be adapted to monitor social standards. Many of the big auditing firms started offering this as a new service. The French retailers also rapidly adopted the SA 8000 framework, a social certification of production plants developed in the US relying on auditing and the certification of production sites (Bartley 2003, 2005). Facing these developments, the campaign-makers needed to find a position and a strategy concerning the issue of code implementation. A workshop organized by the coalition on the topic of the social label in November 1998 pursued this objective. In its announcement, it said:

> Three years of campaigning for the improvement of working conditions in the world have led to an expectation of a solution both by consumers—who want to be able to make choices based on knowledge about the conditions of production of the goods they buy—and by retailers who want to have a credible tool of control for the conditions of production of the goods they sell. At the present moment, where the FCD declares that it wants to commit itself to the improvement of working conditions and their control, it has become urgent to evaluate the existing systems in order to better define our propositions.

Three options were discussed at this workshop: the SA 8000 certification favored by the FCD's initiative, the creation of a norm involving AFNOR (the French agency for the creation of norms), and the development of a monitoring project involving corporations, the campaign coalition, and other civil society actors. SA 8000 was seen as an unsatisfactory solution, although the coalition initially supported the idea of certification and speculated it might be possible to bring civil society actors into the process. The AFNOR track was seen with great enthusiasm, especially because it implied the participation of the state. But the development of a new norm is a very demanding and slow process, requiring the participation of all stakeholders concerned, and no immediate progress could be made on this front. The most promising solution—together with the prospect of being more closely associated with the development of FCD's Initiative Clause Sociale—lay in the experimental monitoring of codes. Such experiments were already under way in a collaboration effort with Auchan.

This collaboration reached back to contacts initiated prior to the FCD's initiative. The Centre français d'information sur les entreprises (Cfie), an organization specialized in gathering information on the social and environmental practices of firms, founded by a former member of Agir Ici, became strongly involved in the CCC coalition at this time and was a driving force behind it. The campaign and Auchan jointly organized training sessions for buyers to teach them about the content of the code and thus put them in a position to understand the social conditions at the factories where they bought products. Auchan also asked the campaign to support a project of code monitoring in Madagascar. Initially, the firm was to do it with its habitual partners for quality auditing (the firm SGS), but they did not have the staff qualified to do so. Missions to Madagascar took place, but they remained limited and did not lead to substantial progress concerning the development of a monitoring initiative going beyond this particular case. Overall, this collaboration was probably the furthest the campaign ever got to realizing its goals. But it eventually failed, for a number of reasons: internal tensions in the campaign coalition, where especially AdM and the CFDT disagreed over their respective roles in the process;[5] a political crisis in Madagascar which jeopardized the conducting of audits; and finally the withdrawal of Auchan, which, in view of the rising Initiative Clause Sociale, preferred the business-driven model of private social audits over collaboration. According to the campaign coordinator,[6] this strategic change was also linked to a change in personnel. The person who had pushed for the collaboration was a high-level manager, on the Board of Auchan, and a former member of a socialist cabinet sympathetic to the CCC cause. When he left the firm, the campaign lost this internal ally (see also Delalieux 2008).

---

5   Interview with Catherine, AdM representative, Paris, May 2008.
6   Interview with P. Erard, Paris, April 2008.

The Road to Escalation

Contrary to what had happened in other countries such as the Netherlands, the UK, Sweden and Switzerland, the French campaign had thus not succeeded in creating an experimental multi-institutional monitoring initiative, in spite of its efforts. After a one-year interruption, it took up public campaigning again. In 2000, the campaign Pour l'école, consommons éthiques combined two tools: on the one hand, it focused on the issue of public procurement policies, by asking municipalities to respect social criteria when buying school material. This part of the campaign would become a sort of side-battle, reaching different targets from the main campaign which focused on big retailers. Administrative actors purchasing goods for school equipment or uniforms, or big firms such as La Poste or SNCF, which later also became associated with this action, do not purchase their clothes in supermarkets, but instead order from specialized firms, a specific niche market for professional equipment. This branch of the campaign enabled reaching these targets, but did not concern the big retailers at all. The retailers were targeted through the first '*carnet de note*' (school grades), also published in the 2000 campaign, evaluating and ranking the major retailers. Taking up the imagery from school grades, the companies received points, and comments on their performance. The ratings were a major tactical innovation, inspired according to the campaign's coordinator by a similar method used in the Swiss CCC in 1999. It broke with the petitions and instead used a consumer action form, with the goal of increasing the pressure on companies by putting them in competition with one another.

The idea of publishing an evaluation also has to be seen within the general dynamic of the campaign and its necessity to innovate and vary the theme. The campaign-makers were aware that they could not just put on identical campaigns every year—one of the reasons why they paused after the 1998 round. Now, this risk of repetition also guided the decision to try a novel action form. A statement from the minutes of a meeting of the piloting committee from November 8, 1999 (at the time of the preparation of the school campaign) makes this reasoning explicit:

> To involve the corporations in this project (of a social label), the pressure of consumers has to remain strong. The identical repetition of campaigns of the type 'Jouez le jeu' contains the risk of tiring the public and our local grassroots coalition. This repetition also runs the risk of giving the impression that things do not progress and that lobbying thus does not have any effect.

The *carnet de note* thus both maintained the pressure *and* was capable of showing that some progress was taking place. Despite this objective, only two of the 14 corporations were evaluated in a somewhat positive light. The reactions of the targeted firms to the first rating were more critical than the campaign-makers had expected. At least this seems to be indicated by a very cautionary internal note (dated May 17, 2001) written in the run-up to the second ranking. In this document, the fear was expressed that, since ranking constitutes a source of 'image risk' to the corporations, it would be perceived negatively by them. This, it was said, is "certainly detrimental to the quality of the bilateral relations that these firms are likely to develop with the campaign coalition."

It is telling that the rankings bothered the corporations (at least those in the FCD) much more than the petitions and postcards. What distinguishes this tool from the others used by the campaign is that firstly, rankings give specific information on each company, while the petitions were always accompanied by a more general discourse. Secondly, rankings use a consumerist approach, taking up and adapting the comparative tests of consumer associations, although in the form of school grades. It seems that the combination of these two attributes—corporate-level information in a consumerist tool—is judged by the companies as a much bigger threat to their public images than petitions and protest tactics (at least those employed by the campaign). What might seem to be a relatively benign action form can be interpreted, in given contexts, as highly contentious and even aggressive.

The second rating was published a year later (in 2001) with the launch of the Exploiter n'est pas jouer campaign round. It was combined with a new and very broad signature campaign, centered on toys but still focusing on the same targets. As a matter of fact, at the same time as the CCC coalition was, more than ever, trying to appeal to the corporations in order to bring them to collaborate, the network of local activists and coalitions kept growing. Internal documents show that the local *collectifs* asked for more participatory campaigns—rating alone, some said, was not the optimal tool in order to mobilize people. The reintroduction of protest tactics, much more than being dictated by the strategic choice of heightening the pressure on corporations, was the result of this organizational dynamic, or more precisely, of the demand of local activists. Participatory tactics were thus reinforced. At this stage the largest mobilization was achieved with the Exploiter n'est pas jouer petition, signed by 180,000 people. The following year, the second phase of this campaign round was designed to decentralize the pressure by targeting local stores and their managers and included yet another ranking.

It was with this third ranking in 2002 that a truly confrontational course between the coalition and its main targets became evident. For this ranking, the coalition changed the scale of the grades, from a scale of 5 to a scale of 20. A comparison of the grades given to firms over the different ratings shows that the third ranking corresponded to an overall downgrading; in fact, all the firms evaluated fared much worse than in the previous ones (Barraud de Lagerie 2010, p. 258). On this scale between 0 and 20, only Carrefour obtained a grade above 10 (10.4 to be precise), while almost all of the firms were given grades of less than 5. This very strict grading was also the result of a strategic decision—the more critical members of the campaign coalition won over their more reformative partners in grading firms (Barraud de Lagerie 2010). Indeed, some of the campaign members, especially from AdM or other, more left-wing, NGOs, were not happy with some interpretations of the rankings in the press or by consumers (as seen in letters the campaign received from consumers). Ranking firms (unless of course the same grade is given to everyone) inevitably means that some fare better than others (which was also the initial goal); however, if consumers read this as "it is ok to buy clothes at firm X because they got the best grade," this was contrary to the CCC coalition's intent, as they felt that in spite of small differences, all firms still did poorly in terms of ethical performance. In other words, the best was only the best of a poor bunch.

Yet it would be inaccurate to 'blame' only the campaign coalition, and in particular its more radical members, for the confrontational turn the campaign took. Rather, the escalation was also provoked by the counter-strategy adopted by the campaigns' targets, in particular the FCD. In the course of the development of the FCD's own system of monitoring (the Initiative Clause Sociale, ICS), it became more and more clear that they were not willing to give the CCC coalition more than just an observatory position. The coalition was informed of the methods and actions by the ICS, and was also invited to some meetings, but they were never permitted to participate actively. In fact, the ICS opted for a system running without any participation by NGOs or unions, let alone the establishment of a multi-stakeholder entity including the coalition. It worked as a strictly business-driven model, relying on social auditing by commercial auditing firms. In other words, while at an earlier moment, there still seemed to be access points or opportunities for the campaign coalition—the contacts with Auchan, the signals of a possible role for the coalition in the ICS—these were gradually shut down. Not only did the FCD shield its initiative from an eventual participation by the campaign, it also started to employ a public counter-strategy of defiance.

In fact, after having constructed its alternative solution without the participation of the CCC, and as a response to steady criticism by the coalition, the FCD engaged in a framing contest. On the very day that the third rating was published, the FCD released a press statement including an open and public letter to the coalition. Unsurprisingly, the letter presented the FCD model as a serious and honest effort to deal with the issue of labor rights in production plants. But it also attempted to disqualify the methods and positions of the campaign coalition. The letter said, for instance, that while the FCD had 'largely included' the coalition in the Initiative Clause Sociale, the campaign didn't return this transparency when establishing the ranking. The FCD, in other words, complained that it had not been involved in the grading process. "It is easy to give lessons but more difficult to work in the field to make things progress," the letter further stated, contrasting the campaign's ideological stance with the companies' pragmatic knowledge of the field. Finally, the letter emphasized the FCD's values, notably its wish not to use ethics as a point of competition between corporations. Implicitly, it thus accused the campaign coalition of pushing corporations to compete on the issue of their ethical records (which was indeed the goal of the coalition), whereas the corporations, allegedly being more ethical on this point, refused such an approach and preferred to make joint efforts. In the same vein, the letter also attacked the coalition for sticking to the idea of a social label applied to particular products, which, the letter stated, was a marketing approach. The general argument thus was that the campaign wanted to make ethics an aspect of the market—that it wanted to marketize ethics— whereas the FCD retailers were treating the issue discreetly, through proper, but not public, auditing and slow improvement.

After this clash, a meeting between coalition members and the FCD might have cleared the situation. Under pressure from the corporations, the coalition first agreed to delay the publication of a fourth *carnet de note* in order not to jeopardize the possibility of a future collaboration. But within the coalition, some pushed for a continued strategy of confrontation, and thus it was eventually decided to do another ranking. This time, the FCD and its Initiative Clause Sociale even went one step further in counter-mobilization tactics. In an attempt to obstruct the evaluation and its publication, the companies that were part of the ICS decided to give a collective answer to the campaign's questionnaire on social records. Since they were in the ICS, the argument went, they shared the same commitment and applied the same methods to the issue of conditions of production. The goal was thus to undermine the campaign's strategy of putting the companies in competition with one another. But the FCD did not achieve its objective. Using other sources of information, the coalition nevertheless produced a ranking, but this time published it in the form of a highly complex 'social barometer.' The FCD's tactic was thus only partially successful, and their position was critically questioned in the media, which contrasted it with the viewpoint of the campaign coalition.[7] However, the FCD's tactic was successful insofar as it helped provoke a serious crisis within the campaign coalition around the attitude to adopt facing the *grande distribution*.

The Dual Strategy in Trouble

What consequences did this effective counter strategy by the main targets have on the campaign? Facing this development, the position of the coalition remained ambivalent: they still wanted to appeal to the corporations and bring them round to collaboration. At the same time, they also had to fight the practice of business-driven social auditing, adopted by corporations as a response to the movement. At this point, the coalition was caught in a strategic dilemma (Jasper 2006). The choice was between denunciation and dialogue; between conflict and collaboration. But while there was a tension between these two strategies throughout the campaign—and while, indeed, a point could be made that this tension can be found in any social movement—the growing counter-mobilization by the targeted firms transformed this strategic issue into a dispute within the coalition, dividing the coalition's organizations.

---

7   When the FCD, in a communication coup, published a press release the day of the launching of a new campaign by the French CCC, the newspaper *Libération* (traditionally close to social movement organizations) not only related the FCD story, but at the same time also ran an interview with the coordinator of the French CCC, giving him the possibility to react. (*Libération*, March 4 2004, "Les vrais problèmes sont-ils détectés?," and "Des marques enquêtent sur l'éthique").

A strategic duality characterized the entire campaign. Putting pressure on companies was only one part of the strategy. This is expressed, for instance, in an interview the coordinator gave to *Libération* in 2001: "We don't wish to denounce the corporations. Our goal is to establish partnerships to put in place a system of social certification."[8] There's a balance to find between denouncing and threatening on the one hand, and the wish to establish partnerships on the other. This duality ran through the whole campaign, but the modalities of its articulation evolved with the dynamic of contentious interaction. In theory, the two are part of the same coin, but fulfill different roles. There is a time for threat and a time for negotiation and partnership. Threat is needed in order to bring opponents to take a movement seriously, to sit down at the negotiating table, to yield to demands. Threat, thus, is an essential part in achieving the stand that could allow the campaign to become a partner. Without threat, it is unlikely that the issue would even appear on companies' agendas, and even less so that it would be taken seriously. Once this *rapport de force* is established, negotiations and forms of collaboration can take place. Early in the campaign, it became apparent that the coalition not only raised claims, but also aspired to form partnerships. The social label as a goal positions the coalition as a player collaborating with corporations (and public authorities) in order to build up such an institution. As long as there were small achievements—companies adopting codes of conduct, willing to launch experimental monitoring projects with the campaign coalition—the dual strategy seemed to pay off. Threat and collaboration were complementary. Their articulation was most of all a matter of dealing with different appearances. Different moments ask for different 'poses' or, to use a Goffmanian metaphor: there was front-stage interaction with companies and with the coalition's public, and there was a backstage of invisible interaction with targets. The strategy, here, is a very common one of speaking to different audiences, of voicing a strong position in public, but signaling an openness behind closed doors. In this articulation between the attitudes of denunciation and negotiation, different visions, reflecting both different organizational cultures and individual trajectories and positions, could sometimes clash. Interpretations, wordings, tactics were controversially discussed. But it was only with the growing confrontation, provoked by the counter-mobilization strategies of the big retailers and by the publication of ratings, that a strategic dispute erupted within the coalition. Facing increasingly closed doors, the strategic issue, latent all along, became a dilemma that divided the coalition.

To some,[9] the lack of results and the counter-mobilization showed that the strategy employed so far was leading nowhere and that a strategic renewal was necessary. The way out had to be through radicalization, stronger public attacks on companies,

---

8   P. Erard in *Libération*, Thursday November 22 2001, "Faire pression sur les distributeurs," interview published for the release of the second ranking.

9   The account of the internal conflict and the dividing lines thereof draws on several interviews conducted with campaign officials present at this time and representatives of different organizations that were involved (AdM, CFDT, CCFD).

and a strategic re-focusing on public (as opposed to private) regulation. This position was especially defended by AdM, symbolically the strongest organization in the coalition (as a founder and official employer of the staff). The opposing pole, on the contrary, considered that the problem was the excessively confrontational attitude the campaign displayed, especially through the ratings. The organization most prominently defending this position was the CFDT. Both positions clashed in the elaboration of the last ranking—the one where the FCD responded with a single voice and that was finally to be published in the form of a 'barometer.'

The counter-strategy by the firms thus provoked this strategic dispute, which expressed a feeling of powerlessness on the part of the campaigners. But to fully understand the reasons for the strategic clash within the coalition, one also needs to account for the broader political context which led to a growing alienation between members of the coalition, and especially between AdM and the CFDT. The retailers' strategy provoked the eruption of these divisions, but in reality, the organizations had already started to drift away from each other for other reasons linked to developments in their respective fields, where they pursued political goals and competed for attention. The field perspective, and in particular the observation that fields are embedded in complex webs of other fields, helps us to understand this. Actions and processes taking place in one field have consequences for other related fields (Fligstein and McAdam 2012). The CCC brings together actors belonging to different fields, and vital changes in these respective environments affected the positions of members of the coalition and increased strategic disputes. Concretely, the most decisive development was the rise of the global justice movement. It brought with it a major reconfiguration of the social movement field, and as such had an impact on the local 'settlement' of the campaign coalition. And two other, more localized, processes and events in related fields contributed further to bringing AdM and the CFDT to occupy progressively antithetical positions on the strategies to be employed and the attitude to be adopted towards retailers.

In the 10 years of the French Clean Clothes campaign, the global justice movement (GJM) became the paramount player in the social movement sector. Unlike in other countries, where professional development NGOs typically dominated this movement (Sommier et al. 2007, Della Porta 2007), France's *altermondialiste* movement was characterized by a coalition of unions and *tiers-mondistes* (Agrikoliansky et al. 2005b, Sommier et al. 2007). The emblematic organization was ATTAC, founded in 1998 after an appeal published in the monthly newspaper *Le monde diplomatique.* This wave of contention, culminating in France in the organization of a European Social Forum in Seine-Saint-Denis in 2003, and the protests against the G8 in Evian the year after, was not only the fruit of rearrangements of different contentious fields (Agrikolansky et al. 2005b) but had also, in turn, led to reconfigurations and the repositioning of social movement actors. As a 'movement of movements' bringing together SMOs from a variety of backgrounds, the French global justice movement in a way resembled the CCC coalition, which was also characterized by a very broad coalition. Many of the coalition's organizations identified with the GJM and were part of it. But the main organizations of the coalition were unevenly committed to it. The division especially concerned AdM and the CFDT. While the former was very strongly involved with the global justice movement, the latter had a very ambiguous position vis-à-vis the *altermondialistes'* goals and propositions (Ancelovici 2008).

The wave of *altermondialiste* contention undoubtedly led to a repoliticization of the fair trade organization Artisans du monde. AdM actively participated in the global justice movement. It was a founding member of ATTAC, and its local member organizations participated in the movement's big events. The organization also sought to bring the campaign coalition closer to the emblematic organizations of the GJM, especially ATTAC.[10] Most importantly, AdM adopted the 'politics against markets frame,' described by Ancelovici (2002) as the characteristic master frame of the French global justice movement. Politics against markets as a master frame unites the diverse claims of the global justice movement in stating the necessity of re-establishing the primacy of politics—democratic processes, public regulations—over the free, neo-liberal market. States should retake control and control globalization and the power of corporations; citizens and public policies rather than consumers, corporations, and financial markets, should define the world's course.

Obviously, this definition of the situation was quite at odds with the orientation the CCC had taken. It targeted corporations directly, built on the mobilization of consumers and advocated a solution based on private regulation. We have seen that this orientation was most of all a result of the mid-1990s failure to impose public regulation on global trade relations: realizing that social clauses had no political viability, movements turned to private and voluntary solutions, using consumer pressure. Pushing for private regulation was thus always a 'second best' solution, and AdM in particular continued to advocate the necessity of giving public actors a role—by insisting, notably, that they be represented on the controlling board of the social label to be created. The fact that public regulation should ideally play an important role was always widely shared by coalition participants, but it was also acknowledged that given prevailing circumstances, public regulation was not a viable option. Hence, the role of public regulation in the claims and actions of the campaign was very limited. Even when the campaign turned to the political arena and targeted elected officials and municipalities, they were addressed in their role as (collective) consumers, not regulators. Legislators should vote in laws that would allow public institutions to take into account the ethical aspects of products they *buy*. The attempts to make public actors participate in the campaign, notably by pushing for the creation of a social norm by AFNOR, did not advance by much, although such attempts were always advocated by the coalition.

With the growing prominence of the global justice movement, private regulation and instruments such as codes of conduct came under increased attack. Private regulation building on market forces—which the CCC clearly did—were viewed

10   Interview with Catherine, AdM representative, Paris, May 2008.

very critically by actors of the global justice movement such as ATTAC. In the internal discussions of the coalition, the effects of this 'politics against markets' master frame can be observed in the discussions about the campaign's orientation plan, documented in files from the internal archives. In 2003, the coalition applied for new funding from the European Union and with this goal discussed the main axes of orientation for the next three-year period. The staff elaborated a plan based on five axes, in strict continuity with the previous actions: awareness-raising among consumers, reinforcing mobilizations of consumers, developing multi-stakeholder monitoring systems, enhancing the information available for consumers, and reinforcing international collaboration. Drafts in the archives show that to these five axes, AdM wanted to add a sixth, on public regulation. The campaign, it maintained, should also address public authorities in order to push for tighter public regulation. AdM thus strongly proposed an explicit strategic re-orientation that would be more in conformity with the global justice movement's general goals and approach. Several interviewees emphasized the eagerness with which the role of public regulation came to be defended by AdM in this period, and the person who represented AdM in the coalition also underlined its importance.[11] In addition to the role the state should play in regulating labor standards, the attitude towards corporations was also re-evaluated in this course. Again, the growing prominence of the politics against market frames affected AdM's general position towards corporations, and in particular big retailers. Rather than actors that could be potential partners, they clearly occupied the role of villains in the rhetoric of many *altermondialistes*.

But AdM's stance vis-à-vis the big retailers was also affected by a change in yet another field of which it was a constituent part, the field of fair trade. The field of fair trade had greatly developed since the CCC had been launched in France. While at that time AdM was almost its sole actor, by 2004 there were many other fair trade actors on the scene, and two poles had developed, one based on labels and the distribution of products in the mainstream market, the other (the AdM model) based on an integrated, alternative distribution system (Diaz Pedregal 2007). The increased competition within the field, and in particular the growing success of Max Havelaar (as well as other, smaller, competitors), whose label was sold by big retailers, had led the actors into battles of distinction and to a sharpening of their positions. In the course of this, AdM had come to strongly criticize the selling of fair trade products in supermarkets, and had gone as far as voting a resolution, in its general assembly, stating that AdM would never integrate big retailers (Dubuisson-Quellier 2013a, Diaz Pedregal 2007). But a strong opposition to the labeling approach, and especially its availability in big supermarkets, had not always been AdM's position: as a matter of fact, the organization itself had plans to launch its own labeling scheme in the early 1990s (before Max Havelaar France was founded by other NGOs) and had for a short time envisioned working with retailers. At this time in the early 1990s, at least, this

---

11   Interview with Catherine, AdM representative, Paris, May 2008.

was an open question (Diaz Pedregal 2007). Thus, field dynamics, or processes of differentiation between actors, also account for the radical opposition to big retailers that came to characterize AdM's position. Changes in the fair trade field and the rise of the GJM reinforced each other. Obviously, it became difficult, in this context, to advocate an approach building on the collaboration between the campaign and big retailers.

The position of the CFDT was also affected through the rise of the GJM. While AdM went through a process of (re-)politicization and possibly radicalization in the course of this movement, the CFDT stood out, having particularly ambiguous relations with the *altermondialistes*. ATTAC, the emblematic organization of the French social justice movement, was joined by most French unions *except* the CFDT. Implicitly, the CFDT thus positioned itself against the social justice movement, and stood outside of the mobilizations around the issue of globalization. Their strategy needs to be put in the context, yet again, of the field of unions, where the CFDT distinguished itself from its competitors. Furthermore, the CFDT attracted the fury of the French left when in 2003, at a crucial moment for the internal crisis of the French CCC, it accepted negotiations on a reform of retirement pensions with (right-wing) prime minister Raffarin, a reform against which the opposition mobilized strongly. Following this episode, the CFDT's image as depicting *any* negotiation as a success per se was magnified, and according to interviews, some of the other members of the CCC coalition made a parallel with the union's enthusiasm for negotiations with retailers. While privileging negotiations was not necessarily a strategic change for the CFDT, whose re-orientation towards a strategy of negotiation rather than confrontation had been under way since the 1980s (Defaud 2009), the global justice movement and the pension reform event exacerbated the gulf that formed within the coalition.

In sum, the positions of the organizations and their mutual perceptions were affected by processes and events in the broader political context of the campaign coalition, and especially in the respective movement fields to which its member organizations belonged. We can compare the this phenomenon to Meyer and Whittier's concept of social movement spillover (Meyer and Whittier 1994) i.e. the impact of one social movement on another through organizational coalitions, overlapping social movement communities, shared personnel, and changes in the external environment. The development of a wave of contention around the issue of globalization spilled over onto the CCC by affecting the positions of the organizations within the coalition. The global justice movement, with its master frame of politics against the market, was like a wave that affected several of the fields that constituted the campaign (international solidarity, unions), and through these reconfigurations, passed over the campaign coalition and shook it up. In this process, moderate responses to globalization using private regulation by corporations became a much less legitimate position, especially for organizations that saw themselves as an active part of the global justice movement.

These developments in the fields constituting the campaign coalition made increasingly tenuous the compromise between denunciation and negotiation, 'oppose and propose,' and between confronting corporations and wanting to collaborate with them. The strategy pursued by the retailers, effectively opposing and even attacking the coalition, made it worse. During this time of strategic crisis, the representatives of the different organizations became much more involved in the campaign and its operating decisions than usual.[12] But because none of the two positions had a clear majority, the result was a compromise that included everything. In the orientation plan, all possible axes were adopted. And in the ratings, the barometer reflected this strategy of inclusion, both wanting to treat companies gently and to set examples. As a consequence, it was so complex that it became unintelligible, or at least it was extremely difficult to transmit a clear message from it; the tool became essentially unusable in the campaign.[13]

Eventually, the campaign dynamics were affected by a different player: the campaign's funders. Over the period from 1995 to 2005, the campaign was financed by public funding amounting to about 50% from the European Commission, and the other half from different French ministries. The above-mentioned fourth request for a three-year funding envelope from the European Commission was refused, bringing the campaign to a (temporary) end. The reasons for this refusal are not officially known. Certainly, the content of the fourth proposal did not substantially differ from the previous ones, consisting of an all-encompassing approach, continuing the actions undertaken so far. One unofficial explanation invokes the potential role played by the corporate players. It is possible that they put pressure on the European Commission to stop funding a campaign that directly targeted them. But the campaign-makers themselves privileged another explanation, completely outside of the coalition's control and even of the policy issues addressed: at the time of the fourth request, the number of member countries and thus of potential initiatives able to apply for funding had increased, following the EU enlargement admitting ten new Eastern European countries. In this context, the money had to be divided among more applicants, and it is possible that priority was given to demands from new member states. Campaign-makers were aware of this increased difficulty. Whatever the explanation is, the accumulation of internal disagreements, external lockout, lack of funding, and the lack of proper organizational structure within the coalition, favored the rapid ceasing of its activities. Given the circumstances, none of the coalition organizations was willing to contribute significantly to its continuation at that time.

Losing Focus? The Swiss Campaign between Raising Claims and Assessing Corporate Reactions

Building on an already established template from the European campaign, the Swiss CCC started by demanding that the targeted companies adopt the Clean

---

12 Interview with Martina, campaign official, Paris, April 2008
13 Interview with Martina, campaign official, Paris, April 2008

Clothes code of conduct. The first campaign round missed its targets: it addressed the most famous sports brands like Nike, Adidas, and Puma, but the campaigners quickly realized that they lacked a clear addressee because those firms were all foreign companies. The Swiss importers or offices of the targeted brands did not have the position within the companies to adopt codes of conduct; and a Swiss campaign was simply not influential enough for the international headquarters to pay attention to it. In analyzing this initial strategic mistake, the Swiss CCC then decided to target primarily Swiss companies, and to focus on the textile industry. The BD conducted a study on the Swiss textile industry to help identify the main players in this market. The resulting list of targets included general retailers (among them Migros and Coop as the two biggest Swiss retailers), specialized Swiss clothing retailers, and a few international brands.

As in the French campaign, the firms were initially addressed through questions sent to the corporate headquarters in the form of a postcard petition. The campaign asked three questions: Do you have a complete code of conduct? Is its application controlled by an independent body? And can workers organize freely and report violations of their rights without taking risks? Before going public, the BD and its allies informed firms of the forthcoming campaign and raised these questions in a letter it sent to them. The campaign consisted of a postcard petition, and the firms' answers were presented in the first campaign newsletter (dated May 1999), together with critical comments and suggestions for (sometimes very complex) further questions. Suggested follow-up questions included "Are you ready to accept an independent control structure?" or "You mention the existence of annual reports by professional organizations and European labor unions. Can you detail for me how their controls work, the main problems revealed by the auditors and the policy of follow-up action if irregularities are discovered?" Through such suggestions, consumers were urged to directly address companies and show that they critically questioned the firms' responses.

The companies reacted quickly to the demands, much quicker than in France. But this was also due to the fact that the Swiss campaign started nearly five years later. The international context had changed, and the most famous clothing brands, especially in the USA, had adopted codes of conduct in the meantime. Of the 15 companies initially targeted by the Swiss campaign, 8 already reported having codes of conduct when they first answered the campaign; 5 more adopted codes rapidly, and only two did not adopt any code over the whole period of investigation. However, in view of the campaign's claims, all codes were judged insufficient. They only very partially fulfilled the demands. Companies also responded to the consumers who sent postcards to them, just as they had responded to the campaign-makers, highlighting their social commitment. An overview of those early responses shows that companies brought to bear all their different initiatives and contributions to social and environmental issues, in order to account for their social commitment. Coop, for instance, put forward its organic clothes under the label 'Natura Line,' while Migros emphasized its eco-label and the fact that it funded schools in India. Switcher, a specialized clothing retailer, spoke of envisioning

SA8000 certifications, and Veillon took pride in its actions against child labor and multiple recognitions thereof (Mach 2001). However, the campaign dismissed these initiatives as not being systematic enough and as sidestepping the issue. In its evaluations, it only commented on the answers relating specifically to the campaign's demands regarding the adoption of a code.

Unlike in the French case, in Switzerland this same campaign round with its postcard petition was continued over several years. During this time, other petitions were launched to address other actors (like UEFA, the IOC, or Triumph), but the main focus remained on the tracking of progress in practices of the initially-targeted companies, regularly updated in the campaign newsletter. All in all, five newsletters were published from May 1999 to May 2002, each time giving an update on the situation, company by company.[14] From the beginning the campaign thus evaluated the different companies comparatively, but it did not rank them in this first stage.

The Pilot Project of Code Monitoring

While the public campaign was ongoing, campaign-makers also engaged in a collaborative initiative with firms. Shortly after the campaign launch, three companies (Switcher, Veillon and Migros) contacted the campaign coalition signaling their readiness to adopt the Clean Clothes code and participate in a project of code verification. At that time, as a representative of one of these companies said in an interview, in spite of the international developments, the concept of codes of conduct was still relatively unknown in Switzerland, and the question of code control in particular was completely new.[15] Faced with the campaign, some companies were willing to conform with demands, but did not know exactly how to do so. As in France, no model for code monitoring existed, especially regarding participation of civil society actors. Campaigners expected firms to react, but had not foreseen that they themselves would become an essential participant in the elaboration of a monitoring system. An interviewee from the campaign put it this way: "Suddenly the corporations respond and say, "ok, what do you propose? We are ready to make a code of conduct but we would like you to help us, we don't really know what it is." We fell a little bit into the trap of the campaign's consequences."[16]

From 2000 to 2002, a pilot project for monitoring took place, involving the three corporations and the Swiss CCC (that is, its member organizations Bern Declaration, Bread for All and Lenten Fund). The project, financed by the corporations, hired a coordinator in order to conduct the independent controls carried out by the newly created body. It was conceived of as an experiment

---

14   The sixth such newsletter from April 2003 does not contain a list of the different companies' practices.

15   Interview with Switcher manager, Lausanne, August 2007.

16   Interview with Martin, Bread for All, July 2007.

that would help find ways to monitor the implementation of the Clean Clothes code of conduct. During this time, the campaign was thus engaged both in campaigning *and* in implementing its demands in collaboration with corporations. The experiment quickly revealed difficulties of the code monitoring process, and led the representatives of the CCC to back away from 'maximalist' demands of code respect to a concept of gradual progress and the application of so-called 'corrective measures.' Concretely, the controls revealed important cases of labor abuses, observations that would have been extremely valuable for a 'shaming' campaign. But how should such revelations be treated within this pilot project, given that the corporations that had agreed to submit to controls were precisely those that had accepted the campaign's demands, contrary to the many others that did not allow independent controlling? This question provoked very controversial debates according to interviewees that had been present in the process. Ultimately, the participants in the pilot project agreed that the campaign should not go public on the first report, but only on a second one, which would evaluate the corrective measures taken following the recommendations following the first control. The participation in this project made movement actors thus change their initial focus on code *verification* to one of code *monitoring* and the acceptance of a dynamic of progress. But not all individual members of the campaign agreed with this. Indeed, it provoked a major clash within the campaign coalition, as it highlighted the inherent problem of a double role of both campaigning and collaborating. Eventually, it was decided to split the coalition: the BD would continue doing campaign work, while Lenten Fund and Bread for All retreated from the coalition and instead continued work on the monitoring project.

This evolution, so far, resembled the dynamics of other, similar campaigns the BD had conducted in the past. A campaign would raise an issue and lead to experiments in solving it, which eventually gave rise to a new and independent institution. The social clause of Del Monte is an early example of this dynamic. Together with two firms, Migros and Switcher (Veillon, the third in the group, had had serious economic difficulties in the meantime and had been acquired by the group Ackermann[17]), the two NGOs turned to the State Secretariat for Economic Affairs (SECO), and more precisely to its office for economic cooperation and development, and successfully applied for funding for the project's continuation. This gave rise to an organization called ISCOM, which was officially established in 2004. It was conceived as a multi-stakeholder initiative of code monitoring, which would attract new firms to join it. For the Swiss government, the promotion of such an initiative fitted into their policy goals of a sustainable development that was market-based, as admitted in the government's 'label strategy.' In the past, the SECO had notably helped to finance the Step label (an industry-wide approach to establish social standards in the rug industry) and the Max Havelaar label.

---

17   Somewhat ironically, Ackermann was the company with the worst social record of all the targeted corporations, having never responded to the campaign's inquiries.

Diversification of Counter-Strategies

While the pilot project and the institution-building that followed was ongoing, campaign work continued and pressure was upheld on the other companies through regular updates in the campaign's newsletter, smaller-scale campaigns (such as for example the actions by small grassroots groups discussed in Chapter 4) and the incentives to consumers to keep sending protest postcards. The existence of the pilot project, and later of ISCOM, meant that the campaign had an even clearer goal than before: firms should join this initiative, which was the only legitimate way of dealing with labor standards in supply chains. But while the campaign built on the pilot project and its successor as the benchmark model of monitoring, and hoped to convince companies to join it, firms increasingly embraced private auditing and business-driven monitoring initiatives. The development that was most relevant for the Swiss firms in this respect was the founding of the Business Social Compliance Initiative (BSCI), created by European retailers in order to establish a common European monitoring system for social compliance. The BSCI's creation goes back to talks beginning in 2002 under the lead of the Foreign Trade Association, an interest group whose members are national trade associations and European companies (Fransen 2012). BSCI was a business-driven social auditing initiative, building on a common code, using commercial auditing firms, and embracing the SA8000 standard. From the beginning, Migros was very involved in the development of the BSCI model, and increasing numbers of Swiss retailers ended up joining it over time, among them the biggest players. In terms of the instrument used (i.e. a business-driven monitoring initiative without 'civil society' participation), this evolution closely resembled the dynamic of the French campaign. But contrary to France, there were no coordinated reactions by the targeted firms in Switzerland and no national business association intervened.

The Swiss companies also used another response which in its turn was notably absent from the French case: ethical labels such as organic or fair trade clothing lines. Of course, this was a very different approach from the demands raised by the Clean Clothes Campaign. Ethical labels only concerned a small amount of clearly designated products, and not, as the code of conduct advocated by the campaign, the whole product range. However, from the point of view of a targeted company, labeling or ethical product lines were seen as a way of dealing with the issue of social responsibility; labels were used as counter-strategies, responding to a consumer demand but also serving to show consumers and the broader public that the company was doing something with regard to conditions of production. Some of those labels preceded the campaign launch, and had already been put forward by companies in their first reactions to the campaign. This was the case of the two biggest retailers, Migros' ecolabel, and Coop's 'Natura Line.' The latter was the result of a partnership of the retailer with a Swiss cotton dealer who, in the early 1990s, had started a project for organic cotton "as a hobby",[18] and would later add social standards to

---

18   Interview with company founder, Risch, October 2007.

it. The project gradually grew to a significant size, without any social movement pressure. But a couple of years later, the label would prove to be a perfect way to respond to social movement demands. When the campaign hit, Coop already had an 'ethical' clothing line, and could build on it as a counter-strategy.

Labeling became an even more viable option when Max Havelaar (MH) Switzerland started developing fair trade cotton. The case of MH most clearly illustrates how the rise of labels challenged campaign-makers and forced a strategic response. MH is the main fair trade labeling organization in Switzerland; from the mid-nineties, fair trade labeled products were increasingly present in major Swiss supermarkets, the most emblematic being bananas and coffee. For MH, certifying cotton was part of a strategy of expansion towards the certification of non-food products at a moment when the label was extremely successful in Switzerland.[19] Ironically enough, Lenten Fund and Bread for All were both founding organizations of MH Switzerland, together with the other major development aid NGOs. They both initially opposed the cotton project. As all campaign members, they saw it as an obstacle to their struggle: their fear was that companies would turn to the (already very well-known) MH label to show their social commitment without having to adopt more cost-intensive monitoring programs.[20] But eventually, they had to give in to the MH majority supporting the development of such a label. In this intricate situation, both sides tried to use the fair trade label to gain leverage over their opponents. Companies could—and one allegedly did[21]—use the uncertainty about their adoption of the label to put pressure on the NGOs in the CCC coalition to present their monitoring reports in a more favorable light. In short, they could threaten to withdraw from the label (and thus jeopardize its existence and the benefits for MH) if they were criticized too heavily by campaign-makers. Since the NGOs had to both back Max Havelaar *and* the campaign, and given the high economic stakes that were behind the Max Havelaar launch, such threats placed them in a strategic dilemma. But not all companies used the MH label in this threatening way. Others, trying to position themselves as genuine ethical corporations, were interested in rigorous controls and public reporting, and at the same time in well-known labeling schemes. From the opposite side, the NGOs also tried to use the MH label to gain leverage over corporations. Their idea was that firms wanting to sell clothes with the MH label should be obliged to join ISCOM, the multi-stakeholder monitoring initiative. This would mean that those firms would have to agree to submit all of their clothes to independent monitoring (not just those with a fair trade certification). But the organizations behind the CCC could not enforce this without facing the resistance of the MH management. Instead, it was simply decided that ISCOM

---

19   Interview with Bernhard, representative of ISCOM, Bern, July 2007.

20   For an NGO-authored study addressing the conflict between product or fair trade approaches and global approaches like the one advocated by the CCC, see Maquila Solidarity (2006).

21   Interview with Bernhard, representative of ISCOM, Bern, July 2007.

should monitor the supply chain of products with the MH label (which guaranteed fair trade only for the production of cotton, not for its processing).

Facing this changed landscape with an abundance of initiatives, some of them legitimized by competing social movement organizations,[22] the campaign adopted a more explicitly consumer-focused strategy. Comparative evaluations had already been part of the strategic repertoire, but now rankings adopting a vocabulary borrowed from consumer associations became the main action form. In 2004, and again in 2006, rankings of companies' social performances were published in a booklet together with Switzerland's biggest consumer organization, the Schweizerische Konsumentenschutz (Swiss consumer protection) and in the French speaking part, the Fédération romande des consommatrices. The ranking classified companies into avant garde, followers, and ignorants. The brochures also featured extensive discussion of the different labels that could be found in the textile market: organic labels, environmental labels, fair trade labels. It even contained a little card to be kept in one's wallet, showing the ranking. The 2006 edition added to this by explicitly recommending that consumers buy organic labels. Claims were still raised (in particular in a pamphlet that was distributed at the same time), but no petition was launched between 2004 and 2008. The centrality of consumer tactics in the Swiss campaign at that time is also clear from the fact that it developed a website where evaluations from all the national CCCs were brought together.[23] The consumerist strategy finally culminated in the publication of the ethical fashion map, an action form that relied almost exclusively on the buycott, i.e. shopping recommendations. However, the last campaign that fell into the time-span of this inquiry featured once again a petition addressed to the whole textile industry, alongside with consumerist tools (a ranking and the selling of a fair t-shirt).

To sum up, one observes a dynamic that goes from a first contentious interpellation and success with a pilot-project to a second stage where different counter-strategies were developed by the targeted firms: in particular, monitoring based on commercial audit firms and ethical labels. Campaign-makers then privileged consumerist action forms and also collaborated with consumer organizations. The campaign became more of a watchdog, an evaluator of the different initiatives, and a guide in the jungle of textile labels, perhaps at the peril of giving voice to its claims. A look inside the campaign reveals the strategic tension that drove this dynamic: between a strategy of shaming and one of rewarding.

---

22   In addition to MH, there was also a big NGO- and government-backed initiative for organic cotton, headed by the development aid organization Helvetas.

23   At the time of the final editing, this website is no longer online. But in the meantime, the campaign has developed an App that contains information on the major brands.

Shaming vs Rewarding, Again and Again

As in the French campaign, one finds a conflict line within the campaign between two (often complementary) strategies, one 'uncompromising,' of shaming and blaming, and one (compromised?) of acknowledging and rewarding even small and partial advances. But unlike in the French case, where this became a disputed issue towards the end of the campaign under the influence of counter-mobilization by the targets and the contentious wave of *altermondialisme*, tensions between a more or less uncompromising attitude already broke out right at the beginning of the Swiss campaign, catalyzed by the participation of the campaign in the monitoring pilot -project. While the coalition split partly resolved this issue, there remained a tension between a repertoire based mostly on threat, and a consumerist repertoire privileging a strategy of rewarding.

The conflict first erupted in the context of the pilot project. This is hardly surprising given the contradictory roles of putting on pressure through campaigning and collaborating with firms. The project revealed differences as to how the term 'collaboration' was to be interpreted. The two officials from the French-speaking BD, who had been the driving force behind the launch of the Swiss CCC, saw their participation in the pilot (and therefore the participation of the campaign) as representing the voice of a concerned public, as an external gaze on the corporations' practices. Hence, for them it was impossible to tolerate a departure from the basic principles of the code, i.e. the respect of the ILO core conventions. But not everybody involved in the campaign shared this basic point of view. The representatives of the other NGOs, notably, saw their role more as supporting the companies to gradually improve working conditions. Organizational cultures were different between the two development aid NGOs and the BD, i.e. between NGOs that were used to working 'on the field,' on concrete development projects, and an advocacy organization specialized in campaign-making. Separating the campaign organization from the monitoring project was an institutional way out of this strategic dilemma. The campaign could then act independently as a watchdog, without compromising the functioning of the monitoring project.

But with regard to strategy, there was also a cleavage between the French-speaking BD and the organization's German-speaking office. Beyond organizational cultures, strategic preferences also reflected individual trajectories. As one of the officials from the French-speaking secretariat expressed it in an interview: "We completely lost on this issue. Everyone except the French-speaking BD agreed to say that (our position) was too demanding."[24] The firm attitude of the two staff members conducting the campaign for the BD—what was perceived by the other members of the campaign as their radicalism—was anchored and reflected in their similar trajectories and political socializations. Contrary to most other protagonists, they both lacked a development aid profile, but studied social sciences and joined the BD as interns, without having any experience in the realm

---

24   Interview with Isabelle, DB, Vevey, July 2007.

of development politics. Politicized to the left and, for one of them, in anarchist and *autonomen* circles, the two women were searching for a professional career where they could put their political convictions into practice, and thus ended up working for the BD. These common features, which distinguished them from the other people working for the campaign, favored their more radical stance, as well as their very strong commitment and self-identification with the campaign. As a matter of fact, once the pilot project ended and it became clear that they could not enforce their strategy, they both quit their jobs.

From then on, the campaign was taken over by the German-speaking secretariat. Prior to this, the staff member from the Zurich office had already played a role in the campaign: he was in charge of the public campaigning part, while the two others took care of the pilot -project and relations with the companies. During this time of collaboration, there was also a divergence of strategy between the French-speaking team and the German-speaking employee, a tension that overlapped with the opposition between the BD and the NGOs. If the position facing the corporations—even those engaged in the pilot project—was to be uncompromising, then the campaign should be intense, its tone sharp and critical. This was the position adopted by the French-speaking team. "Our idea was: we denounce all instances where companies do not even do that [respecting the core conventions of the ILO]";[25] in practice, this position meant that all the companies participating in the pilot -project should have been sharply criticized after the auditing reports. And indeed, for the French-speaking team, the campaign should have made much more out of this—it should have been much more vigorous. The third person in charge, instead, privileged the consumer repertoire, consisting not only of blaming and shaming, but also rewarding companies that were making progress.

The ratings, which were to become the main tactic, were based both on the shaming of those companies that did not meet the standards *and* on rewarding those that did. In the words of the staff member from Zurich, one should not only release negative information and thus end up frustrating consumers, but also show them positive aspects. Without showing consumers that progress had been made and that it was possible to buy clothes that were more socially responsible than others, he feared that consumers would become disinterested in the issue.[26] Thus, the two positions that mostly characterized different organizations in the French case, could be found within the same organization in the Swiss case, although they used different justifications. In France, being 'nice' to corporations was mostly seen as important in order to bring them to collaborate with the campaign; it was a question of being perceived as a potential partner. In Switzerland, this was not really an issue: after all, the pilot-project was launched right away, and after the split between campaign and monitoring program, and the institutionalization of ISCOM, the campaign no longer needed to convince corporations to cooperate with it. The justification in the Swiss case was linked to a different mobilizing

25   Interview with Isabelle, DB, Vevey, July 2007.
26   Interview with campaign coordinator, BD, Zurich, January 2007.

strategy, a strategy that built more on political consumerism than on protest actions. In practice, the rewarding strategy became especially prevalent with the publication of the magazine *'prêt-à-partager'* with the consumer organization. Companies were highlighted in traffic-light colors—red for the 'bad sheep,' yellow for those in between, and green for the good ones. For every category (direct mail selling, retailers, brands), there was at least one, and up to three, good companies (the 'avant-garde'), a majority of 'followers,' and some 'ignorants.' Thus, while using comparative evaluation to put pressure on the badly-rated companies, it also gave consumers advice on what they should buy in order to live up to their ethical standards. By the standards of the French-speaking team, of course, with the exception of one or two companies, none of the recommended companies fulfilled the minimal requirement set.

The trend towards *buycott* (promoting ethical purchases) was reinforced in the campaign dynamic by the ethical shopping map created by a regional group of the BD. It constitutes an interesting insight into the processes driving the campaign dynamic and, more generally, tactical innovation within a campaign. When the group first thought of the map, it was initially projected to be about all kinds of products, but the focus was rapidly narrowed down to clothing, and the map thus directly linked to the CCC. Nevertheless, the initiative and the elaboration of the map were almost fully in the hands of the volunteers from the regional group with which I spent time as a participant observer. The ethical shopping map corresponded to the volunteers' expectations and their approach to politics: it was a project they could pursue autonomously, required a profound intellectual examination of the issue, and at the same time constituted a very concrete tool that could be used by ethical consumers (for a closer analysis, see Balsiger 2014). And in the eyes of the volunteers, it also responded to a demand from consumers. In the words of one of the map's initiators:

> It often happened to me that people told me "yeah, I think fair trade is good. And I think it is good if one is attentive when purchasing clothes, but where can I buy that?" […] Most people would like to behave in a more ethical manner, but they feel they don't know how.

The volunteers observed such a need in their social environment but also, and perhaps even more so, in their own daily practices. They all said they paid attention when shopping for clothes, but often they didn't know where to find garments that respected social standards. They thus reflected the concern voiced by the campaign coordinator: that blaming and shaming alone was not sufficient, but that it was also important to show consumers where to find clothes that respected ethical criteria. For the activists, adapting consumption practices was naturally part of their political participation; it was not sufficient to fight publicly through campaigns, but this political activity had to be accompanied by personal responsibility and, in particular, a changing of private consumption patterns. Theirs was thus a 'personalized politics,' which "combines a concern for broad public issues with an insistence that each individual activist is a locus of political responsibility and efficacy, outside as well as inside activist organizations" (Lichterman 1996, p. 34); public actions and private consumption are two sides of the same medal. The ethical shopping map, therefore, was naturally conceived of as a political tool. Its use was political; shopping 'with a conscience' was a vital part of the personal politics advocated by the regional group.

But it was also true that the ethical shopping map was only about buycotting, only about promoting alternatives and rewarding the firms that had adopted some kind of ethical criteria in their production of clothes. It thus affected the balance between blaming and rewarding. There is a thin line between those two strategic approaches, between consumer action that is still contentious and consumer action that is simply consumerism. The Swiss campaign, with its rankings, had always used both. Despite its media success, the map, stretching the campaign's tactical repertoire very far towards the buycott side, ended up being dismissed by the campaign responsible when the volunteers pressed to create similar maps for other cities. "I have to put pressure on companies! I'm not here to advertise organic cotton!," he said in a meeting which I attended, adding: "the companies can do that very well themselves." However, while the decision was categorical at this time, navigating between promoting alternatives and denouncing corporate practices remained a defining feature of the Swiss campaign. In the campaign round launched in 2008, called 'Revolution in the Fashion Industry,' the campaign sold a T-shirt produced according to its social standards (by the brand Switcher) as a positive example, and continued to put forward certain companies as having good practices, while criticizing others and petitioning the textile industry as a whole.

The episode shows how the tension between shaming and rewarding practices shaped innovation in the campaign's tactical action repertoire. Although the form corresponded to the regional group as well as to a strand of the BD's repertoire consisting of giving advice to consumers, it was ultimately rejected. This rejection was not due to a problem of resources, since the volunteers would do the major part of the work. The rejection had to do with strategic reasons, with regard to achieving the overall goal of the campaign. The campaign-makers estimated that the tactic of buycott could potentially be detrimental to the objective of mobilizing consumers and making retailers change their practices. They feared a process of demobilization, due to the ever-growing existence of alternative offers for ethical consumption. Although tactics of this kind had always been part of the DB's repertoire of market contention, and would remain so, they were always associated with tactics of putting pressure on firms. The sole promotion of alternatives was left to other actors within the social movement field, who could take over the role of publicizing ethical offers.

Oppositions between more or less uncompromising attitudes towards the firms' practices and tensions between contentious action forms and the promoting of ethical consumption practices drove the campaign from the inside. The latter tension was not resolved; instead, it seems to be an inbuilt dialectical contradiction, typical of political consumer campaigns that fluctuate between a contentious approach and the promotion of alternatives. Here one recognizes the tensions encountered in the analysis of the consumer campaigns in the 1970s between public campaigning aiming at the mainstream market, shaming companies in order to make them change their practices, and the retreat to private politics within an alternative society, adopting alternative lifestyles. However, this alternative society in the 2000s was no longer really alternative: the labels, brands and shops promoted on the shopping map were all commercial companies. They were no longer part of a counter-culture, or, for many of them, of the broader social movement community. The alternative had become a specialized niche market, a market that had developed under the influence of previous campaigns, changing consumer preferences, and the rise of labels and brands produced by social entrepreneurs.[27]

Political consumerist campaigns tend to evolve in this field of tension between boycott and buycott, voice and exit, claims-making and retreat to niche markets. The process is usually described as a gradual movement of recuperation or co-optation of movement claims by market actors (Boltanski and Chiapello 1999, Chasin 2000). But such story lines tend to operate through a black-or-white lens. Protesters are all pictured as anti-system and anti-corporate, and whenever market actors incorporate activist demands, those demands lose their transformative power and simply become merchandise. The analysis of the dynamics of the CCC, however, reveals that the campaigners' goals, the back-and-forth between movement demands and corporate reactions, and the back-and-forth between contentious tactics and the promotion and building up of alternative forms of production and consumption, are a great deal more nuanced than that.

---

27   In part, it was also the fruit of a performative action by the makers of the map. By designating stores as ethical, they made them belong to this specialized market, even if the owners of those stores did not think of themselves as motivated by ethical concerns. This was especially visible in the example of some of the second-hand firms that figure on the map; some of them were surprised to be seen as ethical stores, since they were more about luxury vintage clothes than following an anti-consumerism stance. As one of the activists said, "they are about selling last year's Gucci clothes at affordable prices!" For a discussion of the process of "naming the political," see Balsiger (2010).

Chapter 7

Strategic Interactions
and Campaign Outcomes

Common patterns of outcomes can be found in both the Swiss campaign and the French one, as well as in many of the other European Clean Clothes campaigns (Sluiter 2009). The campaigns started by demanding the adoption of codes of conduct; companies more or less rapidly adopted such codes, and the contested issue shifted towards the question of code implementation and the modalities of code monitoring. Campaigns thus quite quickly achieved a first partial success: they got corporations to acknowledge the issue of labor conditions on global value chains and made them adopt formal, albeit voluntary, rules in the form of codes of conduct.

From there on, the issue of code implementation and monitoring moved to the center of campaign demands, where it proved to be much trickier. The partial response of code adoption, which concerns only one aspect of the campaigns' demands, could in the end be a purely cosmetic response; concession costs (Luders 2006) for this measure are low as long as it is not associated with a serious model of control. But concession costs significantly rise as soon as it comes to fully responding to the campaigns' claim to independent control. The campaigns' outcomes in terms of establishing an initiative of code monitoring differed: while such cooperation between campaign makers and three targeted firms took place in Switzerland and was—albeit with many difficulties—institutionalized under the name ISCOM, no similar structure resulted from the French campaign. In spite of initial cooperation with the campaign on the part of individual firms—especially Auchan—it was the retailer association FCD that ended up managing the issue of code monitoring without cooperating with campaign makers. The comparison of the two cases can offer an explanation for this difference in outcomes: distinct characteristics of markets, firms and their supply chains, and previous experiences of collaboration and of stakeholder participation, are factors that differentiate both cases and confirm expectations resulting from existing theories.

This is the first step of the analysis. But it is only part of the story of outcomes. On the one hand, what may appear to be structural differences exposed by the comparison reveal themselves as a set of subsequent decisions that led to an escalating dynamic. Such an iterative perspective proves to be a better explanation of the French campaign's outcomes, with its progressive focusing on big retailers, and the retailers' refusal to yield to the campaign demands. On the other hand, an expansion of the time horizon and a more dynamic perspective on outcomes shows that both campaigns resulted in a kind of outcome 'curb': an early peak (with the adoption of codes of conduct, a few cooperations in France and the monitoring initiative in Switzerland) was followed by a trough where these early gains were lost. While some firms were initially willing to acquiesce to campaign demands, and participated in experimental multi-stakeholder institutions, many also backtracked from initial concessions and developed other strategic responses in reaction to campaign claims. In France, the retailers that cooperated with each other to build up a business-driven initiative of code monitoring ignored many of the campaign's main claims, and ended up publicly defying the campaign-makers. In Switzerland, after the initial success with the pilot project on code monitoring, firms developed a series of alternative responses, in particular by joining a business-driven monitoring initiative rather than the follow-up of the pilot project, and by selling ethical-label clothing lines. The companies' need to conform to legitimate practices can offer an explanation for this outcome. As the campaigns went on, firms developed counter-strategies that built on alternative sources for legitimation. The firms' creative strategic responses thus decisively shaped the impact the campaigns had in both countries.

Bringing Firms to Collaborate

In Switzerland, three firms (Migros, Switcher, and Veillon) agreed to collaborate with the campaign-makers, enabling the joint development of a monitoring initiative. The same attempts in France were not successful. What explains this difference? The main goal of research relating to how social movements create change has been to establish the conditions that favor movement outcomes (Uba 2009). To explain "how movements matter" (Giugni et al. 1999), authors have pointed to the importance of movement characteristics (tactics, organization, resources, or framing strategies) and to the movement's environment (in particular political opportunity structures), as well as to the articulation between these two aspects (Amenta 2006, Amenta and Caren 2004, Amenta and Young 1999, Giugni 2004). Most studies in this field have looked at movements targeting the state, but the recent literature on movements targeting corporations has tended to look at the same factors: movement-internal characteristics, characteristics of targets and of the broader environment (see Chapter 1). In this literature—just as in the general literature on movement outcomes (Uba 2009)—no clear-cut relations have been identified: depending on the cases they study and their theoretical focus, authors tend to point to different factors.

Many of those commonly invoked factors influencing movement outcomes, from movement characteristics and environments, were quite similar in Switzerland and France. This is largely true for the very similar action forms and framings, although there were some notable differences regarding the composition of the coalition and the use of grassroots actions. It comes as more of a surprise that in some respects, the national (and also transnational) political contexts of both campaigns were also very similar. Of course, Switzerland and France have very different political systems and are usually ranged in two very different categories in studies using a comparative political opportunities framework, one being an open and weak state, the other being the paradigmatic case of a strong and closed system (Kitschelt 1986, Kriesi et al. 1995). But these general characteristics of the political system may not be particularly salient in explaining dynamics and outcomes of specific movements, especially if one looks at movements targeting market actors.

Instead, analysis must turn to the relevant aspects of the political environment for the movement under study (Amenta et al. 2002), i.e. the attitudes and actions of the state towards the anti-sweatshop campaign. These relevant domestic and transnational political environments were very similar in France and Switzerland. On the one hand, the campaigns were in part reactions to the perceived closing down of opportunities of regulation at the transnational level, when the introduction of a social clause into the WTO framework failed. This led the organizations to seek private solutions through the use of codes of conduct. On the other hand, the domestic political environment played a sustaining role, as governments were actually, at least to some extent, sympathetic to the campaigns' goals. In France, the support was mostly financial: the campaign was financed by the European and French governments. But the state actors did not get more involved in specific projects of 'private regulation.' The French campaign actively sought out such an involvement, by pursuing different paths for code monitoring. Most notably, it attempted to push the development of a social label through the French agency of normalization, of which the state, as well as civil representatives, are both part. It was the explicit goal of the campaign that the state should play a pivotal role should such a social label emerge. But the label never took form, and the role of the state did not go beyond the financing of the campaign. In Switzerland, the campaign functioned without government funding, and so did the pilot project of code monitoring, which was paid for by the participating companies. But the state ended up funding the follow-up to the pilot, eventually enabling the project to get institutionalized. This subsidy was certainly essential to the pilot project's survival. It is thus clear that in both countries, domestic political contexts for the campaigns were quite favorable, as governments supported the goals of the campaign. But this support was only limited and governments did not actively push for these goals. In this respect, comparisons with other national campaigns would have brought forward more striking differences. The French and Swiss states played less decisive roles than states like Great Britain, where the government supported the British Ethical Trade initiative, the Netherlands with the Fair Wear Foundation, supported by the Dutch state, or the US where the major private regulations of apparel production were in fact driven by government intervention in a framework of neo-liberal policies (Bartley 2007b). In both Switzerland and France, the state played a considerably less active role.

Political opportunities and movement tactics therefore cannot explain different outcomes. Instead, it was differences in the market arena which were decisive: the crucial factors to explain divergent outcomes are to be found in characteristics of the market, its organization and participants. The comparative analysis reveals three main differences in this regard: the relationship between activists and their corporate targets, the role of consumer demand, and the divergent characteristics of the targeted firms themselves.

In Switzerland, there is a history of precedents involving the same actors at the time of the campaign launch. This is particularly the case with the firm Migros. Migros had been the target of a number of campaigns since the late 1970s, and initially reacted to them with aggressive counter-strategies. However, the group gradually changed its policies and a first collaboration between Migros and a development aid NGO (Bread for All) took place in the 1980s with the social clause on pineapple production. Bread for All was later also part of the Swiss Max Havelaar label, together with other Swiss development aid NGOs, and Max Havelaar products were introduced in Migros supermarkets from early on. In other words, when the Clean Clothes Campaign was launched, there was already a history of successful collaboration between Migros and NGOs. These historic precedents favored collaboration at the time of the CCC launch. Corporations and activists were already used to each other; they had been socialized to the idea of cooperating.

In France, the situation was very different. The Clean Clothes Campaign was arguably the first time a social movement coalition explicitly targeted corporations with regard to their social responsibility over an extended period of time. Even more so, in addition to the lack of previous experience and of personal ties,[1] the relationship between campaign makers and their targets was also characterized by a growing cultural distance. The *grande distribution* had an increasingly bad public image. In the early years of the 2000s, a number of anti-retailer publications attacked the big retailers for their policies regarding manufacturers (Jacquiau 2000, Lugos 2003, Tinard and Tinard 2003). The big retailers were increasingly pictured as villains, destroying small neighborhood shops and dictating ever-lower prices to farmers and producers. The publication of rankings was part of this logic, as it individually named and blamed retailers for their social performances. This negative image affected the possibility of collaboration insofar as it further alienated the campaign coalition from its targets. On the side of the campaigners, it was difficult, especially for the organizations positioned to the left of the political spectrum (for example Artisans du monde), to defend a collaborative approach vis-à-vis their traditional public. This difficulty was even greater, as we saw in Chapter 6, due to the rise of the global justice movement with its framing in terms of politics-against-markets, which contributed to paint a negative picture of big retailers. For the big retailers, hostile public opinion was likely to affect their interpretation of the rankings as an aggressive, merely denunciatory strategy and to have an effect on the firms' defensive attitude, combined with a strategy of counter-mobilization. This hypothesis is supported, for example, by a post on the blog of the retailer Leclerc, by its director. He called the campaign coalition's practice "blackmailing" and speaks of

---

1   Except for the case of the internal ally the campaign had at Auchan, which favored the early collaboration between the two. Significantly, his departure also brought about the end of this collaborative project (see Chapter 6)

people who, without guarantee of competence, without preliminary approval, without any other argument or justification other than their own affirmations evaluate, criticize, and even denigrate firms [...] depending on whether or not they accept to collaborate with them.[2]

Schurman and Munro (2009) argue that the cultural meaning attributed to commodities or industries affect the likely reactions of corporations to movement demands. In the French case, the cultural meaning attributed to the industry—one that pictured them as extremely powerful Goliaths making money off consumers' and producers' backs—did not favor cooperation from either side. Thus, cultural opportunities for collaboration were reduced, too. By contrast, the public image of Swiss retailers was not nearly as negative—on the contrary. The biggest retailers Migros and Coop were both credibly presenting themselves to the public as corporations preoccupied not only with their own profit, but also with driving a wider social and environmental agenda which would benefit the general public.

The second point concerns the timing of the campaigns with regard to the existence or not of a market for ethical goods. The broader question of corporate social responsibility and ethical initiatives by companies was completely new in the French context, and developed later compared to the Swiss market. In Switzerland, both major retailers (Migros and Coop) started selling fair trade-labeled products in 1992;[3] the same early introduction can be found with organic products, where Coop in particular took a leading role.[4] In France, the presence of fair trade in supermarkets was extremely marginal and only increased in the early 2000s,[5] and retailers only let organic products enter their shelves somewhat faintheartedly. Thus, Carrefour launched its first organic products in 1997 while almost all its main competitors (with the exception of Monoprix) were still hesitating.[6] Finally, one also observes a slight difference in reporting on environmental and social concerns: while Migros and Coop started publishing 'environmental reports' (treating the subject as one of social responsibility) in 1996, similar reports appeared much later in France.[7] This evidence suggests that ethical issues were probably perceived as more marginal and less pressing by the companies targeted in France than those in Switzerland. Despite the mobilization by the campaign and the studies it quoted on consumer interest in ethical products, the rise of the citizen-consumer as a public figure and a potential market did not happen until the early 2000s in France, much later than in Switzerland. In the Swiss case, the

---

2   The blog is cited by Barraud de Lagerie (2010, p. 255) (my translation).

3   The first MH certified coffee in 1992 was available at both Coop and Migros: *Neue Zürcher Zeitung*, May 8 1992, "In der Schweiz erforlgreicher Max Havelaar Kaffee."

4   *Neue Zürcher Zeitung*, April 19 2000, "Coop steht in Blüte."

5   *Le Monde*, May 5 2007, "La grande distribution flaire un nouveau marché."

6   *Le Monde*, June 16 1997, "Grandes manœuvres sur le marché des produits bio."

7   They became compulsory for publicly traded firms with the Nouvelle regulation *économique* law, voted by the Jospin government in 2001.

Swiss consumer culture's disposition to embrace ethical initiatives and goods was already demonstrated by their purchase behavior (see Schurman and Munro (2009) for a similar argument for the British retail sector). Ethical commitment, thus, might pay off; beyond the signals given by those citizens sending protest postcards within the campaign framework, there were other strong signals in the market that showed that ethical strategies could be beneficial for the bottom line, too. This made market-based counter-strategies such as ethical product lines and labels potentially rewarding for firms, but also meant that there was a general public awareness of ethical issues firms needed to take into account.

Finally, the third point concerns the particular characteristics of the firms themselves. For each of the Swiss firms that joined the pilot project, one can find certain firm-level and industry-level characteristics that made them more likely than their competitors to react favorably. The first one, Switcher, a specialty chain, was a characteristic 'challenger' firm (Fligstein 2001) that decided to follow an 'ethical' corporate policy. In the clothing market, the firm was a relatively small player compared with the big retailers; positioning itself as a company with an ethical approach may have been viewed as a strategic asset to gain new market shares. Switcher was thus a firm combining high commitment to change with high capacity of organization, which, according to Zald et al. (2005), should favor its responsiveness to movement campaigns. The founder and CEO of Switcher had become one of the best-known social entrepreneurs in Switzerland. Before the Clean Clothes Campaign, the company was involved in some philanthropic projects in the towns where they manufactured. At the end of the 1990s, the director hired an economist who previously worked for the Swiss Ministry of Economy, in order to deal with the rising demands of codes of conduct. From the beginning, the issue of codes of conduct and of ethical trade was thus incorporated at the firm's management level.[8] Finally, the firm's integrated business model also strongly facilitated participation in the pilot and the adoption of strong social standards in general. Contrary to the dominant functioning of the clothing market, Switcher did not rely on middlemen and always produced in the same production plants. Their global supply chain was thus different from those of the bigger retailers and clothing brands who often manufacture in many more countries and factories,

---

8   The first explanation in terms of market politics and the second in terms of corporate culture are of course variants of the distinction between interests vs values. In one instance, Switcher turns ethical because the firm (that is, its founder) believes in ethical trade as an important value; in the other instance, it does so for strategic and instrumental reasons. Both motivations are likely to be at play, but are not equally legitimate. When addressing consumers, the media, or sociologists, firms arguably prefer to speak about values rather than market interests. Thus, in an interview, the CSR spokesperson insisted that CSR policies had nothing to do with gaining market shares, and gave a number of reasons for this: according to market research conducted by the firm, only about 5% of their customers are aware of the company's ethical initiatives, and the firm does not undertake notable communication campaigns on the subject.

and frequently change their sites of production. This integrated model favored the participation in the pilot insofar as the company already had an overview of its production sites, and their limited number, and the long-term commitment, made it easier to guarantee the respect of labor standards.

The second firm, Veillon, was already pursuing a strategy of social philanthropy, centered on actions against child labor (Mach 2001), when the CCC was launched. This pre-campaign commitment to labor rights is likely to have played a role in Veillon's participation in the pilot. Again, evidence suggests that there was a mixture of corporate culture and Veillon's interest in (further) positioning itself as an ethical company. Mach (2001) quotes the CEO of Veillon saying (in May 2000) "We realized that our endeavors were being well perceived and this has made us more aggressive on the public relations front." Migros, finally, was (and still is) an incumbent firm. Together with Coop, Migros is one of the leaders of the Swiss general retailing market. In fact, the retail market structure in Switzerland is very particular, as it is dominated by two players both having between 35 and 40% of the market share (Mueller and Tinguely 2007), thus controlling nearly 80% of the market together. Another particularity of the Swiss retailing market is that Migros and Coop both originated as cooperatives and still partly maintain these structures today. Migros, in addition, prides itself on pursuing ethical goals since its foundation: for example, it bans the selling of alcohol and tobacco for moral and health-related reasons. Its bylaws also oblige it to use one percent of its sales volume to fund cultural activities. More recently, Migros had successfully integrated organic and fair-trade products in its supermarkets. In fact, the particular configuration of the Swiss retail market signifies that one player, in a classic mimetic process, usually follows innovations by its competitor immediately. Since the two of them control almost 80% of the market, this means that very quickly, a broad share of the market is concerned with the innovation in question. This 'ethical competition' is likely to have driven Migros to participate in the pilot project, too, for Coop already had its 'ethical' clothing line. Coop therefore probably had less interest in participating in the pilot project, since they already had a strategy, albeit one which built on a single product line. But they could put forward these efforts and thus appear as an ethically conscious firm. Migros lacked such a positioning but collaborating with NGOs through participation in the pilot project would put it again at the forefront of this ethical competition. Thus, the structure of the Swiss retail market and the strategic reasoning of the two competitors seem to have played a role in explaining the adherence of one of them to the pilot project.

Compared to the Swiss corporate targets, the French ones were quite different. It was a more homogeneous group—general retailers and sports retailers. The firms were generally much bigger than the ones targeted in Switzerland. Carrefour was already the second largest retailer worldwide, and many of the other French retailers had annual sales figures significantly higher than the biggest firms targeted in Switzerland, i.e. Migros and Coop. In addition, because they were all retailers, they also had supply chain structures that were complex and built on a variety of subcontractors. None of them was comparable to the Swiss firm Switcher with its direct control over factories.

But there were, of course, also differences between the individual firms that the French campaign targeted. What further distinguished the French campaign dynamic from the Swiss case is the role played by business associations. The individual firms actually ended up delegating this issue to the business associations, which ultimately responded with one voice for all the companies and refused to include the campaign makers in its monitoring initiative. The Fédération des entreprises du commerce et de la distribution's (FCD) part in addressing this issue built on the role the organization already played in the managing of other collective action problems. Not only did the FCD act as a political lobbyist for the retailing sector, but its responsibility also extended to industrial relations with workers' unions and to tasks of quality control and standardization in the realm of product security. The importance of business associations in France is striking when compared to Switzerland, but less so when compared to other countries. Business associations were often addressees of the petitions and campaigns. In France, petitions were explicitly addressed to the Conseil national du commerce and to the Federation of sports retailers (FPES). Both in pilot projects in the Netherlands and in Germany, business associations were involved; a business association (the Foreign Trade Association) was also at the origin of the European BSCI standard that was launched in 2003. The fact that business associations played no role in Switzerland is rather a sign of the low organizational level of the textile and retailing sector in that country.[9]

In sum, the comparison points to a number of structural differences between the French and Swiss cases. Many of the factors that shaped outcomes have also been proposed in other studies as favoring corporate responsiveness to movement demands. The relationship between activists and their targets points to the importance of the establishment of mutual trust in order to form a collaborative initiative. Internal advocates (Raeburn 2004) can help create this, but so do positive previous experiences of collaboration which create proximity between movement actors and their targets. The role of consumer demand has been stressed by Schurman and Munro (2009) as crucial for the responsiveness of companies; it means that ethical practices also have 'pragmatic legitimacy' and are viable (den Hond and de Bakker 2007, p. 907). The last point, finally, contains various aspects of 'corporate opportunity structures' that have been revealed by other studies on movement impact on corporations: most notably, differences in corporate cultures (Schurman 2004) and supply chain structures (Schurman and Munro 2009) differentiate the firms that participated in the pilot project in Switzerland. Organizational cultures stemming from the nationally distinct form of capitalism may have favored the development of a multi-stakeholder

---

9   The Textilverband is the association of firms in the textile industry—manufacture and production, rather than retailing. The association Swiss Fashion Stores, formerly Association suisse des détaillants en textile, assembles independent stores selling textiles.

monitoring initiative in Switzerland too: Swiss firms evolving in an environment of a coordinated economy are more used to procedures of collective bargaining and thus to directly negotiating contentious issues with stakeholders. In addition to this, forms of private- or self-regulation are quite common and often serve to prevent more all-encompassing state regulation (Mach et al. 2007). French companies, on the other hand, are part of a state-led economy where regulation of capitalism is usually a prerogative of the state, and direct negotiations with stakeholders are not common. Different varieties of capitalism could thus also be part of the explanation of the different fate of the monitoring projects in both countries (Bair and Palpacuer 2012).

Interactions and Outcomes

From this comparison one could conclude that the opportunity structure for the campaign was more favorable in the Swiss context than in the French one, and this difference explains the 'success' of the Swiss campaign compared to its French counterpart. Those stable factors are certainly important in explaining divergent outcomes. But operating with hindsight, the comparative perspective may lead observers to give too much importance to broad structural differences at the expense of neglected turning points—moments where things could have gone different ways—as well as strategic responses and interactions, which mean that outcomes can change over time. Strategic decisions and interaction dynamics played an important role in the focusing of the campaigns on specific targets, in dynamics of escalation, and in the backtracking of corporations from initial concessions and thus the loss of certain early gains for the campaigns.

In the French case, the very targets that occupied the center stage of the campaign and became the co-protagonists of the arena of contention that was created by the campaign, were the result of a process that was highly path-dependent. The campaign came to target essentially the players of the *grande distribution*—the biggest general retailers. This was not the case at the outset. In the first two rounds of campaigning, a broader range of targets was addressed. The clothing sector consisted of a wide range of different business models, each one defining a socially distinct market: specialized branded retailers, hyper- and supermarket stores, mail-order companies, sports stores, and department stores (Aspers 2010). The campaign started with an analysis of the transformations of the clothing sector, pointing to the growing control of retailers over global commodity chains, as retailers (general or specialized) gain market shares over the traditional independent clothing stores which used to dominate the market. In fact, this transformation was seen as one of the reasons for the deterioration of production conditions and the 'race to the bottom' to ever lower wages and cheaper production costs. This analysis led the campaign makers to identify clothing retailers as responsible for this problem and to target them. Although in the first campaign round, three specific targets were picked out, it was clearly stated that the campaign actually meant to target the whole sector. The second campaign followed this pattern by choosing three different companies as individual targets, representing the categories of mail-order, specialized chain and sports retailers, and addressing a petition to the Conseil national du commerce. From the third campaign round on, however, big retailers—sports retailers on the one hand, and general retailers on the other—were targeted almost exclusively.

This choice had to do with strategic considerations that were partly fed by the very dynamic the campaign set in motion. The big retailers sold the biggest volume of clothes, and their adoption of codes of conduct and participation in independent monitoring thus potentially had the biggest impact on developing countries. But some retailers were also the first ones to react, to adopt codes of conduct and to signal their willingness to address the issue. This was the case of Carrefour and Auchan, and then also with the FCD who invited the campaign to participate in its meetings. Thus, there seemed to be a perceived opening—an opportunity—with the *grande distribution*, which further convinced the campaign makers to keep targeting these actors. Strategic decisions and interaction were thus crucial in the progressive focusing on one type of target rather than another. In this respect, the Swiss campaign differed. There was no such progressive channeling. As in France, the idea was to target the whole sector and not to single out one company over another. But the Swiss campaign mostly stuck to the list of 15 main targets it had identified in the beginning, representing different retailing formats.

Focusing on the big retailers to the detriment of other clothing firms turned out to be crucial for the French campaigns' outcomes. For one thing, it channeled interactions towards a particular type of firm, not necessarily characterized by features such as small to medium size, relatively simple supply chains or 'ethical' corporate cultures that distinguished firms in other countries that had yielded to campaign demands. Instead, they were big, sometimes publicly traded firms with a strong business association. Nonetheless, the launching of the Initiative Clause Sociale, an industry-wide initiative by the FCD, did not rule out collaboration per se, as the comparative assessment might conclude; rather, it was a combination of the structural factors with the interaction dynamic that made it increasingly unlikely. At different moments, there were openings and possibilities to create a collaborative initiative. Auchan's collaboration with campaign makers in code monitoring is the most striking argument against a structuralist explanation of the difference between the Swiss and French case. Favored by the presence of an internal ally, there was the possibility that a collaborative project could develop, and had it succeeded, one would be writing a different account. But the decision of the FCD to start a business-driven monitoring initiative, and Auchan's subsequent retreat from the experiment, changed this.

Yet even the creation of an initiative by the business association FCD might have played into the hands of the French CCC, since in its beginnings, a closer collaboration between the FCD and the campaign seemed possible. The FCD sent encouraging signals, but the participation of campaign makers in the retailers' monitoring initiative never materialized. In other words, it was not an unchallengeable structural characteristic of the FCD that impeded collaboration, it was the strategy the organization came to rely on, and the following growing antagonism, which ruled it out. It led to a dynamic of escalation which could not be foreseen.

After the retailers started their ICS, the campaign resumed direct contentious targeting of corporations when it published its first ranking, giving bad grades to almost all the big retailers that were part of the newly created monitoring initiative. The corporations organized in the FCD interpreted this move as a radicalization of the campaign—a reaction that campaign makers had partly anticipated. But they estimated that the advantages of putting the different corporations in competition with one another were greater. However, the FCD then started to undermine the campaign coalition strategy. On the various occasions of subsequent ratings, and under the pressure of an ever more mobilizing campaign, the FCD started deploying a more offensive counter-strategy, defused 'ethical competition' by responding with one voice, and ended up not taking into account any of the claims of the campaign. The negative mutual perceptions campaign makers and retailers had of each other were aggravated by this increasingly conflicting exchange of moves. Campaigners resented retailers for their uncompromising attitude and strategic coups such as the publication of an open letter on the same day a ranking was published. Interviewees perceived this move as a provocation. Retailers, for their part, perceived campaigners as 'lecturers disconnected from reality.'[10] The back and forth between campaigners and retailers had contributed to creating this mutual perception; in turn, it made breaking the escalation dynamic very difficult, in spite of the campaign makers' wish to stick to a dual strategy with the goal of collaboration.

Early Gains, Readily Lost: Outcome Curbs and Legitimacy Strategies

When looking at both the Swiss and French campaigns, it is striking that they both came closest to achieving their goals at an early stage. The experiments on code monitoring in France happened after only a few years of campaigning, and the pilot project in Switzerland was started shortly after the campaign launch. Subsequently, these early gains got lost again: targeted companies found other, less costly ways to react to movement demands.

The field perspective can be helpful in conceptualizing an alternative perspective on outcomes that can explain such dynamics. When movements protest and manage to get public attention for their demands, they open up new arenas of contention (Duyvendak and Jasper 2014) or strategic action fields (Fligstein and McAdam 2012), and force their targets to react. All players that are part of a contentious struggle—as an initiator or as a target—are actors with agency, deploying strategies to influence the further course of interaction. In the case of contention in markets with corporations as targets, legitimation becomes

---

10   According to an interview with an official of a firm targeted by the French CCC quoted by Delalieux (2008).

a defining issue of such struggles. As institutional theory suggests, firms are driven by concerns of legitimacy (Oliver 1991). Struggles between corporations and social movement organizations are thus forms of 'legitimation politics' (Fransen 2012), driven by the quest of companies for conformation with social norms, values and expectations (Palazzo and Scherer 2006) and the attempts of movements to publicly question corporations' conformity with norms and/or to establish new norms.

In the two cases at hand, firms used a series of strategies to respond to the challenges to their legitimacy. Those strategies went from ignorance to compliance, from different forms of 'sidestepping' to confrontation and defiance. At first, they ignored challenges and then reacted with some concessions or even acquiescence; but at a later stage, they also developed counter-initiatives of code monitoring and ethical labels that sidestepped campaign demands, and in France, they directly confronted and defied campaign-makers. In sum, firms have a broad strategic *repertoire* that they can use to respond to campaign demands, and these responses are significant in shaping campaign outcomes.

The analysis suggests that in the early stages of the campaign, campaign-makers had an advantage because they were the first ones to raise the issue of working conditions in supply chains and monopolized expertise and legitimacy on the question. The targeted companies had to seek legitimacy in view of the campaigns' accusations. But they did not know how to react to the campaign and were looking for solutions. As we have seen, at this time there were no established and institutionalized ways of dealing with this topic. Some firms therefore turned to campaign makers and accepted their offer for collaboration because of the lack of alternatives. At this early stage, campaign-makers appeared as the only, or at least the main, conveyors of legitimacy if firms were willing to address the problem of sweatshops. The newness and the absence of established solutions was an advantage for the campaigns. But as time went by, companies could develop alternative solutions and build up other sources of legitimacy and backtrack from initial concessions.

Business-driven monitoring programs building on traditional audits were the main source of this. After a few experimental collaborations, organized retailers in France succeeded in significantly shaping the outcome of the campaign with their Initiative Clause Sociale. Rather than having a 'social label,' based on a strict control of the codes of conduct involving organizations from 'civil society,' the big retailers stuck to a very light version of control through social audits. But the firms had to use additional strategies to respond to the on-going criticism by the campaign coalition. They could not just build an initiative that disregarded most of the campaign's main claims. On the one hand, the companies stressed their own expertise in matters of supply chain management and the efficiency of the Initiative Clause Sociale; they thus emphasized aspects of legitimacy where they had more credibility than the campaigners (Quack 2010). But to further defend their legitimacy, they also had to develop an ever more political response with the goal of delegitimizing opponents and obstructing the campaign. Concessions were thus paralleled by an effort to openly attack the campaign makers. The FCD's communication, especially its open letter questioning the coalition's methods, motivations and competence, were strategic moves to dismiss demands for an *independent* monitoring initiative and make their own, business-driven initiative appear more legitimate.

In Switzerland, the apparent success of the multi-stakeholder pilot did not last all that long either. Companies started to develop alternative counter-strategies that constituted limited concessions and sidestepped campaign demands. Eventually, this meant that the pilot project could not decisively shape how the issue of production conditions was dealt with. Instead, firms took the upper hand and shaped outcomes through their own strategic responses, firstly through the building-up of the Business Social Compliance Initiative (BSCI), a business-driven alternative to the multi-stakeholder project. Migros was a driving force behind BSCI, and eventually opted out of the project with the Swiss CCC. Many more Swiss companies joined BSCI in the years after its founding. The BSCI constitutes a response of the corporations to the campaign, as it takes up a number of the claims, while controlling the whole process of monitoring itself. BSCI proceeds using a very similar model to the French Initiative Clause Sociale, built on social auditing.

Nevertheless, its growing prominence in Switzerland did not lead to an increase in confrontation between the campaign and its targets, although the campaign explicitly refuted and rejected this approach, and uses, just as its French counterpart, rankings. Why not? One of the reasons for this different dynamic may be that Swiss clothing retailers used, in parallel, another strategy that allowed them to shape the campaign outcomes. They developed market-based responses such as the adoption and promotion of social and environmental labels. Such labels certify the respect of ethical criteria for a limited range of products, for a given issue (fair trade, ecology), and usually also only for a limited part of the commodity chain (the growing of cotton, in particular). In other words, they do not cover all the clothes sold by a given retailer, as the campaign demanded. They cater to a specific segment of 'conscious' consumers, and at the same time they allow retailers, in a way, to distract attention from the conditions of production of the other textile products they sell. Ethical labels often originated in collaboration with competing movement actors, i.e. movement actors that were not part of the campaign, as in the case of Max Havelaar fair trade cotton or organically certified cotton. From the point of view of firms, the activity of these competing movement actors thus produced opportunities for firms to broaden their repertoire of strategic responses by sidestepping the campaign demands (Balsiger 2012). Thus, in the Swiss case too, movement outcomes were strongly shaped by strategic interactions and, in particular, by corporations' strategic responses to counter the campaign.

The Open-Ended Character of Movement Outcomes in Markets

These diverse strategies—from some concessions to sidestepping campaign demands to open confrontation—allowed firms to counter movement demands and to 'get away with' outcomes that were far from meeting the main claims. 'Legitimation politics' (Fransen 2012) was a defining part of this struggle. Campaign makers had succeeded in challenging firms' positions by questioning the legitimacy of their practices. One way to regain legitimacy was by acquiescing to movement demands—for campaign makers, the preferred solution, and in the beginning this is also what happened in some cases. But mostly, firms made limited concessions and developed compensating strategies to make up for a loss in legitimacy. In the French case, the strategy of defiance served the firms to defend the legitimacy of the ICS facing their challengers. In the Swiss outcome dynamics, legitimation politics was an equally important issue, and the case of Migros shows how legitimacy issues were at the center of balancing interests. According to a former official of the pilot project, Migros hoped to associate a civil society organization, if possible the CCC and its monitoring project, with the BSCI: "they hoped that another organization from the outside would give the BSCI an independent label. Their problem was always that they lacked legitimacy, because it is a business-driven initiative. What they were looking for was legitimacy."[11] Using sources from the BSCI, Fransen (2012) has documented how the organization tried to find support from civil society organizations to gain more legitimacy for its approach. Migros eventually decided to quit the multi-stakeholder monitoring initiative, although there was still no civil society organization involved in the alternative, BSCI. Instead, legitimacy was provided through other sources. On the one hand, the label strategies facilitated the firm's dismissal of multi-stakeholder initiatives to the benefit of less costly alternatives. Labels for specific product lines were thus one source of legitimacy, often enhanced thanks to NGO participation. On the other hand, the fact that more and more Swiss corporations joined BSCI meant that this compromise strategy became the new norm, set by the firms and shared by most of them. Given that all the main competitors were betting on the same horse, legitimacy issues became less prevalent.

With changing configurations and contexts, and depending on their individual characteristics, firms will adopt different strategies to oppose movement demands. The comparison has revealed some core differences that can explain the different responsiveness of firms in France and Switzerland, with some Swiss firms being more open to acquiescing to the campaign demands. It is within this general contextual background—especially the greater proximity between campaign actors and firms in Switzerland, and the earlier development of markets for ethical goods in that country—that these interactions took place. But the more dynamic perspective also reveals that in the course of the campaign, firms developed different strategic responses through interaction with challengers and other actors. Over

---

11   Interview with Bernhard, representative of ISCOM, Bern, July 2007.

time, outcomes can therefore change, as corporate targets organize themselves and develop new strategies and forms of legitimation, to counter demands. This is what happened in the case of the CCC in both countries.

Movements targeting the state often demand legislative change; when they achieve their goals, they bring about new legislation which is characterized by its relative durability.[12] When targeting corporations, it is arguably more difficult to achieve durable outcomes, unless they are a) authoritatively implemented through the law or b) locked into institutional arrangements with positive feedback effects, which makes exit difficult and costly (Pierson 2000). If this is not the case, we find instances of competing solutions and strategies, and outcome dynamics may switch from early successes to increasing drawbacks—firms manage to draw on different sources of legitimacy and may pull out of initial concessions. Indeed, it is likely that the open-ended character of social movement outcomes is particularly prevalent in cases where movements are targeting corporations.

---

12   This is also a simplified picture of course. The adoption of new legislation does not necessarily mean that legislation is implemented, and movements can have divergent outcomes regarding the different stages of the legislative process (Burstein et al. 1995)

Conclusion
Contention, Consumers, and Corporations

Markets have been, and are, sites for protest; firms are shamed and blamed by civil society groups who fight for more effective regulation and its implementation in transnational supply chains. Struggles span continents and take place on local, national and global scales. The anti-sweatshop movement is by no means the only concerted effort to push companies to change their practices with regard to labor rights, the environment, or other issues put forward by social movements. In industries as varied as biotechnology, electronics or mining, movement campaigns mobilize citizens and consumers to target corporations and fight against the negative social and environmental consequences of the global market economy. The campaigns fighting for 'ethical fashion' have been among the most visible ones in the recent past and have led to the establishment of new forms of private regulation and the rise of new markets for ethical fashion. This study has compared the rise, interactions and consequences of the global anti-sweatshop movement as it was carried out in two European countries, Switzerland and France. Building on the comparison of these two cases, I have attempted to gain some general insights into the rise of consumer campaigns and the dynamics of protest in markets.

The study has shown that the Clean Clothes Campaign's origins can be traced back to the late 1960s/early 1970s, when social movement organizations started to develop a repertoire of actions mobilizing consumers on which the anti-sweatshop campaigns would later build. In the course of the mobilization cycle of the 1970s, when many of the so-called new social movements emerged and thrived, some groups came to link production and consumption to political issues, especially development politics and the environmental cause. Firms and global markets were identified as responsible for the exploitation of workers and the environment, and as the main cause of poverty and underdevelopment in the 'Third World.' Groups like the Bern Declaration in Switzerland or Artisans du monde in France were fighting for more social justice in markets: fair trade, production in cooperatives, or the promotion of locally owned businesses and autonomous development were seen as instrumental in bringing about a world with less inequality and poverty. Advocacy organizations carried out campaigns and built up networks of production and distribution to raise awareness for the politics of development and to put in place alternatives and promote them. Changing consumption practices was an integral part of this strategy: as a consumer, each individual could personally contribute to changing the economic world order by buying fair trade products, jute bags and coffee from Tanzania, or by consuming less meat, to take examples from BD campaigns. Changing consumption and building up alternative markets also resonated well with the counter-cultural climate of the seventies and its ideology of 'everything is political'—it meant anticipating the new order by directly putting it in place, a form of prefigurative politics not unlike the recent forms of alternative exchange promoted by sustainable community movements (Graziano and Forno and 2012, Forno and Graziano 2014). But gradually, consumption also came to be used in a more contentious way, as a weapon to put pressure on the companies that were viewed as responsible for the exploitation of workers and the environment in developing countries. Consumer power was expressed in campaigns that used petitions and, later on, rankings, to put pressure on corporations.

The adoption and dissemination of consumer campaigns and protest targeting corporations had to do with the increasingly global economy and the possibility of linking distant issues to everyday practices, but it was also a matter of strategy. The rise of consumption campaigns was favored by strategic struggles within the fields of development politics. In Switzerland, the use of consumer campaigns allowed the BD to position itself as different from the traditional development aid organizations while at the same time as also distinct from more radical groups opposing capitalism. In France, the rise of a new category within the field of development—the French doctors and their humanitarian interventionism—jeopardized the dominant position of traditional development aid organizations and advocacy groups and public campaigning with petitions was a way for them to regain a more visible profile. The launch of the French CCC was also part of this tactical innovation.

Strategy also matters in the choice of targets and arenas where claims are made. Bypassing the political arena by advocating personal change and targeting firms directly was just as much a strategic choice as a form of activism in agreement with the worldviews of the activists. That changing consumer behavior was part of the solution was obvious for them—individual change was an important step towards social change—but the activists also perceived its limits. The 'alternative lifestyles' of the counterculture were unable to reach a broader public and seriously challenge the functioning of the global economy. The early promoters of consumer campaigns never dismissed political solutions—protest in markets and protest in the political arena were complementary. Whether the focus was on actions in political arenas, or 'private' arenas such as markets or consumption, was mostly a strategic question. In the case of the launch of the CCC, both public and private regulation were envisioned, but the specific conjuncture of the mid 1990s made campaign makers choose to target companies directly. Activist groups had long sought to implement a social clause at the international level of the global agreement on trade and taxes (GATT), but ultimately failed to do so. In this context where public regulation was no longer an option, anti-sweatshop advocates focused their attention on the market arena where they fought for the adoption of codes of conduct. This kind of 'private politics,' using consumer force to promote sustainability, had also become a preferred public policy instrument for national governments, and at the EU level. It was a soft form of regulation that corresponded to the neoliberal policies of deregulation that prevailed in Europe.

The campaigns were, in a way, also part of these policies, especially in France where the CCC was publicly financed. However, they came to it from a different perspective: for them, it was the only way to address the working conditions in the global clothing industry at all. Given that the path of national or transnational regulation was closed, only consumer power and public shaming and blaming could bring firms to respect labor standards in supply chains.

To bring companies to adopt codes of conduct and accept their independent monitoring, the campaigns used a tactical action repertoire adapted to the marketplace where the demands were raised. Postcard petitions, but even more so evaluations and rankings, were tactical instruments that took advantage of the market situation to increase the pressure on targeted companies. Market competition was astutely used to pit the retailers against each other. At the same time as shaming non-cooperative companies, the tactics and framing strategies rewarded those firms that yielded to the movement's demands. The campaigns raised consumer awareness for ethical issues in fashion production and produced tools that could orient concerned consumers' purchases. Thus, the campaigns tried to influence both sides of market exchanges in parallel: the supply side by publicly shaming companies (but also rewarding those complying with demands) and the demand side by raising consumer awareness and giving them instruments to guide their consumption behavior. As the analysis has shown again and again, the interplay between these two approaches was not without friction. Campaigners constantly struggled to find the right mix between shaming companies and promoting alternatives.

This was a strategic dilemma that became especially prominent as retailers developed strategies to counter movement demands. An interactionist perspective focusing on strategies proved useful to understand the changing movement outcomes over time. The French and Swiss cases provide two contrasting dynamics in this regard—dynamics that seem to be typical for how movement-corporate interactions can evolve. In France, rewarding the companies that responded positively was hardly an option, as retailers were unwilling to yield to core demands, and counter-attacked. Equally problematic for campaign-makers were the Swiss retailers' market-based counter-strategies around the building up of niche products that took up movement demands. While the campaigners rewarded this because it partially responded to campaign demands, it was also a form of side-stepping on the part of companies and risked undermining the ultimate campaign goals. In sum, this study points out the significance of the corporate targets' tactics and counter-strategies for any understanding of movement dynamics and outcomes on markets. Beyond the yes/no, one/zero question of movement outcomes—were the movements a success or a failure?—one needs to look at the grey areas. With their counter-strategies, companies managed to shape the impact of movements decisively. To some extent, they complied with demands, but most of the time, compliance was at best partial, and concerned the less costly part of demands: the adoption of codes of conduct and monitoring by audit firms, not by the independent 'civil society' organizations that the campaigners had in mind.

Furthermore, specifically designated ethical products drew attention away from the far bigger section of the clothing industry in which nothing changed in the production process.

The targeted firms thus developed a diversity of responses. While in France the concerted response by retailers, together with the weak appeal of 'ethical' markets in other sectors, prevented the rise of a new category of 'ethical fashion' over the period of this inquiry, the development of fair trade and organic labels in Switzerland meant that consumers increasingly had the option to buy clothes that respected social and/or environmental standards. Once the campaigns had set the ball rolling with their demands, a new category of 'ethical fashion' could emerge and become the basis of a niche market. The analysis of contention in markets can thus give an insight into the processes of both market change and also market creation, as new moral or political issues can become the basis for the establishment of categories of worth within markets (Beckert and Aspers 2011). Studying social movements, in other words, yields great promise for scholars interested in the dynamics of market innovation, especially when looked at from an interactionist perspective, where the development of new categories is the result of the interplay between movements and firms.

Acknowledging and further analyzing the broad range of repertoires used by firms to respond to movement demands is also crucial from a perspective of social movement studies and of political sociology more generally. This study has mainly focused on the movement side, but the analysis reveals how important it is to look closely into the strategies and tactics used by companies when they face challenges from social movement campaigns. Their repertoire is not limited to economic activities: to name but a few tactics and strategies, corporations also engage in efforts of counter-framing and develop media strategies, strategically seek out partners and allies to sidestep demands, carefully analyze their opponents (and sometimes spy on them) in order to develop ways to undermine their legitimacy and/or demands, and so forth. Risk analysis, lobbying and corporate social responsibility departments specialize in such political activities, and a whole range of intermediary actors such as consulting firms or private security agencies participate in it. Especially in a world where market economies are increasingly liberalized and largely shape national societies, firms play a core political role that calls for greater scholarly attention if we are to understand current social and political processes. This study constitutes a first step in this direction.

References

Afonso, A. (2013) *Social Concertation in Times of Austerity: European Integration and the Politics of Labour Market Governance in Austria and Switzerland.* (Amsterdam: Amsterdam University Press).

Agir Ici (1994) *La mouche du coche. Groupes de pression et changement social: l'expérience d'Agir ici* (Paris: Fondation pour le progrès de l'homme).

Agrikoliansky, E. (2005) Du Tiers-mondisme à l'altermondialisme: genèse(s) d'une nouvelle cause, in E. Agrikoliansky, O. Fillieule and N. Mayer (eds), *L'altermondialisme en France. La longue histoire d'une nouvelle cause*, pp. 43–74 (Paris: Flammarion).

Agrikoliansky, E., Fillieule, O., and Mayer, N. (2005a) Aux origines de l'altermondialisme français, in E. Agrikoliansky, O. Fillieule and N. Mayer (eds), *L'altermondialisme en France. La longue histoire d'une nouvelle cause* (Paris: Flammarion).

Agrikoliansky, E., Fillieule, O., and Mayer, N. (2005b) *L'altermondialisme en France. La longue histoire d'une nouvelle cause* (Paris: Flammarion).

Aldridge, A. (1994) The Construction of Rational Consumption in *Which?* Magazine: The More Blobs the Better?, *Sociology*, 28, 4, 899–912.

Allan Michaud, D. (1990) *L'avenir de la société alternative. Les idées 1968–1990 ...* (Paris: L'Harmattan).

Almond, G.A., and Verba, S. (1963) *The Civic Culture: Political Attitudes and Democracy in Five Nations* (Princeton, NJ: Princeton University Press).

Amenta, E. (2006) *When Movements Matter: The Townsend Plan and the Rise of Social Security* (Princeton: Princeton University Press).

Amenta, E., and Young, M.P. (1999) Making an Impact: Conceptual and Methodological Implications of the Collective Goods Criterion, in M. Giugni, D. McAdam and C. Tilly (eds), *How Social Movements Matter*, pp. 22–41 (Minneapolis: University of Minnesota Press).

Amenta, E., and Caren, N. (2004) The Legislative, Organizational, and Beneficiary Consequences of State-Oriented Challengers, in D.A. Snow, S.A. Soule and H. Kriesi (eds), *The Blackwell Companion to Social Movements*, pp. 461–488 (Malden, MA: Blackwell Publishing).

Amenta, E., Caren, N., Fetner, T. and Young, M.P. (2002) Challengers and States: Toward a Political Sociology of Social Movements, *Research in Political Sociology*, 10, 47–83.

Ancelovici, M. (2002) Organizing against Globalization: The Case of ATTAC in France, *Politics & Society*, 30, 3, 427–463.

Ancelovici, M. (2008) *Between Adaptation and Resistance: Labor Responses to Globalization in France*, PhD dissertation, Department of Political Science, Massachussetts Institute of Technlogy.

Armstrong, E.A., and Bernstein, M. (2008) Culture, Power, and Institutions: A Multi-Institutional Politics Approach to Social Movements, *Sociological Theory*, 26, 1, 74–99.

Aspers, P. (2010) *Orderly Fashion. A Sociology of Markets* (Princeton, NJ: Princeton University Press).

Bair, J. and Palpacuer, F. (2012) From Varieties of Capitalism to Varieties of Activism. The Antisweatshop Movement in Comparative Perspective. *Social Problems*, 59, 4, 522–543.

Balsiger, P. (2010) Making Political Consumers: The Tactical Action Repertoire of a Campaign for Clean Clothes, *Social Movement Studies*, 9, 3, 311–329.

Balsiger, P. (2012) Competing Tactics: How the Interplay of Tactical Approaches Shapes Movement Outcomes on the Market for Ethical Fashion, *MPIfG Discussion Paper* 12/9.

Balsiger, P. (2014) Between Shaming Corporations and Promoting Alternatives: The Politics of an Ethical Shopping Map, *Journal of Consumer Culture,* 14, 2, 218–235.

Balsiger, P., and Lambelet, A. (2014) Participant Observation, in D. Della Porta (ed.) *Methodological Practices in Social Movement Research* (Oxford: Oxford University Press).

Barraud de Lagerie, P. (2010) *Les patrons de la vertu. Entrepreneurs de morale et instruments de mesure dans la construction de la responsabilité sociale des entreprises*, PhD dissertation, CSO, Science Po, Paris.

Bartley, T. (2003) Certifying Forests and Factories: States, Social Movements, and the Rise of Private Regulation in the Apparel and Forest Products Fields, *Politics & Society*, 31, 3, 433–464.

Bartley, T. (2005) Corporate Accountability and the Privatization for Labor Standards: Struggles over Codes of Conduct in the Apparel Industry, *Research in Political Sociology*, 14, 211–244.

Bartley, T. (2007a) How Foundations Shape Social Movements: The Construction of an Organizational Field and the Rise of Forest Certification, *Social Problems*, 54, 3, 229–255.

Bartley, T. (2007b) Institutional Emergence in an Era of Globalization: The Rise of Transnational Private Regulation of Labor and Environmental Conditions, *American Journal of Sociology*, 113, 2, 297–351.

Bartley, T., and Child, C. (2011). Movements, Markets and Fields: The Effects of Anti Sweatshop Campaigns on US Firms, 1993–2000. *Social Forces*, 90, 2, 425–451.

Beckert, J., and Aspers, P. (eds) (2011) *The Worth of Goods. Valuation and Pricing in the Economy* (Oxford, New York: Oxford University Press).

Berger, S. (1985) Religious Transformation and the Future of Politics, *European Sociological Review*, 1, 1, 23–45.

Bernstein, M. (1997) Celebration and Suppression: The Strategic Uses of Identity by the Lesbian and Gay Movement, *American Journal of Sociology*, 103, 3, 531–565.

Béroud, S., and Mouriaux, R. (1998) La CFDT, les aventures du modernisme, *Regards sur l'actualité*, sept.–oct., 25–36.

Boltanski, L. (1993) *La souffrance à distance* (Paris: Editions Métailié).

Boltanski, L., and Chiapello, E. (1999) *Le nouvel esprit du capitalisme* (Paris: Gallimard).

Bothwell, R.O. (2001) Philanthropic Funding of Social Change and the Diminution of Progressive Policymaking, in M.D. Montilla and E. Reid (eds), *Exploring Organizations and Advocacy: Strategies and Finances*, pp. 67–82 (Washington DC: The Urban Institute).

Bourdieu, P. (1985) Social Space and the Genesis of Groups, *Theory and Society*, 14, 6, 723 744.

Bourdieu, P. (1989) Social Space and Symbolic Power, *Sociological Theory*, 7, 1, 14–25.

Bourdieu, P. (1991) Political Representation: Elements for a Theory of the Political Field, in P. Bourdieu, *Language and Symbolic Power*, pp. 171–202 (Cambridge: Polity Press).

Braunschweig, P. (1978) Wo stehen wir in der Lebensstildebatte?, *Schritte in Offene*, 3/1978.

Brooks, E.C. (2009) *Unraveling the Garment Industry. Transnational Organizing and Women's Work* (Minneapolis: University of Minnesota Press).

Bruneau, I. (2004) La Confédération paysanne et le "mouvement altermondialiste": L'international comme enjeu syndical, *Politix*, 17, 68, 111–134.

Brunner, U. (1999) *Bananenfrauen* (Frauenfeld: Huber).

Burstein, P., Einwohner, R.L., and Hollander, J.A. (1995). The Success of Political Movements: A Bargaining Perspective, in J.C. Jenkins and B. Klandermans (eds), *The Politcs of Social Protest. Comparative Perspectives on States and Social Movements,* pp. 275–295. Minneapolis: University of Minnesota Press.

Chasin, A. (2000) *Selling Out. The Gay and Lesbian Movement Goes to Market* (Houndmills, Basingstoke: Palgrave McMillan).

Chatriot, A., Chessel, M.-E., and M. Hilton (eds) (2006) *The Consumer Expert: Associations and Professionals in Consumer Society* (Farnham, Burlington VT: Ashgate).

Chessel, M.-E. (2004) Consommation et réforme sociale à la Belle Epoque. La Conférence internationale des Ligues sociales d'acheteurs en 1908, in M.-E. Chessel, F. Cochoy, Marché et politique. Autour de la consommation engagée, *Sciences de la société*, 62, 45–68.

Clarke, N., Barnett, C., Cloke, P., and Malpass, A. (2007a) Globalising the Consumer: Doing Politics in an Ethical Register, *Political Geography*, 26, 3, 213–249.

Clarke, N., Barnett, C., Cloke, P., and Malpass, A. (2007b) The Political Rationalities of Fair Trade Consumption in the United Kingdom, *Politics & Society*, 35, 4, 583–607.

Cohen, L. (2003) *A Consumers' Republic: The Politics of Mass Consumption in Postwar America* (New York: Knopf).

Contamin, J.-G. (2001) *Contribution à une sociologie des usages pluriels des formes de mobilisations: l'exemple de la pétition en France*, PhD dissertation, Université Paris I Sorbonne.

Crossley, N. (2003) From Reproduction to Transformation: Social Movement Fields and the Radical Habitus, *Theory, Culture & Society*, 20, 6, 43–68.

Curtis, R.L., and Zurcher, L.A. (1973) Stable Resources of Protest Movements: The Multi-Organizational Field, *Social Forces*, 52, 53–61.

Davis, G.F., and Thompson, T.A. (1994) A Social Movement Perspective on Corporate Control, *Administrative Science Quarterly*, 39, 1, 141–173.

Davis, G.F., McAdam, D., Scott, W.R., and Zald, M.N. (2005) *Social Movements and Organization Theory* (Cambridge: Cambridge University Press).

Defaud, N. (2009) *La CFDT (1968–1995). De l'autogestion au syndicalisme de proposition* (Paris: Presses de Sciences Po).

Delalieux, G. (2008) Influence des ONG dans la construction des pratiques de RSE et développement durable. Une étude de cas, *Mondes en Développement*, 36, 4, 45–62.

Della Porta, D. (2007) *The Global Justice Movement: Cross-national and Transnational Perspectives* (Boulder, CO: Paradigm Publishers).

Della Porta, D. (2008) Comparative Analysis: Case-oriented versus Variable-oriented Research, in D. Della Porta and M. Keating (eds), *Approaches and Methodologies in the Social Sciences. A Pluralist Perspective*, pp. 198–222 (Cambridge: Cambridge University Press).

Della Porta, D., and Diani, M. (2004) *Social Movements. An Introduction* (Oxford: Blackwell).

Della Porta, D., and Rucht, D. (1995) Left-Libertarian Movements in Context: A Comparison of Italy and West Germany, 1965–1990, in B. Klandermans and C. Jenkins (eds), *The Politics of Social Protest: Comparative Perspectives on States and Social Movements*, pp. 229–272 (Minneapolis: University of Minnesota Press).

Della Porta, D., and Rucht, D. (2002) The Dynamics of Environmental Campaigns, *Mobilization*, 8, 1, 1–14.

den Hond, F., and de Bakker, F.G.A. (2007) Ideologically Motivated Activism: How Activist Groups Influence Corporate Social Change Activities, *Academy of Management Review*, 32, 3, 901–924.

Diaz Pedregal, V. (2007) *Le commerce équitable dans la France contemporaine. Idéologies et pratiques* (Paris: L'Harmattan).

DiMaggio, P.J., and Powell, W.W. (1983) The Iron Cage Revisited: Institutional Isomorphism and Collective Rationality in Organizational Fields, *American Sociological Review*, 48, 147–160.

Donati, P.R. (1989) Dalla politica al consumo. La questione ecologica e i movimenti degli anni settanta, *Rassegna Italiana di Sociologia*, 30, 321–345.

Dubuisson-Quellier, S. (2013a) *Ethical Consumption* (Winnipeg: Fernwood Publishing).

Dubuisson-Quellier, S. (2013b). A Market Mediation Strategy: How Social Movements Seek to Change Firms' Practices by Promoting New Principles of Product Valuation. *Organization Studies*. 34, 5–6, 683–703.

Duyvendak, J.W. (1995) *The Power of Politics, New Social Movements in an Old Polity: France 1965–1989*, Boulder, CO: Westview Press).

Duyvendak, J.-W., and Jasper, J.M. (forthcoming) *Players and Arenas: The Interactive Dynamics of Protest* (Amsterdam: University of Amsterdam Press).

Eliasoph, N., and Lichterman, P. (2003) Culture in Interaction, *American Journal of Sociology*, 108, 4, 735–794.

Epstein, S. (1996) *Impure Science* (Berkeley, Los Angeles, London: University of California Press).

Featherstone, L. (2002) *Students against Sweatshops* (London: Verso).

Fillieule, O. (1997) *Stratégies de la rue* (Paris: Presses de Sciences Po).

Fillieule, O. (2006) Requiem pour un concept. Vie et mort de la notion de "structure des opportunités politiques," in G. Dorronsoro (ed.), *La Turquie conteste* (Paris: Presses du CNRS).

Fillieule, O. (2008) Travail militant, action collective et rapports de genre, in O. Fillieule and P. Roux (eds), *Le sexe du militantisme* (Paris: Presses de Sciences Po).

Fillieule, O. (2009) De l'objet de la définition à la définition de l'objet. De quoi traite finalement la sociologie des mouvements sociaux?, *Politique et société*, 28, 1, 15–36.

Fillieule, O., and Tartakowsky, D. (2008) *La manifestation* (Paris: Presses de Sciences Po).

Fillieule, O., Agrikoliansky, E., and Sommier, I. (eds) (2010) *Penser les mouvements sociaux* (Paris: La Découverte).

Fillieule, O. and Sommier, I. (2013) The Emergence and Development of the "No Global" Movement in France: A Genealogical Approach, in C. Flesher Fominaya and L. Cox. (eds), *Understanding European Movements: New Social Movements, Global Justice Struggles, Anti Austerity Protest*, pp. 47–60 (London and New York: Routledge).

Fisher, D.R. (2007) Outsourcing Activism in America, *APSA Annual Meeting*, Chicago, 2007.

Fligstein, N. (1996) Markets as Politics: A Political-Cultural Approach to Market Institutions, *American Sociological Review*, 61, 656–673.

Fligstein, N. (2001) *The Architecture of Markets: An Economic Sociology of Twenty First Century Capitalist Societies* (Princeton Oxford: Princeton University Press).

Fligstein, N., and McAdam, D. (2012) *A Theory of Fields* (Oxford, New York: Oxford University Press).

Forno, F. (2006) La protesta nei consumi: nuove forme (e luoghi) di partecipazione, in S. Tosi (ed.), *Consumi e partecipazione politica. Tra azione individuale e mobilitazione colletiva* (Milano: FrancoAngeli).

Forno, F., and Ceccarini, L. (2006) From the Street to the Shops: The Rise of New Forms of Political Actions in Italy, *South European Society & Politics*, 11, 2, 197–222.

Forno, F. and Graziano, P. (2014) Sustainable Community Movement Organisations, *Journal of Consumer Culture*, 14, 2, 139–157.

François, B., and Neveu, E. (1999) Pour une sociologie politique des espaces publics contemporains, in B. François and E. Neveu (eds) *Espaces publics mosaïques*, pp. 13–58 (Rennes: Presses universitaires de Rennes).

Frank, T. (1997) *The Conquest of Cool. Business Culture, Counterculture, and the Rise of Hip Consumerism* (Chicago, IL: University of Chicago Press).

Fransen, L. (2012) *Corporate Social Responsibility and Global Labor Standards* (New York: Routledge).

Freire, P. (2000 [1968]) *Pedagogy of the Oppressed* (New York: Continuum).

Friedman, M. (1997) *Consumer Boycotts: Effecting Change through the Marketplace and Media* (New York: Routledge).

Friedman, E. (2009) External Pressure and Local Mobilization: Transnational Activism and the Emergence of the Chinese Labor Movement, *Mobilization* 14, 2, 199–218.

Gamson, W.A. and Meyer, D.S. (1996) Framing Political Opportunity, in D. McAdam, J.D. McCarthy, and M. Zald (eds) *Comparative Perspectives on Social Movements: Political Opportunities, Mobilizing Structures, and Cultural Framing* (Cambridge: Cambridge University Press).

Gaxie, D. (1977) Économie des partis et rétributions du militantisme, *Revue française de science politique*, 47, 1, 123–154.

George, A., and Bennet, A. (2005) *Case Studies and Theory Development in the Social Sciences* (Cambridge, MA: MIT Press).

Gereffi, G., and Korzeniewicz, M. (eds) (1994) *Commodity Chains and Global Capitalism* (Westport, CT: Praeger).

Gerhards, J., and Rucht, D. (1992) Mesomobilization: Organizing and Framing in Two Protest Campaigns in West Germany, *American Journal of Sociology*, 98, 3, 555–596.

Ghaziani, A. (2008) *The Dividends of Dissent: How Conflict and Culture Work in Lesbian and Gay Marches on Washington* (Chicago, IL: University of Chicago Press).

Giamporcaro-Saunière, S. (2004) L'investissement socialement responsable en France. Un outil au service d'une action politique par la consommation?, *Sciences de la société*, 62, 169–188.

Giugni, M.G. (2004) *Social Protest and Policy Change: Ecology, Antinuclear, and Peace Movements in Comparative Perspective* (Lanham: Rowman & Littlefield).

Giugni, M.G., and Eggert, N. (2006) The Global Justice Movement in Switzerland: The Heritage of the New Social Movements, in D. Della Porta (ed.) *The Global Justice Movement: Cross-National and Transnational Perspectives*, pp. 184–209 (Boulder, CO: Paradigm).

Giugni, M.G., and Passy, F. (1998) Contentious Politics in Complex Societies: New Social Movements between Conflict and Cooperation, in M. Giugni, D. McAdam and C. Tilly (eds), *From Contention to Democracy* (Lanham, Boulder, New York, Oxford: Rowman & Littlefield).

Giugni, M.G., and Passy, F. (1999) *Zwischen Konflikt und Kooperation: die Integration der sozialen Bewegungen in der Schweiz* (Chur, Zürich: Rüegger).

Giugni, M.G., McAdam, D., and Tilly, C. (eds) (1999) *How Social Movements Matter* (Minneapolis: University of Minnesota Press).

Glickman, L.B. (2005) "Make Lisle the Style": The Politics of Fashion in the Japanese Silk Boycott, 1937–1940, *Journal of Social History* 38, 3, 573–608.

Glickman, L.B. (2009). *Buying Power. A History of Consumer Activism in America*. (Chicago, IL: Chicago University Press).

Goodwin, J., and Jasper, J.M. (1999) Caught in a Winding, Snarling Vine: The Structural Bias of Political Process Theory, *Sociological Forum*, 14, 1, 27–54.

Goodwin, J. and Jasper, J.M. (eds) (2011) *Contention in Context: Political Opportunities and the Emergence of Protest* (Stanford, CA: Stanford University Press).

Goul Andersen, J., and Tobiasen, M. (2004) Who are these Political Consumers Anyway? Survey Evidence from Denmark, in M. Micheletti, A. Follesdal and D. Stolle (eds), *Politics, Products, and Markets. Exploring Political Consumerism Past and Present*, pp. 203–222 (New Brunswick, London: Transaction Publishers).

Graziano, P., and Forno, F. (2012) Political Consumerism and New Forms of Political Participation: The Gruppi di Acquisto Solidale in Italy, *Annals AAPSS*, 644: 121–133.

Griggs, S., and Howarth, D. (2002) An Alliance of Interest and Identity? Explaining the Campaign against Manchester Airport's Second Runway, *Mobilization*, 7, 1,43–58.

Grignon, C. (1977) Sur les relations entre les transformations du champ religieux et les transformations de l'espace politique, *Actes de la recherche en sciences sociales*, 16, 3–34.

Guilhot, N. (2005) *The Democracy Makers: Human Rights and the Politics of Global Order* (New York: Columbia University Press).

Gusfield, J.R. (1981) *The Culture of Public Problems: Drinking-Driving and the Symbolic Order* (Chicago, IL: University of Chicago Press).

Gupta, D. (2009) The Power of Incremental Outcomes: How Small Victories and Defeats Affect Social Movement Organizations, *Mobilization*, 14, 4, 417–432.

Hall, P.A., and Soskice, D. (2001) *Varieties of Capitalism: The Institutional Foundations of Comparative Advantage* (Oxford, New York: Oxford University Press).

Hannerz, U. (2003) Being There ... and There ... and There!: Reflections on Multi-Site Ethnography, *Ethnography*, 4, 2, 201–216.

Harrison, R., Newholm, T., and Shaw, D. (2005) *The Ethical Consumer* (London, Thousand Oaks: Sage).

Hatton, J.-M. (2006) Note sur la structuration progressive des OSI dans leur relation avec les pouvoirs publics, http://www.coordinationsud.org/spip.php?article12009

Hiatt, S.R., Sine, W.D., and Tolbert, P.S. (2009) From Pabst to Pepsi: The Deinstitutionalization of Social Practices and the Creation of Entrepreneurial Opportunities, *Administrative Science Quarterly*, 54, 635–667.

Hilgartner, S., and Bosk, C L. (1988) The Rise and Fall of Social Problems: A Public Arenas Model, *American Journal of Sociology*, 94, 1, 53–78.

Holenstein, A.-M. (1976) Ein anderer Lebensstil?, *Schritte in Offene*, 3/1976.

Holenstein, A.-M., Renschler, R., and Strahm, R. (2009) *Entwicklung heisst Befreiung. Erinnerungen and die Pionierzeit der Erklärung von Bern* (Zürich: Chronos).

Holenstein, R. (1998) *Was kümmert uns die Dritte Welt. Zur Geschichte der internationalen Solidarität in der Schweiz* (Zürich: Cronos).

Holt, D. (2002) Why Do Brands Cause Trouble? A Dialectical Theory of Consumer Culture and Branding, *Journal of Consumer Research* 29, 1, 70–90.

Jacquiau, C. (2000) *Les coulisses de la grande distribution* (Paris: Albin Michel).

Jasper, J.M. (1997) *The Art of Moral Protest: Culture, Biography, and Creativity in Social Movements* (Chicago, IL: University of Chicago Press).

Jasper, J.M. (2004) A Strategic Approach to Collective Action: Looking for Agency in Social Movement Choices, *Mobilization*, 9, 1, 1–16.

Jasper, J.M. (2006) *Getting Your Way: Strategic Dilemmas in the Real World* (Chicago, IL: Chicago University Press).

Jasper, J.M. (2011) Introduction: From Political Opportunity Structures to Strategic Interaction, in J. Goodwin and J.M. Jasper (eds), *Contention in Context: Political Opportunities and the Emergence of Protest*, pp. 1–33 (Stanford, CA: Stanford University Press).

Jasper, J.M., and Poulsen, J. (1993) Fighting Back: Vulnerabilities, Blunders, and Countermobilization by the Targets in Three Animal Rights Campaigns, *Sociological Forum*, 8, 4, 639–657.

Johnston, H. (2009) Protest Cultures: Performance, Artifacts, and Ideations, in H. Johnston (ed.), *Culture, Social Movements, and Protest* pp. 3–29 (Aldershot, England, Burlington, VT: Ashgate).

Johnston, H., and Mueller, C. (2001) Unobtrusive Practices of Contention in Leninist Regimes, *Sociological Perspectives*, 44, 3, 351–375.

Jordan, G., and Maloney, W.A. (2007) *Democracy and Interest Groups: Enhancing Participation?* (Basingstoke: Palgrave Macmillan).

Kalt, M. (2010) *Tiersmondismus in der Schweiz der 1960er und 1970er Jahre. Von der Barmherzigkeit zur Solidarität* (Bern: Peter Lang).

Kellogg, K.C. (2011) *Challenging Operations: Medical Reform and Resistance in Surgery* (Chicago, IL: University of Chicago Press).

King, B.G. (2008a) A Political Mediation Model of Corporate Response to Social Movement Activism, *Administrative Science Quarterly*, 53, 395–421.

King, B.G. (2008b) A Social Movement Perspective of Stakeholder Collective Action and Influence, *Business & Society*, 47, 1, 21–49.

King, B.G., and Pearce, N.A. (2010) The Contentiousness of Markets: Politics, Social Movements, and Institutional Change in Markets, *Annual Review of Sociology*, 36, 249–267.

King, B.G., and Soule, S.A. (2007) Social Movements as Extra-institutional Entrepreneurs: The Effect of Protest on Stock Price Returns, *Administrative Science Quarterly*, 52, 413–442.

Kitschelt, H. (1986) Political Opportunity Structures and Political Protest: Anti- Nuclear Movements in Four Democracies, *British Journal of Political Science*, 16, 1, 57–85.

Klandermans, B. (1984) Mobilization and Participation: Social Psychological Expansions of Resource Mobilization Theory, *American Sociological Review*, 49, 583–600.

Klandermans, B. (1997) *The Social Psychology of Protest* (Oxford: Blackwell).

Klawiter, M. (2008) *The Biopolitics of Breast Cancer: Changing Cultures of Disease and Activism* (Minneapolis, London: University of Minnesota Press).

Klein, N. (2002) *No Logo* (New York: Picador).

Kriesi, H., Koopmans, R., Duyvendak, J.W., and Giugni, M. (1995) *New Social Movements in Western Europe: A Comparative Analysis* (Minneapolis: University of Minnesota Press).

Kuhn, K.J. (2005a) Das Produkt als Aufhänger für Information und Schulungsarbeit: Die entwicklungspolitische Konsumentenaktion Jute statt Plastic 1976–1979, *Traverse*, 3, 27–39.

Kuhn, K.J. (2005b) *Fairer Handel und Kalter Krieg. Selbstwahrnehmung und Positionierung der Fair Trade Bewegung in der Schweiz 1973–1990* (Bern: Edition Soziothek).

Lahusen, C. (1996) *The Rhetoric of Moral Protest: Public Campaigns, Celebrity Endorsement, and Political Mobilization* (Berlin, New York: W. de Gruyter).

Le Velly, R. (2006) Le commerce équitable : des échanges marchands contre et dans le marché, *Revue française de sociologie*, 47, 2, 319–340.

Le Velly, R. (2007) Is Large-scale Fair Trade Possible?, in E. Zaccai (ed.) *Sustainable Consumption, Ecology and Fair Trade* (London: Routledge).

Lichterman, P. (1996) *The Search for Political Community: American Activists Reinventing Commitment* (Cambridge, New York: Cambridge University Press).

Lounsbury, M. (2005) Institutional Variation in the Evolution of Social Movements: Competing Logics and the Spread of Recycling Advocacy Groups, in G.F. Davis, D. McAdam, W.R. Scott and M.N. Zald (eds) *Social Movements and Organizational Theory* (Cambridge: Cambridge University Press).

Lounsbury, M., and Ventresca, M.J. (2002) Social Structure and Organizations Revisited, *Research in the Sociology of Organizations*, 19, 3–36.

Lounsbury, M., Ventresca, M., and Hirsch, P.M. (2003) Social Movements, Field Frames and Industry Emergence: A Cultural-Political Perspective on US Recycling, *Socio-Economic Review*, 1, 1, 71–104.

Luders, J. (2006) The Economics of Movement Success: Business Responses to Civil Rights Mobilization, *American Journal of Sociology*, 111, 4, 963–998.

Lugos, T. (2003) *Grande distribution: vérités et mensonges* (Latresne: Le Bord de l'eau).

Mach, A. (2001) Swiss Business and Human Rights: Confrontations and Partnerships with NGOs, *Documents de travail de l'IIEDH*, No.2 (Fribourg: Université de Fribourg).

Mach, A. David, Th., Schnyder, G., and Lupold, M. (2007) Transformations of Self- Regulation and New Public Regulations in the Fields of Swiss Corporate Governance (1985–2002), *World Political Science Review*, 3, 2.

Maney, G., Kutz-Flamenbaum, R.V., and Rohlinger, D.A. (eds) (2011) *Strategies for Social Change* (Minneapolis: University of Minnesota Press).

Maquila Solidarity Network (2006) Is Fair Trade a Good Fit for the Garment Industry? *Online working paper*.

Martin, A.W. (2010) Movement Publications as Data: An Assessment of an Underutilized Resource, *Research in Social Movements, Conflict and Change*, 30, 271–299.

Mathieu, L. (2008) *L'espace des mouvements sociaux. Eléments pour une sociologie de l'action collective protestataire*, Mémoire pour l'habilitation à diriger des recherches, Lyon, Ecole normale supérieure.

Mathieu, L. (2012) *L'espace des mouvements sociaux* (Paris: Editions du Croquant).

McAdam, D. (1995) "Initiator" and "Spin-off" Movements: Diffusion Processes in Protest Cycles in M. Traugott (ed.), *Repertoires and Cycles of Collective Action* (Durham, NC, London: Duke University Press).

McAdam, D., McCarthy, J.D., and Zald, M.N. (1996) *Comparative Perspectives on Social Movements* (Cambridge: Cambridge University Press).

McCarthy, D. (2004) Environmental Justice Grantmaking: Elites and Activists Collaborate to Transform Philanthropy, *Sociological Inquiry*, 74, 2, 250–270.

McCarthy, J.D., and Zald, M.N. (1977) Resource Mobilization and Social Movements: A Partial Theory, *American Journal of Sociology*, 82, 1212–1241.

Melucci, A. (1985) The Symbolic Challenge of Contemporary Movements, *Social Research*, 52, 4, 789–916.

Melucci, A. (1989) *Nomads of the Present: Social Movements and Individual Needs in Contemporary Society* (Philadelphia, PA: Temple University Press).

Melucci, A. (1996) *Challenging Codes: Collective Action in the Information Age* (Cambridge: Cambridge University Press).

Meyer, D.S. (2006) Claiming Credit: Stories of Movement Influence as Outcomes, *Mobilization*, 11, 3, 201–218.

Meyer, D.S., and Whittier, N. (1994) Social Movement Spillover, *Social Problems*, 41, 2, 277–298.

Micheletti, M. (2003) *Political Virtue and Shopping: Individuals, Consumerism, and Collective Action* (Houndmills, Basingstoke, New York: Palgrave Macmillan).

Micheletti, M., Follesdal, A., and Stolle, D. (2004) *Politics, Products and Markets, Exploring Political Consumerism Past and Present* (New Brunswick: Transaction Publishers).

Mueller, N., and Tinguely, D. (2007) *Enjeux de la Grande Distribution Helvétique: Analyse socio-economique et strategique de l'évolution des acteurs de la grande distribution alimentaire en Suisse*, Mémoire de licence, Université de Genève.

Offerlé, M. (1988) Le nombre de voix, *Actes de la recherche en sciences sociales*, 71, 1, 5–21.

Offerlé, M. (1998) *Sociologie des groupes d'intérêt* (Paris: Montchrestien).

Oliver, C. (1991) Strategic Responses to Institutional Processes, *The Academy of Management Review*, 16, 1, 145–179.

Ollitrault, S. (2008) *Militer pour la planète: sociologie des écologistes* (Rennes: Presses universitaires de Rennes).

Palazzo, G., and Scherer, A.G. (2006) Corporate Legitimacy as Deliberation: A Communicative Framework, *Journal of Business Ethics*, 66, 1, 71–88.

Passy, F. (1998) *L'action altruiste* (Genève, Paris: Librairie Droz).

Passy, F. (2001) Political Altruism and the Solidarity Movement, in F. Passy and M. Giugni (eds), *Political Altruism? Solidarity Movements in International Perspective* (Lanham, Boulder, New York, Oxford: Rowman & Littlefield).

Péchu, C. (2006) *Droit au logement, genèse et sociologie d'une mobilisation* (Paris: Dalloz).

Pelletier, D. (1996) 1985–1987: une crise d'identité du tiers-mondisme catholique?, *Le mouvement social*, 177, 89–109.

Pierson, P. (2000) Increasing Returns, Path Dependence, and the Study of Politics, *American Political Science Review*, 94 (2): 251–267.

Polanyi, K. (1985 [1944]) *The Great Transformation* (Boston, MA: Beacon).

Polletta, F. (1999) Free Spaces in Collective Action, *Theory and Society*, 28, 1, 1–38.

Quack, S. (2010) Law, Expertise and Legitimacy in Transnational Economic Governance, *Socio-Economic Review*, 8, 1, 3–16.

Raeburn, N.C. (2004) *Changing Corporate America from Inside Out. Lesbian and Gay Workplace Rights* (Minneapolis, London: University of Minnesota Press).

Rao, H. (2009) *Market Rebels. How Activists Make or Break Radical Innovations* (Princeton, Oxford: Princeton University Press).

Rao, H., Morrill, C., and Zald, M.N. (2000) Power Plays: How Social Movements and Collective Action Create New Organizational Forms, *Research in Organizational Behavior*, 22, 239–282.

Raynolds, L.T., Murray, D.L., and Wilkinson, J. (2007) *Fair Trade. The Challenges of Transforming Globalization* (London: Routledge).

Rist, G. (2007) *Le développement, histoire d'une croyance occidentale* (Paris: Presses de Sciences Po).

Rochon, T.R. (1998) *Culture Moves. Ideas, Activism, and Changing Values* (Princeton, NJ: Princeton University Press).

Rojas, F. (2007*) From Black Power to Black Studies. How a Radical Social Movement Became an Academic Discipline* (Baltimore, MD: The Johns Hopkins University Press).

Rucht, D. (2000) Distant Issue Movements in Germany: Empirical Description and Theoretical Reflection, in J.A. Guidry, M.D. Kennedy, M.N. Zald (eds), *Globalizations and Social Movements. Culture, Power, and the Transnational Public Sphere*, pp. 76–105 (Michigan: University of Michigan Press).

Rucht, D., Koopmans, R., and Neidhart, F. (1999) *Acts of Dissent: New Developments in the Study of Protest* (Lanham, MD: Rowman & Littlefield).

Schmidt, V.A. (2003) French Capitalism Transformed, Yet Still a Third Variety of Capitalism, *Economy and Society*, 32, 4, 526–554.

Schneiberg, M. and Lounsbury, M. (2008) Social Movements and Institutional Analysis, in R. Greenwood, C. Oliver, R. Suddaby and K. Sahlin (eds) *The SAGE Handbook of Organizational Institutionalism*, pp. 650–672 (Los Angeles, London, New Dehli, Singapore: Sage**).**

Schurman, R. (2004) Fighting "Frankenfoods": Industrial Opportunity Structures and the Efficacy of the Anti-Biotech Movement in Western Europe, *Social Problems*, 51, 2, 243–268.

Schurman, R., and Munro, W. (2009) Targeting Capital: A Cultural Economy Approach to Understanding the Efficacy of Two Anti-Genetic Engineering Movements, *American Journal of Sociology*, 115, 1, 155–202.

Scott, W.R. (1995) *Institutions and Organizations* (Thousand Oaks, London, New Dehli: Sage Publications).

Scully, M., and Segal, A. (2002) Passion with an Umbrella, *Research in the Sociology of Organizations*, 19, 125–168.

Siméant, J., and Dauvin, P. (2004) *Le travail humanitaire* (Paris: Presses de Sciences Po).

Sine, W.D., and Lee, B.H. (2009) Tilting at Windmills? The Environmental Movement and the Emergence of the U.S. Wind Energy Sector, *Administrative Science Quarterly*, 54, 123–155.

Skocpol, T. (1999) Advocates without Members: The Recent Transformation of American Civic Life, in T. Skocpol and M.P. Fiorina (eds), *Civic Engagement in American Democracy*, pp. 461–509 (Washington DC, New York: Brookings Institution Press, Russell Sage Foundation).

Skocpol, T. (2003) *Diminished Democracy: From Membership to Management in American Civic Life* (Norman: University of Oklahoma Press).

Skocpol, T., and Fiorina, M.P. (1999) *Civic Engagement in American Democracy* (Washington DC, New York: Brookings Institution Press; Russell Sage Foundation).

Sluiter, L. (2009) *Clean Clothes. A Global Movement to End Sweatshops* (London, New York: Pluto Press).

Snow, D.A. (2004) Framing Processes, Ideology, and Discursive Fields, in D.A. Snow, S.A. Soule and H. Kriesi (eds), *The Blackwell Companion to Social Movements*, pp. 380–412 (Malden, MA, Oxford, Victoria: Blackwell).

Snow, D.E., and Benford, R.D. (1988) Ideology, Frame Resonance, and Participant Mobilization, *International Social Movement Research*, 1, 197–217.

Snow, D.E., Rochford, B., Worden, S., and Benford, R.D. (1986) Frame Alignment Processes, Micromobilization, and Movement Participation, *American Sociological Review*, 51, 4, 464–481.

Sommier, I. (2001) *Les nouveaux mouvements contestataires à l'heure de la mondialisation.* (Paris: Flammarion).

Sommier, I., and Crettiez, X. (eds) (2006) *France Rebelle* (Paris: Michalon).

Sommier, I., Agrikoliansky, E., and Fillieule, O. (2007) *La généalogie des mouvements antiglobalisation en Europe. Une perspective comparée* (Paris: Karthala).

Soule, S.A. (2004) Diffusion Processes Within and Across Movements, in D.A. Snow, S.A. Soule and H. Kriesi (eds), *The Blackwell Companion to Social Movements*, pp. 294–310 (Malden, MA, Oxford, Victoria: Blackwell).

Soule, S.A. (2009) *Contention and Corporate Social Responsibility* (Cambridge: Cambridge University Press).

Soule, S.A. (2012) Social Movements and Markets, Industries, and Firms, *Organization Studies*, 33, 12, 1715–1733.

Soule, S.A., and King, B.D. (2008) Competition and Resource Partitioning in Three Social Movement Industries, *American Journal of Sociology*, 113, 6, 389–394.

Staggenborg, S. (1988) The Consequences of Professionalization and Formalization in the Pro-Choice Movement, *American Sociological Review*, 53, 4, 585–605.

Staggenborg, S., and Lecomte, J. (2009) Social Movement Campaigns: Mobilization and Outcomes in the Montreal Women's Movement Community, *Mobilization*, 14, 2, 163–180.

Steinberg, M.W. (1999) *Fighting Words: Working-Class Formation, Collective Action, and Discourse in Early Nineteenth-century England* (Ithaca, NY: Cornell University Press).

Steinberg, M.W. (2002) Toward a More Dialogic Analysis of Social Movement Culture, in D.S. Meyer, N. Whittier and B. Robnett (eds), *Social Movements. Identity, Culture, and the State* (Oxford: Oxford University Press).

Stolle, D., Hooghe, M., and Micheletti, M. (2005) Politics in the Supermarket: Political Consumerism as a Form of Political Participation, *International Political Science Review*, 26, 5, 245–269.

Strahm, R. (1975) *Überentwicklung—Unterentwicklung. Ein Werkbuch mit Schaubildern und Kommentaren über die wirtschaftlichen Mechanismen der Armut* (Stein/Nürnberg).

Suh, D. (2004) Outcome Framing and Movement Dynamics: Korean White-Collar Unions' Political Mobilization and Interunion Solidarity, 1987–1995, *Mobilization*, 9, 1, 17–37.

Tarrow, S. (1998) *Power in Movement* (Cambridge: Cambridge University Press).

Tarrow, S. (2005) *The New Transnational Activism* (Cambridge: Cambridge University Press).

Taylor, V. (1989) Social Movement Continuity: The Women's Movement in Abeyance, *American Sociological Review*, 54, 5, 761–775.

Taylor, V., and Van Dyke, N. (2004) "Get Up, Stand Up": Tactical Repertoires of Social Movements, in D.A. Snow, S.A. Soule and H. Kriesi (eds), *The Blackwell Companion to Social Movements*, pp. 2672–293 (Malden, MA, Oxford: Blackwell Publishing).

Tilly, C. (2008) *Contentious Performances* (Cambridge: Cambridge University Press).

Tinard, C., and Tinard, Y. (2003) *La grande distribution française: bouc émissaire ou prédateur?* (Paris: Litec).

Trentmann, F. (ed.) (2006) *The Making of the Consumer: Knowledge, Power and Identity in the Modern World* (Oxford, New York: Berg).

Turner, F. (2006) *From Counterculture to Cyberculture: Stewart Brand, the Whole Earth Network, and the Rise of Digital Utopianism* (Chicago, IL: The University of Chicago Press).

Uba, K. (2009) The Contextual Dependence of Movement Outcomes: A Simplified Meta-analysis, *Mobilization*, 14, 4, 433–448.

Van Dyke, N., Soule, S.A., and Taylor, V. (2004) The Targets of Social Movements: Beyond a Focus on the State, *Research in Social Movements, Conflict and Change*, 25, 27–51.

Vasi, I.B. (2009) Social Movements and Industry Development: The Environmental Movement's Impact on the Wind Energy Industry, *Mobilization*, 14, 3, 315–336.

Wahlström, M., and Peterson, A. (2006) Between the State and the Market: Expanding the Concept of "Political Opportunity Structure," *Acta Sociologica*, 49, 4, 363–377.

Walker, E.T. (2012) Social Movements, Organizations, and Fields: A Decade of Theoretical Integration, *Contemporary Sociology*, 41. 5, 576–587.

Walker, E.T., Martin, A.W., and McCarthy, J. (2008) Confronting the State, the Corporation, and the Academy: The Influence of Institutional Targets on Social Movement Repertoires, *American Journal of Sociology*, 114, 1, 35–76.

Walsh, E.J. (1981) Resource Mobilization and Citizen Protest in Communities around Three Mile Island, *Social Problems*, 29, 1, 1–21.

Weber, K., Heinze, K.L., and Michaela, D. (2008) Forage for Thought: Mobilizing Codes in the Movement for Grass-fed Meat and Dairy Products, *Administrative Science Quarterly*, 53, 529–567.

Weber, K., Thomas, L.G., and Rao, H. (2009) From Streets to Suites: How the Anti-biotech Movement Affected German Pharmaceutical Firms, *American Sociological Review*, 74, 1, 106–127.

Whittier, N. (2009) *The Politics of Child Sexual Abuse: Emotion, Social Movements, and the State* (Oxford, New York: Oxford University Press).

Wicki, M. (1984) Die Erklärung von Bern, in H. Kriesi (ed.), *Bewegung in der Schweizer Politik. Fallstudien zu politischen Mobilisierungsprozessen in der Schweiz* (Frankfurt a.M.: Campus Verlag).

Wiedenhoft, W.A. (2008) An Analytical Framework for Studying the Politics of Consumption: The Case of the National Consumers' League, *Social Movement Studies*, 7, 3, 281–303.

Wilkinson, J. (2007) Fair Trade: Dynamic and Dilemmas of a Market Oriented Global Social Movement, *Journal of Consumer Policy*, 30, 3, 219–239.

Zaccai, E. (2007) *Sustainable Consumption, Ecology and Fair Trade* (London: Routledge).

Zald, M.N., Morrill, C., and Rao, H. (2005) The Impact of Social Movements on Organizations, in G.F. Davis, D. McAdam, W.R. Scott and M.N. Zald (eds), *Social Movements and Organization Theory* (Cambridge: Cambridge University Press).

Zietsma, C., and Winn, M.I. (2008) Building Chains and Directing Flows: Strategies and Tactics of Mutual Influence in Stakeholder Conflicts, *Business & Society*, 47, 1, 68–101.

Index

For Product Safety Concerns and Information please contact our EU
representative GPSR@taylorandfrancis.com
Taylor & Francis Verlag GmbH, Kaufingerstraße 24, 80331 München, Germany

www.ingramcontent.com/pod-product-compliance
Ingram Content Group UK Ltd.
Pitfield, Milton Keynes, MK11 3LW, UK
UKHW020952180425
457613UK00019B/642